THE NATURE PRINCIPLE

THE NATURE PRINCIPLE

Human Restoration and the End of

Nature-Deficit Disorder

Richard Louv

ALGONQUIN BOOKS OF CHAPEL HILL | 2011

Published by
Algonquin Books of Chapel Hill
Post Office Box 2225
Chapel Hill, North Carolina 27515-2225

a division of
Workman Publishing
225 Varick Street
New York, New York 10014

Excerpt from "The Peace of Wild Things" from *The Selected
Poems of Wendell Berry*, © 1998 by Wendell Berry.
Reprinted by permission of Counterpoint.

Library of Congress Cataloging-in-Publication Data
Louv, Richard.
The nature principle : human restoration and the end of nature-deficit
disorder / by Richard Louv.—1st ed.
p. cm.
Includes bibliographical references and index.
ISBN 978-1-56512-581-0
1. Nature—Psychological aspects.   I. Title.
BF353.5N37L69 2011
128—dc22   2011003626

10 9 8 7 6 5 4 3 2 1
First Edition

The search which we make for this
quality, in our own lives, is the central search of any person,
and the crux of any
individual person's story. It is the search
for those moments and situations
when we are most alive.

—Christopher Alexander,
"The Timeless Way of Building"

When despair for the world grows in me
and I wake in the night at the least sound
in fear of what my life and my children's lives may be,
I go and lie down where the wood drake
rests in his beauty on the water, and the great heron feeds.
I come into the peace of wild things . . .
I rest in the grace of the world, and am free.

—Wendell Berry

ACKNOWLEDGMENTS

FOR THE CONSTRUCTION of this book and the notions it contains, my wife, Kathy, deserves enormous credit, not only for her kindness and help with the writing, but for her intellectual contributions and her artistic mind, which reveals itself often in these pages. Similar gratitude is due my sons. Jason, an urbane writer and editor, helped with much of the early research and contributed his formidable knowledge of philosophy, religion, and advertising; Matthew offered keen insights and wit, often while casting from the middle of a stream. My friend Dean Stahl offered expert editorial support, along with wisdom and humor. Robyn Bjornsson also provided gritty editorial assistance. James Levine is as good a friend as he is an agent. I often say that in Algonquin, I have the best publisher in the world. The brilliant Elisabeth Scharlatt is now giving seminars on patience, or should. Throughout this book, you will find the fingerprints of the supportive Algonquin team, including my persistent and wise editor Amy Gash, Ina Stern, Brunson Hoole, Michael Taeckens, Craig Popelars, Kelly Bowen, and Cheryl Nicchitta. Special thanks to Peter Workman, and to Jackie Green, who handles the universe. Since the publication of *Last Child in the Woods*, I've been blessed with a growing family of colleagues who created or now nurture the Children and Nature Network (C&NN), including Cheryl Charles, Amy Pertschuk, Martin LeBlanc, Mike Pertschuk, the late John Parr, Brother Yusuf Burgess, Marti Erickson, Howard Frumkin, Betty Townsend, Fran Mainella; and at the grassroots: Juan Martinez, Avery Cleary, John Thielbahr, Nancy Herron, Mary Roscoe, Bob Peart, Sven Lindblad, and many others who have contributed ideas to this book and encouragement to its author. So have my brother, Mike Louv, and my friends (not all of them listed here, of course), including Karen Landen, Peter and Marti Kaye, Anne Hocker

Pearse, John Johns, Neal Peirce, Bob Burroughs, Peter Sebring, Jon Funabiki, Bill Stothers, Cyndi Jones, Jon Wurtmann, Gary Shiebler, John Bowman, Conway Bowman, Steve Bunch, Don Levering, and the extended family called Chapter One. I am also grateful to Bob Perkowitz and ecoAmerica, who helped create Nature Rocks, and to *Orion Magazine* and the *San Diego Union-Tribune*, in which I first floated some of these concepts. This book is also, in part, a result of the pioneering work of a growing network of biophilic thinkers, including Stephen Kellert, who invited me to a pivotal conference on biophilic design, attended by E. O. Wilson, David Orr, Tim Beatley, Robert Michael Pyle, and others on the cutting edge of that new world.

THE NATURE PRINCIPLE

Nature-Deficit Disorder for Adults

Listen: there's a hell of a good universe next door; let's go.
—E. E. Cummings

W E TRAVELED DOWN a dirt road through the melting adobe village of Puerto de Luna, New Mexico, crossed a low bridge over the shallow Pecos River and entered a valley of green chili fields held by red-rimmed sandstone bluffs. Jason, our older son, then three, was asleep in the backseat.

"Is it this turn?" I asked my wife.

"The next one," Kathy said.

I got out of the rental car and unhooked the gate, and we drove onto the land owned by our friends Nick and Isabel Raven. They were away working in Santa Fe that year, and their farm and house were vacant. We had come to know them before Jason was born. Kathy and I had lived two summers in nearby Santa Rosa, where she had worked in a local hospital.

Now, after a stressful period of our lives, we were back for a couple of weeks. We needed this time for ourselves, and we needed it for Jason.

We entered the dusty adobe house. I inspected the room addition that I had helped Nick build during one of those summers. I turned on the electricity and the water (indoor plumbing had finally come to the Raven homestead), walked into the kitchen, and opened the faucet. A foot-long centipede leapt out of the drain, its tail whipping toward my face. I don't know who was more startled, the centipede or me, but I was the one holding the steak knife.

Later, as Kathy and Jason took naps, I walked outside in the heat, found Nick's rusted folding chair, and set it in the shade of a tree next to the adobe. Nick and I had rested under the branches of this tree between bouts of mixing adobe mud in a pit filled with straw, sand, earth, and water. I thought about Nick, about our political arguments, about the green-chili stew that Isabel heated on a wood stove and served in tin bowls, even in the hottest hours.

Now I sat alone and looked out over the field toward a line of distant cottonwoods that rimmed the Pecos. I watched the afternoon thunderheads rise above the high desert to the east and the layers of sandstone across the river. The field of chili shivered in the sun. Above me, leaves rattled and tree limbs scratched. My eyes settled on a single cottonwood at the river, its branches and upper leaves waving in a slow rhythm above all the others. An hour, perhaps more, went by. Tension crawled up and out of me. It seemed to twist in the air above the green field. Then it was gone. And something better took its place.

Twenty-four years later, I often think about the cottonwood at the river's edge, and similar moments of inexplicable wonder, times when I received from nature just what I needed: an elusive *it* for which I have no name.

We have thought about moving to New Mexico ever since. Or rural Vermont. But we are reminded daily that *it* also occurs where we already live — and even within the densest cities, where the urban wild still exists in the most unexpected places. It can be restored or even created where we live, work, and play.

We're not alone in feeling this hunger.

ONE DAY IN SEATTLE, a woman literally grabbed my lapels and said, "Listen to me, *adults* have nature-deficit disorder, too." She was right, of course.

In 2005, in *Last Child in the Woods*, I introduced the term *nature-deficit disorder*, not as a medical diagnosis, but as a way to describe the growing gap between children and nature. After the book's publication, I heard many adults speak with heartfelt emotion, even anger, about this separation, but also about their own sense of loss.

Every day, our relationship with nature, or the lack of it, influences our lives. This has always been true. But in the twenty-first century, our survival—or thrival—will require a transformative framework for that relationship, a reunion of humans with the rest of nature.

In these pages, I describe a future shaped by what I call the Nature Principle, an amalgam of converging theories and trends as well as a reconciliation with old truths. This principle holds that a reconnection to the natural world is fundamental to human health, well-being, spirit, and survival.

Primarily a statement of philosophy, the Nature Principle is supported by a growing body of theoretical, anecdotal, and empirical research that describes the restorative power of nature—its impact on our senses and intelligence; on our physical, psychological, and spiritual health; and on the bonds of family, friendship, and the multispecies community. Illuminated by ideas and stories from good people I have met, this book asks: *What would our lives be like if our days and nights were as immersed in nature as they are in technology? How can each of us help create that life-enhancing world, not only in a hypothetical future, but right now, for our families and for ourselves?*

Our sense of urgency grows. In 2008, for the first time in history, more than half of the world's population lived in towns and cities.[1] The traditional ways that humans have experienced nature are vanishing, along with biodiversity.

At the same time, our culture's faith in technological immersion seems to have no limits, and we drift ever deeper into a sea of circuitry. We consume breathtaking media accounts of the creation of synthetic life, combining bacteria with human DNA; of microscopic machines designed to enter our bodies to fight biological invaders or to move in deadly clouds across the battlefields of war; of computer-augmented reality; of futuristic houses in which we are surrounded by simulated reality transmitted from every wall. We even hear talk of the "transhuman" or "posthuman" era in which people are optimally enhanced by technology, or of a "postbiological universe" where, as NASA's Steven Dick puts it, "the majority of intelligent life has evolved beyond flesh and blood intelligence."[2]

This book is not an argument against these concepts or their proponents—at least not the ones who are devoted to the ethical use of technology to expand human capacities.[3] But it does make the case that we're getting ahead of ourselves. We have yet to fully realize, or even adequately study, the enhancement of human capacities through the power of nature. In a report praising higher-tech classrooms, one educator quotes Abraham Lincoln: "The dogmas of the quiet past are inadequate to the stormy present. The occasion is piled high with difficulty, and we must rise with the occasion. As our case is new, so we must think anew and act anew." That we should; but in the twenty-first century, ironically, an outsized faith in technology—a turning away from nature—may well be the outdated dogma of our time.

In contrast, the Nature Principle suggests that, in an age of rapid environmental, economic, and social transformation, the future will belong to the nature-smart—those individuals, families, businesses, and political leaders who develop a deeper understanding of nature, and who balance the virtual with the real.

In 2010, *Avatar* became the most-watched film in history. The success had less to do with the movie's advanced 3-D technology than with the hunger it tapped—our instinctive knowledge that the endangered human species is paying an awful price as it loses touch with nature. Describing the core message of the movie, the film's maker, James Cameron, said: "It asks questions about our relationship with each other, from culture to culture, and our relationship with the natural world at a time of nature-deficit disorder." This collective disorder threatens our health, our spirit, our economy, and our future steward-ship of the environment. Yet, despite what seem prohibitive odds, trans-formative change is possible. The loss that we feel, this truth that we already know, sets the stage for a new age of nature. In fact, because of the environmental challenges we face today, we may be—we had better be—entering the most creative period in human history, a time defined by a goal that builds on and extends a century of environmentalism, which includes but goes beyond sustainability to the re-naturing of ev-eryday life.

Seven overlapping precepts, based on the transformative powers of nature, can reshape our lives now and in the future. Together they form a singular force:

- The more high-tech our lives become, the more nature we need to achieve **natural balance.**
- The mind/body/nature connection, also called **vitamin N** (for nature), will enhance physical and mental health.
- Utilizing both technology *and* nature experience will increase our intelligence, creative thinking, and productivity, giving birth to the **hybrid mind.**
- **Human/nature social capital** will enrich and redefine commu-nity to include all living things.
- In the new **purposeful place,** natural history will be as important as human history to regional and personal identity.
- Through **biophilic design,** our homes, workplaces, neighbor-hoods, and towns will not only conserve watts, but also produce human energy.
- In relationship with nature, the **high-performance human** will conserve and *create* natural habitat—and new economic poten-tial—where we live, learn, work, and play.

Young, old, or in between, we can reap extraordinary benefits by con-necting—or reconnecting—to nature. For the jaded and weary among us, the outdoor world can expand our senses and reignite a sense of awe and wonder not felt since we were children; it can support better health, enhanced creativity, new careers and business opportunities, and act as a bonding agent for families and communities. Nature can help us feel fully alive.

In these pages, which offer a sampling of the emerging research, I have not knowingly excluded any studies that would dispute my central thesis. But I do hope this book will raise useful questions for future inquiry. I should add: my view is not based solely on science, but also on the long human experience of nature, on the stories of everyday people, and on my own reflection.

The skeptic will say the nature prescription is problematic, given our quickening destruction of nature, and the skeptic will be right. The natural world's benefits to our cognition and health will be irrelevant if we continue to destroy the nature around us. However, that destruction is assured without a human reconnection to nature. This is why the Nature Principle is about conservation, but also about restoring nature while we restore ourselves; about creating new natural habitats where they once were or never were, in our homes, workplaces, schools, neighborhoods, cities, suburbs, and farms. It's about the power of living in nature—not *with* it, but *in* it. The twenty-first century will be the century of human restoration in the natural world.

Martin Luther King Jr. often said that any movement—any culture— will fail if it cannot paint a picture of a world that people will want to go to. The first brushstrokes are already visible.

This book is about the people creating that world, in their daily lives and beyond, and about how you can, too.

PART ONE

Nature Neurons

Intelligence, Creativity, and the Hybrid Mind

The lover of nature is he whose inward and outward senses

are still truly adjusted to each other.

—Ralph Waldo Emerson

The natural world is not only a set of constraints

but of contexts within which we can more fully realize our dreams.

—Paul Shepard

CHAPTER I

Singing for Bears

Discovering the Full Use of the Senses

There's another world, and it's in this one.
—Susan Casey, "The Devil's Teeth"

As a species, we are most animated when our days and nights on Earth are touched by the natural world. We can find immeasurable joy in the birth of a child, a great work of art, or falling in love. But all of life is rooted in nature, and a separation from that wider world desensitizes and diminishes our bodies and spirits. Reconnecting to nature, nearby and far, opens new doors to health, creativity, and wonder. It is never too late.

My younger son, Matthew, then twenty, and I were hiking upstream on Alaska's Kodiak Island. Joe Solakian, our guide, was teaching us how to sense the presence of Kodiak brown bears, the largest grizzlies, the ones that can run thirty-five miles per hour.

"Never surprise them, that's the main thing," Joe said.

And, keeping in mind the fate of Timothy Treadwell, documentary filmmaker—and meal—never try to be their new best friend.

In the shallow green pools, bracketed between two walls of forest, the salmon—chum, sockeye, and pink—come here to spawn and die; this is a bear kitchen. So we talked, sang, and shook the bear bells on our vests, watched for tracks, and sniffed the air for the distinctive, mingled odors of musk and rotted salmon. Now and then during the week that fragrance would suddenly fill the air and the hair on the backs of our necks would stand up. That meant a bear was watching us from the thickets, or just around the bend, or had just left.

One afternoon, we did see a bear. It was upwind from us, beyond our hearing distance. It came out of the forest and lumbered across a gravel bar, raised its muzzle, hesitated, then turned and loped across the creek and into the trees.

Singing for bears puts the risks of everyday life in perspective.

So does being on this island. In 1964, a tsunami wave thirty feet high destroyed shoreline villages. An even greater cataclysm occurred in 1912, when Mount Katmai erupted on the mainland.

"About three o'clock in the afternoon, as we emerged from the forest, we saw, for the first time, a huge, fan-shaped cloud directly west of the village," wrote Hildred Erskine, a Kodiak survivor. "It was the blackest and densest cloud that I have ever seen. Lightning frequently flashed through . . . electrical storms just do not happen in Alaska. Static was so bad that radio operators did not dare go near their instruments." It grew dark, strange for June in Kodiak, when daylight is almost continuous. "We began thinking of the fate of the people of Pompeii."

Lakes filled with the ash; ptarmigan were killed in their nesting season; trout were destroyed, and most of the island biota was, indeed, buried alive. But soon, from that ash, life began again. With the help of winds from the mainland, which brought the seeds of trees and plants that had never grown there, the island was reborn. In geologic terms, then, the surface and life of Kodiak is brand-new, a reminder that creation is the other face of death.

After Hurricane Katrina, some people said that New Orleans should be allowed to revert to its natural wetland state; the population resettled in surrounding cities on higher ground; perhaps a Bourbon Street amusement park, easily evacuated, built in that drowning pool. The wetland reversion approach is sensible, because to a degree it restores natural, protective habitat. But when people say, as they often do, that other humans are fools if they live in a natural disaster zone, they base this on the assumption that ultimate high ground exists. Should people—you and I—be marched out of any habitat threatened by natural disaster? I don't think so. Where would we go? Where no flood ever runs or fire ignites? To the seemingly safe boot heel of Missouri, which happens to be located on a fault that once changed the course of the Mississippi River?

Nearly a century after that Katmai eruption, my son and I leave our footprints in this dark volcanic soil of renewal. Life edges back from the brink, then pushes forward again. So Matthew and I press on, up the stream, awake, more careful than we would ever be in our daily lives, listening, watching, lifting our heads to sense what the wind carries. Something is coming. So we ring the bells. And we sing.

More Senses Than We Sense

Singing for bears, or smelling them, may not be your idea of a good time, but it hints at the sensory capabilities that are in our nature, if seldom used.

Many of us desire a fuller life of the senses.

By its broadest interpretation, nature-deficit disorder is an atrophied awareness, a diminished ability to find meaning in the life that surrounds us, whatever form it takes. This shrinkage of our lives has a direct impact on our physical, mental, and societal health. However, not only can nature-deficit disorder be reversed, but our lives can be vastly enriched through our relationship with nature, beginning with our senses. In *A Natural History of the Senses*, Diane Ackerman writes: "People think of the mind as being located in the head, but the latest findings in physiology suggest that the mind doesn't really dwell in the brain but travels the whole body on caravans of enzyme, busily making sense of the compound wonders we catalogue as touch, taste, smell, hearing, vision."[1] We city dwellers marvel at the seemingly superhuman or supernatural abilities of Australian aborigines and other "primitive" people, but consider such talents vestigial, like that remnant tailbone. Here's another view. Such senses are not vestigial but latent, blanketed by noise and assumptions.

Ever wonder why you have two nostrils? Researchers at the University of California–Berkeley did. They published their findings in the journal *Nature Neuroscience*. Jay Gottfried, a professor of neurology at Northwestern University, wrote: "What this study highlights most for me is that the human sense of smell is a lot better than many people think it is. It's true that narrow visual and auditory streams comprise the primary sensory currents of our lives. But all of our senses are capable of more than what we assume." The researchers fitted college undergraduates with taped-over goggles, earmuffs, and work gloves to block other senses, then set them loose in a field; most of the students could follow a thirty-foot-long trail of chocolate perfume and even changed direction precisely where the invisible path took a turn. The subjects also were able to smell better with two functioning nostrils, which researchers likened to hearing in stereo.[2] One researcher postulated that the brain gathers odor "images" from each nostril to construct a composite picture of the trail. The students found themselves zigzagging, a technique employed by dogs as they track.

The study also found that the students' olfactory tracking abilities improved with practice, suggesting that humans could develop the ability to match the tracking talents of many other animals. According to researcher Noam Sobel, part of the reason dogs are better at this than humans is that dogs sniff quickly. Very quickly. "We interpret these results to suggest that, as subjects increased their speed, it was necessary for them to sniff more quickly to get the same quality of information," reported Sobel. "We found that not only are humans capable of scent-tracking, but they spontaneously mimic the tracking pattern of [other] mammals."[3]

What else can we do that we have forgotten? What do we miss seeing, hearing, and knowing because we allow the tangle of technology's wire to tighten around us a little more each day? And how can we develop these natural but obscured abilities and make them applicable to the lives we live today?

Perhaps you recall a time when you took in more of the world—you just *did* it. You were new and the world was new. As a boy, I would go out in the woods and sit under a tree, wet my thumb, and then wipe each nostril with it. I had read somewhere that people—pioneers or Indians—would do this in order to keen their sense of smell for approaching game, or even danger. I did this and held perfectly still, my back against rough bark, waiting. And, slowly, the animal life returned. A rabbit appeared under a bush, birds swooped low, an ant went on a walkabout over my knee to see what was on the other side. And I felt intensely alive.

Most scientists who study human perception no longer assume that we have five senses: taste, touch, smell, sight, and hearing. The current number ranges from a conservative ten senses to as many as thirty, including blood-sugar levels, empty stomach, thirst, joint position, and more. The list is growing.

In 2010, scientists at University College in London published the results of a study suggesting that human beings may be hardwired with an inner sense of direction.[4] Another related sense is called proprioception: the awareness of your body's position in space, including movement and balance; this sense makes it possible for us to touch our noses when our eyes are closed. Dolphins and bats might teach us a thing or two about a latent talent we share with them: echolocation, the ability to locate objects by interpreting sounds bouncing off of them. In 2009, researchers at Madrid's University of Alcalá de Henares showed how people could identify objects around them, without needing to "see" them, through the echoes of human tongue clicks. According to the lead researcher, echoes are also perceived through vibrations in ears, tongue, and bones.[5] This refined sense has been learned by trial and error by some blind people and even by some sighted individuals.

"In certain circumstances, we humans could rival bats in our echo-location or biosonar capacity," said Juan Antonio Martínez Rojas, lead author of the study. "Lots of things, like an empty room, don't make a sound, but they do structure it. They give it shape, which people can see without seeing. I have had students listen to sounds broadcast between two boards and be able to tell me whether there was enough space between the boards for them to fit through." Human echoloca-tion can be done without technology or "without having to develop any new mental processes," according to Lawrence D. Rosenblum, a professor of psychology at University of California–Riverside. To him, it's all about "hearing" a world that exists beyond what we nor-mally mistake for silence.[6]

Karen Landen hears that world. A former newspaper editor, Landen had been a birder many years when, on field trips, she noticed a few people had an uncanny knack for detecting and identifying birds. These "superbirders," as she calls them, were, in a sense, seeing with their ears. How? They had taken Seattle Audubon's Birding by Ear course, taught by professional birding-tour leader Bob Sundstrom. Landen had studied singing and languages, so she thought "bird" would be easy.

She soon understood why most students were repeaters: "Unlike human language, birds don't have rules. We studied pages of song types—think whistle, squawk, whinny, rattle, chatter, trill—and qualities—clear, liquid, metallic, raspy, burry, sweet. You listen for a pattern: number of beats, duration, simplicity/complexity, repeated phrases. Are notes ascending or descending? Are there pauses, or one long breath? The songs of a robin and black-headed grosbeak sound alike until you notice that the robin's notes are distinct and the gros-beak's slurred (hence the grosbeak's song described as 'drunk robin')."

She also learned that some birds are instrumentalists, others are composers: "Woodpeckers drum, and a hummingbird's wings 'hum.' A young song sparrow may sing a basic phrase, but an older one with prime territory will throw in extra flourishes to advertise his status. On top of that, species' sounds vary by region and by individual, just like us." What Landen learned was that birding starts with one sense, which leads to an opening up of other senses. A superbirder learns to see birds first, then learns to hear them, and then to "see" them by hearing them. "When you bird by ear, you learn that there's a whole life story going on out there. Calls warn of predators. A male sings 'no trespassing' to other males but also, 'hey, ladies, here's a handsome, successful guy who'll make a great family man.' " She laughs. "You know how when you wake up at the tail end of a dream, if it was a good one, its memory creates a rich extra layer that hovers over your day? Well, birding by ear creates this luscious extra layer in life that just rises above the day-to-day. I can't imagine a life without birds, without their beauty, their spiritedness, and their song. That would be a poverty of the senses."

This brings us to the so-called sixth sense, which to some means intuition, to others extrasensory perception, and to still others, the human's ability to unconsciously detect danger.

In December 2004, as the devastating Asian tsunami approached, Jarawa tribespeople, along with some animals, reportedly sensed or detected sounds from the approaching wave, or other unusual natural activity, long before the water struck the shore. They fled to higher ground. The Jarawa used tribal knowledge of nature's warning signs, explained V. R. Rao, director of the Anthropological Survey of India, based in Kolkata. "They got wind of impending danger from biological warning signals, like the cry of birds and change in the behavioral patterns of marine animals."[7] In the Jarawa's case, the simplest explanation may be that the sixth sense is the sum of all the other senses put together, combined with everyday nature-knowledge.

Researchers at Washington University in St. Louis point to the anterior cingulate cortex, the brain's early warning system, which is better at picking up subtle warning signs than scientists had previously thought. Joshua W. Brown, director of the Cognitive Control Lab, Indiana University–Bloomington, coauthored a study reported in 2005, in the journal *Science*.[8] "It makes sense that this mechanism exists because there are plenty of situations in our everyday lives that require the brain to monitor subtle changes in our environment and adjust our behavior, even in cases where we may not necessarily be aware of the conditions that prompted the adjustment," he wrote. "In some cases, the brain's ability to monitor subtle environmental changes and make adjustments may actually be even more robust if it takes place on a subconscious level."

Ron Rensink, an associate professor in both psychology and computer science at the University of British Columbia, has investigated the sixth sense, which he calls "mindsight," as a way to understand how people can have accurate "intuition" that something is about to happen. "In a way, it's like a 'first strike' system . . . that we use without conscious thought," Rensink told the *Monitor*, the journal of the American Psychological Association.[9] His research suggests that vision is, in fact, a collection of abilities, not just one sense—and that the brain can receive, through light, a kind of pre-image vision. In the University of British Columbia's monthly newspaper, *UBC Reports*, he explained: "There is something there—people do have access to this other subsystem. . . . It turns out these are two very different subsystems— one of them is conscious, one of them is non-conscious—and they actually work slightly differently. . . . In the past, people believed that if light came into your eyes, it would have to result in a picture. If it didn't result in a picture, it must mean that it can't be vision." On the contrary, he wrote, light can enter your eyes and be employed by other perceptual systems. "It's just another way of seeing."[10]

In separate research, the U.S. military has studied how some soldiers and marines can apparently use their latent senses to detect roadside bombs and other hazards in war zones in Afghanistan and Iraq. "Military researchers have found that two groups of personnel are particularly good at spotting anomalies: those with hunting backgrounds, who traipsed through the woods as youths looking to bag a deer or turkey; and those who grew up in tough urban neighborhoods, where it is often important to know what gang controls which block," reported Tony Perry of the *Los Angeles Times*.[11]

A common factor seemed to be at work: plenty of experience outside the home and outside the electronic bubble, in an environment that *demands* better use of the senses. Army Sgt. Maj. Todd Burnett, who has served in Iraq and Afghanistan, conducted the research. The eighteen-month-long study of eight hundred military personnel at several bases found that the best bomb-spotters were rural people, familiar with hunting, who signed on with the South Carolina National Guard. According to Burnett, "They just seemed to pick up things much better. . . . They know how to look at the entire environment." And the other young soldiers, the ones who were raised with Game Boys and spent weekends at the mall? By and large, these enlistees lacked the ability to see nuances that might enable a soldier to spot a hidden bomb. Even with perfect vision, they lacked the special ability, that combination of depth perception, peripheral vision, and instinct, if you will, to see what was out of place in the environment. Their focus was narrow, as if they were seeing the world in a set format, "as if the windshield of their Humvee [was] a computer screen," Perry wrote. Sgt. Maj. Burnett put it this way: The gamers were "focused on the screen rather than the whole surrounding."

The explanation may be partly physiological. Australian researchers suggest that the troubling increase in cases of myopia—nearsightedness—is linked to children and young people spending less time outdoors, where eyes are conditioned to focus on longer distances.[12] But more is probably going on here. Vision, including mindsight; more acute hearing; an attuned sense of smell; a sense of where one's body is in space—all of these abilities could be operating simultaneously. In a natural environment, this advantage offers practical applications and benefits: one is an increased ability to learn; another is an enhanced capability to avoid danger; and still another, perhaps the most important application of all, is the measurement-defying ability to more fully engage in life.

Beyond proprioception, that awareness of our body's position through movement and balance, nature also offers us the opportunity to realize an even larger sense—the position of our body and spirit in the universe and in time.

One day, my son Matthew wondered, "Is faith a sense?"

"What do you mean?" I asked.

"You know, as in sensing a higher power?"

This is a wonderful question, and it leads to other questions: Could a literal sense of spirit exist on the far edge of our senses, out where the flat earth stops and all that is beyond and within begins? Might this particular sense be activated by the other senses, when they're working at full throttle—which often occurs when we are in nature?

Perhaps this sense, if it is one, is why so many of us use religious terminology as we talk about our experience of nature, even if we're not religious in a formal way.

Nature writer Robert Michael Pyle, who coined the elegant phrase "the extinction of experience," asks: "What happens to a species that loses touch with its habitat?" Our sensitivity to nature, and our humility within it, are essential to our physical and spiritual survival. Yet, our growing disconnection from nature dulls our senses, and eventually blunts even the sharpened sensory state created by man-made or natural disaster. Spending time in nature, particularly in wilderness, can pose physical dangers, but rejecting nature because of those risks and discomforts is a greater gamble.

The Humility Sense

On that Alaska stream, where the red sockeye moved against the current and the forest leaned inward over cut banks, the potential of a bear in those bushes presented a danger. At the same time, our awareness gave us protection and excited our senses to everything around and above and in that stream. It offered us something larger, too: a sense of natural humility.

Far across an open plain, a bear was running toward us. Joe suggested that we stand together. "We'll look like one big animal with a lot of legs," he said. This seemed a sensible recommendation. It was not lost on me that the Kodiak brown bear, isolated on the Kodiak Archipelago for twelve thousand years, is the world's largest land carnivore, weighing up to seventeen hundred pounds.

"Let's back away from the water," said Joe.

The bear crossed in front of us and leaped into the bend of the river where we had just crossed. We watched in awe. Young but impressive, the bear pounced and swiped at the migrating salmon, and occasionally lifted his nose and bobbed his head and looked our way, then went back to his fishing.

"He has to make a living, too," Joe said.

I glanced at Matthew, who clutched his can of pepper spray. Irrationally, I felt a surge of joy that outweighed any concern about safety. How fine it is, I thought, for Matthew to experience this moment, with its beauty and imposed natural humility. The pleasure of being alive is brought into sharper focus when you need to pay attention to *staying* alive. Alive in the larger universe, alive in time.

Kodiak Island, with more bears than human residents, is one of the last wild places on the planet where human beings can feel that peculiar constriction of flesh on the back of the neck that occurs only when one is in another predator's environment. Even those who live in less-developed areas of the world know such moments are growing rare. In his 2003 book *Monsters of God*, David Quammen predicts that by the year 2150, all the world's top predators will either be wiped out or in zoos, their genetic pool dwindling, their fierce possibility caged. Then, he writes, people "will find it hard to conceive that those animals were once proud, dangerous, unpredictable, widespread and kingly.... Children will be startled and excited to learn, if anyone tells them, that once there were lions at large in the very world." And tigers, and bears.

In rare cases, large predators are on the rebound. After being decimated by hunters in the 1940s, and subsequent efforts to protect it, the Kodiak bear population is stable and possibly increasing. In Southern California, the number of mountain lions has grown dramatically since the state banned lion hunting in 1990. However, an accurate mountain lion count grows more elusive because of the "shoot, shovel, and shut up" mentality of ranchers who sometimes conduct their own kind of animal control. Wolves reintroduced in Yellowstone face a similarly questionable future. We no longer hear much about human population control, just wildlife control.

In wilderness, and in natural cases or even natural urban parks, we find our senses—but can we come to them in time? Even if human beings never encounter predator species (other than humans), their protection of wildlife preserves or restores part of our humanity. It nourishes the remnants of our deeper senses, especially the sense of humility required for true human intelligence.

On Kodiak, a piece of that frontier survives—a kind of Jurassic Park with salmon. Another day, my son and I watched a different bear move quickly up a small ridge, straight for a cluster of the island's wild, or feral, horses. Perhaps it hoped to take the little white colt from them. Remarkably, the horses (more dangerous to people than were the bears, Joe told us), led by a strong palomino, ran directly at the bear. As the horses raced forward, tails flying like flags, the bear considered a different plan.

The wild horses stopped and stood together and watched, and so did we, as the bear ambled along the beach and disappeared into the fog. The horses went their own way, into the same fog. Then we were alone on the plain.

CHAPTER 2

The Hybrid Mind

Enhancing Intelligence through the World Outdoors

L ET'S BE REALISTIC. Even if we're lucky enough to sing for bears in Alaska or to have bonded with nature when we were young, keeping that bond or establishing an evolved relationship with nature is no easy thing.

My office in San Diego is a sea of distraction. Two computers, two printers, a fax/answering machine/scanner, a negative and slide scanner, a radio, and four hard drives sit on my desk; beneath it, a tangle of wires that has baffled me for years. I half expect this mess of ganglia to creep up the stairs one night, like a serial-killer Slinky, and strangle me where I sleep. Right now, however, I see a movement in the bushes beyond the sliding glass door. A spotted towhee dances in the leaves, doing its comical back-kick as it searches for bugs, calling *to-wheeeee*. Recently, our son Matthew, who has taken up birding with a passion, gave my wife and me a set of 10×42 binoculars and *The National Audubon Society Field Guide to Birds: Western Region*. He has marked pages of the book with yellow tags to show which birds frequent our territory.

The binoculars and the book are on my desk. The desk is vibrating. I reach for the iPhone.

Robert Michael Pyle would be the first to say that finding a balance isn't easy. In 2007, Pyle announced in his *Orion Magazine* nature column that he was thinking about going cold turkey on e-mail. "Time will tell whether I can make a living without e-mail," he wrote. "In the meantime, I'm going back to the post, and the virtues of patience and silence. My loss, you'll say. Maybe so. We'll see . . ."[1]

Two years later, I e-mailed Bob and asked him how his life was going since he swore off e-mail. It was a bad sign when he answered, quickly. "I have backslid," he wrote. "You could say I had a hiatus, but I haven't yet fully succeeded in achieving the ideal. I try to spend as little time as I can on the machine away from writing, however, and do as little as possible on the web." When he must spend time before a screen to do his daily work of writing, he gets up and goes outside as soon as possible.

Sometimes, even Pyle — as hopeful and energetic a man as you'll ever meet — gets discouraged about the odds against a human/nature reunion.

Unctuous personalities squawk at us from flat-panel TVs on gas pumps. Billboard companies replace pasted paper with flashing digital screens. Screens pop up in airports, coffeehouses, banks, and grocery-store checkout lines, even in restrooms, above the urinal or mounted on hand dryers. On some airlines, advertising messages reach out to us from the seatback dining tables and motion-sickness bags. Disney advertises DVDs for preschoolers on the paper liners of examination tables in pediatricians' offices. Perhaps this is our punishment for using the DVR to skip the commercials. "We never know where the consumer is going to be at any point in time, so we have to find a way to be everywhere," Linda Kaplan Thaler, chief executive at the ad agency Kaplan Thaler Group, tells the *New York Times*. "Ubiquity is the new exclusivity."[2]

This info-blitzkrieg has spawned a new field called "interruption science" and a newly minted condition: continuous partial attention.[3]

Maggie Jackson, author of *Distracted: The Erosion of Attention and the Coming Dark Age*, reports that a distracted worker takes nearly a half hour to get back to and continue a task; 28 percent of a typical worker's day is taken up by interruptions and recovery time; constant electronic instrusions leave interrupted workers feeling frustrated, pressured and stressed, and less creative.[4] We text more, communicate less. At the UCLA Center on Everyday Lives of Families, Elinor Ochs, a linguistic anthropologist, and a team of twenty-one researchers, have been using the tools of ethnography, ecology, archaeology, and primatology to videotape and study the routines of thirty-two families in the Los Angeles area. The team found that restless family members moved quickly, gathering in the same room only 16 percent of the time; they tended to grunt more than talk; they walked past one another without greeting, barely looking up from the video game, television, or computer. "Returning home at the end of the day is one of the most delicate and vulnerable moments in life. Everywhere in the world, in all societies, there is some kind of greeting." But not in these families.[5]

Larry Hinman, professor of philosophy and director of the Values Institute at the University of San Diego, has studied the evolution of robots. One scientist he interviewed remarked that machines are "without entanglements," and he considered that a positive feature. "Nature is a complex world, and you are born with entanglements, starting with the umbilical cord," says Hinman. Notwithstanding electric cords, "the technological world is the world of the blank slate; you can redo it without the messiness of reality. A false dream, but that's what captures the imagination of some people who work in the field of robotics." This is particularly true in Japan, where demonstration robots are becoming eerily humanlike. "One robot 'newscaster' read the news one night on television, and virtually no one noticed," he says. "Another scientist created a basic prototype with the features of his own young son, who commented, 'Aren't I enough, Dad?' It was devastating to him."

Taken to its extreme, a denatured life is a dehumanized life. As the American naturalist and writer Henry Beston put it, when the wind in the grass is "no longer a part of the human spirit, a part of very flesh and bone, man becomes, as it were, a kind of cosmic outlaw." There's no denying the benefits of the Internet. But electronic immersion, without a force to balance it, creates the hole in the boat—draining our ability to pay attention, to think clearly, to be productive and creative. The best antidote to negative electronic information immersion will be an increase in the amount of *natural* information we receive.

The more high-tech we become, the more nature we need.

Nature Smart

During a visit to the Galapagos Islands in 2010, I spent an afternoon at the Tomas de Berlanga School on the island of Santa Cruz. Scalesia Foundation, a nongovernment organization created in 1991 to provide an education alternative for residents of the archipelago, supports the school, which serves the islands' growing number of children whose parents moved there in pursuit of ecotourism jobs. Even here, on these extraordinary islands—where you must be careful where you put your feet, lest you step on an iguana, lava lizard, sea lion, or blue-footed booby—children know little about their own bioregion.

Not so at this school. With the exception of courses requiring computers, classes are conducted under rough shelters with no walls. Such "forest schools," particularly popular in Europe, can range from traditional schools that send the students outdoors a few hours a week, to ones that have no buildings at all. Their effectiveness is supported by several studies.

The director of the Berlanga School, Reyna Oleas, is a vivacious former environmental consultant from Ecuador, who, in her former life, helped design more than twenty environmental funds in Latin America and the Caribbean. Now in her late thirties, she moved to the Galapagos in 2007 to open this school. I asked her how the natural world had influenced her way of thinking. Had it made her smarter?

"I'd prefer the word *sharpness*. I have more sharpness and perpetual awareness," she said. "Before I came here, my life was . . . dormant."

She offered an interesting definition of dormant: not asleep, but driven to distraction. "You're writing e-mail, watching TV, answering the phone. You've got your head in so many channels. Your body could collapse and you wouldn't even realize it. I was smoking two packs of cigarettes a day. I was stressed out. I wasn't well. Here, I healed, I quit smoking." And here, her thinking cleared. "When there is something you have to deal with, you go do it. Solutions come more naturally. I can separate the real problem from the static. Before, it was—you have a problem, and everything is huge. And now, if something happens, okay, this is what it is, how are we going to deal with it?"

This seems clear enough: When truly present in nature, we do use all our senses at the same time, which is the optimum state of learning.

At lunch that day, I met Celso Montalvo, a naturalist and expedition leader in his early forties who worked with Lindblad National Geographic Expeditions. Celso spent part of his childhood in the Galapagos. A graduate of the Ecuadorian Naval Academy, he studied computer science in New York but decided to return to the islands he loved. As Oleas and I talked about natural intelligence—or as she put it, sharpness and awareness—Celso jumped into the conversation. He defined natural intelligence as "knowing the signs of nature."

"I see a kind of a general animal intelligence. I can see this in the fish, I can see this in the birds," he said. "We all are born with it. It can be triggered again. It's not that hard. It helps to know biology, but this knowledge becomes much deeper. Every time I step out on the deck or out of the house, I can feel the direction of the breeze; I feel what animals can feel. They can feel the sun rise and the sun set. The plants point in one direction when it is wet and then the other direction when it is dry. Connecting dots. It's as simple as that. Off the Internet, everything is connecting you with the world. *Everything.*"

The natural world helps us perceive connections; it can also help us fine-tune knowledge.

Wolf Berger, Distinguished Research Professor at the Geosciences

Research Division of the Scripps Institution of Oceanography and a friend, hikes to clear his mind and to focus. Usually, he walks along the beach at La Jolla, up the paths of Torrey Pines State Park, along the gnarled mud sculptures of the sandstone cliffs frozen hard by time, through California coastal sage where rattlesnakes sun themselves, through groves of the rarest pine in North America, a remnant of an ancient coastal forest. He looks out to sea and follows the porpoises with their curved backs stitching the waves, the dipping gulls.

One day, as he and I walked along a plateau farther inland, he explained the way his scientific mind processes nature. "Soils and plants have a plethora of different hues of browns and greens, and by noting these carefully, one can guess what to expect in terms of rocks and plants when coming closer," he said. "As I get older, my hearing suffers, but I still enjoy the whispering of the pines and firs in the breeze, and the song of birds. I try to guess the size of each bird from the frequency distribution in its acoustic emissions—perhaps not a very romantic approach. Even more than my senses, my *thinking* is enhanced in nature."

Our society seems to look everywhere *but* the natural domain for the enhancement of intelligence. Gary Stix, writing in *Scientific American*, reports a boom in pill popping to build brain performance. Many people already take "natural" supplements to enhance or calm the brain—*Ginkgo biloba* for increased blood flow to the brain, Saint-John's-wort for depression, and so on. And psychoactive substances have been used for thousands of years to enhance the human ability to envision and then create. As any baby-boom survivor of the 1960s can attest, though, results may vary. Now we're taking the next leap. "The 1990s, proclaimed the decade of the brain by President George H. W. Bush, have been followed by what might be labeled 'the decade of the better brain,'" writes Stix. College students and business executives are downing stimulant drugs for routine mental performance, though the drugs were never approved for that purpose.

Called neuroenhancers, nootropics, or smart drugs, the smart pills of choice currently include methylphenidate (Ritalin), the amphetamine Adderall, and modafinil (Provigil). "On some campuses, one quarter of students have reported using the drugs," according to Stix.[6] Some people need such medication, of course, but reliance on these drugs remains a massive experiment, with long-term side effects yet to be determined. Beyond drugs, the news media's imagination is captured by the potential of artificial neural networks — the reproduction or extension of the biological nervous system — to boost human intelligence. Yet an immediately available, low-cost intelligence-enhancing supplement already exists.

The study of the relationship between mental acuity, creativity, and time spent outdoors is a frontier for science. But new research suggests that exposure to the living world can enhance intelligence for some people. This probably happens in at least two ways: first, our senses and sensibilities are improved through our direct interaction with nature (and practical knowledge of natural systems is still applicable in our everyday lives); second, a more natural environment seems to stimulate our ability to pay attention, think clearly, and be more creative, even in dense urban neighborhoods. This research has positive implications for education, for business, and for the daily lives of young and old.

Foundational work in this arena was begun in the 1970s by environmental psychologists Rachel and Stephen Kaplan.[7] Findings from their nine-year study for the U.S. Forest Service and later research suggested that direct and indirect contact with nature can help with recovery from mental fatigue and the restoration of attention. In addition to supporting the theory that nature experience can improve psychological health, they also found that it helped restore the brain's ability to process information. They followed participants in an Outward Bound–like wilderness program, which took people into the wilds for up to two weeks. During these treks or afterward, subjects reported experiencing a sense of peace and an ability to think more clearly; they also reported that just being in nature was more restorative than the physically challenging activities, such as rock climbing, for which such programs are mainly known.

Over time, the Kaplans developed their theory of directed-attention fatigue. As described in a paper by Stephen Kaplan and Raymond DeYoung: "Under continual demand our ability to direct our inhibitory processes tires. . . . This condition reduces mental effectiveness and makes consideration of abstract long-term goals difficult. A number of symptoms are commonly attributed to this fatigue: irritability and impulsivity that results in regrettable choices, impatience that has us making ill-formed decisions, and distractibility that allows the immediate environment to have a magnified effect on our behavioral choices."[8] The Kaplans hypothesize that the best antidote to such fatigue, which is brought on by too much directed attention, is involuntary attention, what they call "fascination," which occurs when we are in an environment that fulfills certain criteria: the setting must transport the person away from their day-to-day routine, provide a sense of fascination, a feeling of extent (enough available space to allow exploration), and some compatibility with a person's expectations for the environment being explored. Furthermore, they have found that the natural world is a particularly effective place for the human brain to overcome mental fatigue, to be restored.

The Kaplans' work suggests that nature simultaneously calms and focuses the mind, and at the same time offers a state that transcends relaxation, allowing the mind to detect patterns that it would otherwise miss. Yes, some people might achieve a similar state while walking the streets of New York, or through advanced meditation, or perhaps someday from a pill. The natural world, though, offers its own supplements. "Our work has focused on the many ways in which nearby nature, whether experienced directly or indirectly, can contribute to well-being," says Rachel Kaplan. "Tending houseplants, the view of a tree from the window, gardening, street trees, planters with flowers at bus stops . . . there are so many ways in which the natural world may benefit people."

Subsequent research supported the Kaplans' findings. The researchers Marlis Mang and Terry Hartig, at the University of California–Irvine, compared three groups of backpacking enthusiasts. One group went on a wilderness-backpacking trip and showed improved proofreading performance, while those who went on an urban vacation or took no vacation showed no improvement in this task.[9] At the University of Michigan, researchers demonstrated that participants' memory performance, and attention spans improved by 20 percent after just an hour of interacting with nature, according to results published in *Psychological Science* in 2008.[10] Marc Berman, a psychologist at the University of Michigan, and lead author of the study commented: "People don't have to enjoy the walk to get the benefits. We found the same benefits when it was 80 degrees and sunny over the summer as when the temperatures dropped to 25 degrees in January. The only difference was that participants enjoyed the walks more in the spring and summer than in the dead of winter."

Meanwhile, at the Human-Environment Research Laboratory at the University of Illinois, researchers have discovered that children show a significant reduction in the symptoms of attention-deficit disorder when they engage with nature.[11] Since grown-ups can exhibit the symptoms of attention-deficit disorder, too, one might speculate that this research is also relevant to the lives of adults.

Most research on how nature experience can improve learning has been conducted with young people. But nature-smart education appears to work for everyone involved, including the teachers. A Canadian study showed that greening school grounds not only improved academic performance of students; it also lowered exposure to toxins and increased teachers' enthusiasm for being teachers, in part due to fewer classroom discipline problems.[12]

Schools with greened grounds experience reduced absenteeism.

School gardening can improve students' learning and behavior; students participating in gardening had improved school attitude and teamwork and expanded learning opportunities. Natural views from high schools can positively impact students' academic achievement and behavior. A study that investigated 101 public high schools in Michigan found that students in schools with larger windows and more views of nearby nature—from classrooms, lunchrooms, and outdoor eating areas—had both higher standardized test scores and higher graduation rates, and a greater percentage of those students planned to attend college. (There were also fewer reports of criminal behavior.)[13] Real field trips offer better learning environments than virtual field trips. This isn't to say virtual field trips (via webcams, for example) aren't useful, but a real field trip provides a chance for students to use all their senses, spontaneity, and instigative learning—what the researchers called a superior learning environment that goes beyond specific curriculum-based learning.[14] So-called at-risk students who have not had much experience in nature show a marked improvement of 27 percent in test scores, related to mastery of science, when they learn in weeklong residential outdoor education programs. They also showed enhanced cooperation and conflict-resolution skills; gains in self-esteem; gains in positive environmental behavior; and improvements in problem solving, motivation to learn, and classroom behavior.[15] Typically, these studies controlled for socioeconomic status, racial/ethnic makeup, building age, and size of enrollment.

More research is needed on adult learning, but the studies and theories related to the young are relevant in any discussion of intelligence, no matter what the age of the student.[16]

Got dirt? A study conducted by Dorothy Matthews and Susan Jenks at the Sage Colleges in Troy, New York, has found that a bacterium given to mice helped them navigate a maze twice as fast. The bacterium in question is *Mycobacterium vaccae*, a natural soil bacterium commonly ingested or inhaled when people spend time in nature. The effect wore off in a few days, but, Matthews said, the research suggests that *M. vaccae* may play a role in learning in mammals. She speculated that creating outdoor learning environments where *M. vaccae* is present may "improve the ability to learn new tasks."[17] Smart pill, meet smart bug.

Even if the bacteria research turns out to be on the mark, don't expect anyone to start handing out smart bugs in the classroom or the boardroom. But, whether conducted on adults or children, the growing body of research associating learning ability with time spent in nature does have implications for teaching methods at all levels, as well as implications for the design of school grounds and buildings. This thinking extends to colleges and universities, and to how educational institutions and businesses might offer extended or continuing education programs. One can imagine a nature-based trend in education that would rival the explosion of high-tech virtual education. This research also suggests that individuals can proceed on their own to gain a natural intellectual and creative advantage by tapping into nature.

Still, most people need a little help from their friends to sharpen their minds in nature. Jon Young, a longtime wilderness-tracking teacher, works with adults and children in the Bay Area through the Regenerative Design Institute in Bolinas, California. "You almost never find one person being connected to nature and the whole community not being connected to nature," he says. "There are cultural practices that get the whole community involved in what amounts to 'nature-connection practice.'" He works with up to two hundred adults a year, teaching them how to become nature-connection mentors. In his courses, Young applies the methods outlined in *Coyote's Guide to Connecting with Nature*, a book he coauthored with Ellen Haas and Evan McGown. Among the exercises and rituals: body radar, the six arts of tracking, mapping, mind's eye imagining, listening for bird language, and plant concentration. His school teaches navigation skills, the awareness of time of day, understanding that certain birds have returned from their migration, the anticipation of seasonal change, knowing where the mushrooms are going to pop up on the hillside because of the rain patterns. "All that is deeply embedded in our—can I call it software? I hate to use that analogy. It's the operating system our hardware is designed to run with, if you will. . . . And when we are connected to nature, all those functions turn on by themselves. We play outside, we track, we wander around. And a couple months into it, there's a light that turns on in their eyes and they suddenly say, 'Ah, this is great. I haven't felt this way since I was nine.' It's as if there's some sort of neurological phenomenon happening when that reawakening happens. Some adults feel guilty about that; they think learning has to hurt. The educational systems that we are used to are about information transfer." If that approach is used exclusively, people tend to hold the information in their short-term memory, bring it out for a test, "and then they let it go—it's not going to fill the memory banks long-term." At the other end of the spectrum of learning environments is what Young calls "full connection." He offers this example: "An eleven-year-old girl who has made a deep connection with a horse can tell you an extraordinary amount of information about horses, and she won't even know where it's coming from. She'll be able to tell you this information through animated, engaging storytelling. I always remind people that if we do nature connection effectively, the information will come along for the ride."

The word *intelligence* gives Young pause. "I think of the nature connection as more nutritive, in an emotional, intellectual, spiritual sense. It's such a profoundly deep part of who we are as human beings, and our potential." Thus, Young wonders if we're talking about intelligence or something he would call innate awareness. "Intelligence may be in the context of this larger awareness, a subset of a larger perceptual body. It's the big container, larger than the collection of intelligences. It's the background system."

Natural Creativity—Because Man Does Not Live by Dread Alone

Creative genius is not the accumulation of knowledge; it is the ability to see patterns in the universe, to detect hidden links between what is and what could be. *To connect the dots*, as Celso Montalvo from the Galapagos school put it. Ralph Waldo Emerson, in a speech at Henry David Thoreau's funeral service, described his friend's many talents: "He was a good swimmer, runner, skater, boatman, and would probably out-walk most countrymen in a day's journey. . . . The length of his walk uniformly made the length of his writing. If shut up in the house he did not write at all."[18] These walks not only stimulated his creativity, but had practical, day-to-day application: Thoreau's outdoor experiences made him a sought-after land surveyor; he could not only outline boundaries with exactitude, but could explain the ecological workings of an area in great detail. An amateur stream-watcher and river-gazer, he knew the secrets of local waters long before professional hydrologists took their measures.

When NPR commentator John Hockenberry reported the research that revealed greater mental acuity after a nature walk, he pointed out that Albert Einstein and the mathematician and philosopher Kurt Gödel, "two of the most brilliant people who ever walked the face of the earth, used to famously, every single day, take walks in the woods on the Princeton campus." Well, we're not all Einsteins. But we've all experienced that *eureka* moment when the brain is relaxed in a positive state.

As with the studies of learning ability, most research on the relationship between nature experiences and creativity involves young people. In 2006, for example, a Danish study found that outdoor kindergartens were better than indoor schools at stimulating children's creativity. The researchers reported that 58 percent of children who were in close touch with nature often invented new games; just 16 percent of indoor kindergarten children did.[19] One explanation, for adults as well as children, is suggested by the "loose parts theory" in education, which holds that the more loose parts there are in an environment, the more creative the play. A computer game has plenty of loose parts, in the form of programming code, but the number and the interaction of those parts is limited by the mind of the human who created the game. In a tree, a woods, a field, a mountain, a ravine, a vacant lot, the number of loose parts is unlimited. It's possible, then, that exposure to the loose but related parts of nature can encourage a greater sensitivity to patterns that underlie all experience, all matter, and all that matters.

In 1977, the late Edith Cobb, a noted proponent of nature-based education, contended that geniuses share one trait: transcendent experience in nature in their early years.[20] Environmental psychologist Louise Chawla of the University of Colorado offers a broader view. "Nature isn't only important to future geniuses," she says. Her work explores "ecstatic places." She uses the word *ecstatic* carefully. Rather than applying the contemporary definition of delight or rapture, she prefers the word's ancient Greek roots—*ek stasis*—meaning "outstanding" or "standing outside ourselves." These ecstatic moments are "radioactive jewels buried within us, emitting energy across the years of our lives," as Chawla puts it. Such moments are often experienced during formative years. But, because of the brain's plasticity, and individual sensitivities, they can happen throughout life.

And so can the creation of new neurons, the brain cells that process and transmit information. It's reasonable to speculate, then, that time spent in the natural world, by both restoring and stimulating the brain, may lead to bursts of new neurons—"nature neurons," as my wife puts it.

Time awareness may also be a factor. As noted in the report "Healthy Parks, Healthy People," issued by the Deakin University School of Health and Social Development, in Melbourne, Australia:

"City life is dominated by mechanical time (punctuality, deadlines, etc.) yet our bodies and minds are dominated by biological time." We know that conflict between biological and mechanical time—jet lag comes to mind—can lead to irritability, restlessness, depression, insomnia, tension, and headaches. In addition, "the experience of nature in a neurological sense can help strengthen the activities of the right hemisphere of the brain, and restore harmony to the functions of the brain as a whole," the university report explains.[21] "This is perhaps a technical explanation of the process that occurs when people 'clear their head' by going for a walk in a park. . . . Furthermore, in the act of contemplating nature, researchers have found that the brain is relieved of 'excess' circulation (or activity), and nervous system activity is also reduced."[22]

Whatever the process, creative people are often aware of being drawn to the outdoors for refreshment and ideas. "I always work outside, if I can. It's important to grab the instant thought," says writer Hilary Mantel, the 2009 winner of the prestigious Booker Prize.[23] American painter Richard C. Harrington continues in the tradition of artists who gain inspiration from being outdoors. He writes: "For me, to be removed from the environment, not to be outside on a regular basis, leaves me stressed, depressed, and generally unhappy."[24]

Sculptor David Eisenhour, who is in his fifties, lives in a small town in Washington State. I met him one day in 2009 at the other side of the continent, at the Chautauqua Festival in upstate New York, where his art was featured. As a boy, he lived in a trailer with his father in a northern Pennsylvania farming community. He spent most of his free time in the wild, but he also kept aquariums filled with frogs, fish, crayfish, and insects. A good microscope took him deep into another world. Today, his cast-metal pieces express natural forms that seem familiar, yet his inspiration often comes from objects or creatures so small they escape notice. Lichens or beetles take on surprising shapes in his hands. His Chautauqua display was a large and unlikely sculpture of a dung beetle's helmet; it looked rather like a Triceratops, and it was beautiful. As he sat on a rock wall near the display, he talked about the link between nature and inspiration.

"The reason my career seems to be progressing is that the imagery I'm doing isn't sentimental but it is very organic and very primordial looking. It's coming into its time because people are wanting this connection to the natural world. It opens up that childhood fascination again," he said. "I search for the imagery that, on a macro- or a microscopic level, is repeated. You're looking more at the building blocks of life. Somewhere in our simian brain, subconscious, we have all that information. We've just lost access to it . . . the fact that the spiral of a snail shell and the spiral of the Milky Way galaxy are the same thing."

But the main reason he chooses this imagery, he says, is because "being in nature quiets my mind and out of that quietness is where the real art happens."

In the summer of 2009, several colleagues and I were invited to actor Val Kilmer's Pecos River Ranch, in New Mexico, to speak with him about his plans to create a sort of art museum/creativity center on his property. What struck me most during the visit was not the actor's vision, but a small black-and-white photograph on the fireplace mantel. The image was of a thunderhead above water. Under it, in Kilmer's cramped handwriting, was this inscription written for his son: "Inspiration is confirmation . . . xox Dad." In the bottom corner of the photo, he added a P.S. *"But if you ever run out of ideas, just go outside."*

Hybrid Thinking

One more thought before we move on to physical and emotional health. While still considering the arena of nature and intelligence, let's punch some holes in the false dichotomy of nature and technology.

When my sons were growing up, they spent a lot of time outdoors, but they also played plenty of video games—more than I was comfortable with. Every now and then, Jason and Matthew would try to convince me that their generation was making an evolutionary leap; because they spent so much time texting, video-gaming, and so forth, they were wired differently. In response, I pointed out that my generation had said something similar about drugs, and that didn't work out so well. Chances are, neither will electronic addiction, which is why the nature balance is so necessary. What's different now is not the presence of technology, but the pace of change—the rapidity of the introduction of new media and adoption of new electronic devices.

Gary Small, a neuroscientist at the University of California–Los Angeles, suggests that the pace of technological change is creating what he calls a "brain gap" between the generations. "Perhaps not since early man first discovered how to use a tool has the human brain been affected so quickly and so dramatically," he writes in his book, *iBrain: Surviving the Technological Alteration of the Modern Mind.*[25]

If Small is right, then my response to my sons—that evolution doesn't work that fast—may be overstated.

Small and his colleagues used MRI imaging to study the dorsolateral area of the prefrontal cortex, which integrates complex information and short-term memory and is instrumental in decision making.[26] Two groups were tested: experienced, or "savvy," computer users; and inexperienced, or "naïve" users. While doing Web searches, the savvy users' dorsolateral area was quite active, while in the naïve users, the dorsolateral area was quiet. As the Canadian magazine *Macleans* reported: "On day five, the savvy group's brain looked more or less the same. But in the naïve group, something amazing had happened: as they searched, their circuitry sprang to life, flashing and thundering in exactly the same way it did in their tech-trained counterparts."[27] After this short period of time, had the naïve subjects "already rewired their brains?" People over thirty, whose brains were fully formed when they first came to the Web, can also become proficient in the virtual universe. But teenagers' brains are particularly malleable, more apt to be shaped by technological experience.

One view is that people who experience too much technology in the formative years will stunt the maturation of normal frontal lobe development, "ultimately freezing them in teen brain mode," as *Macleans* puts it. "Are we developing a generation with underdeveloped frontal lobes, unable to learn, remember, feel, control impulses?" Small writes. "Or will they develop new advanced skills that poise them for extraordinary experiences?"[28]

Optimistic researchers suggest that all this multitasking and texting is creating the smartest generation ever, freed from the limitations of geography, weather, and distance—all those pesky inconveniences of the physical world. But Mark Bauerlein, an English professor at Emory University, in his book, *The Dumbest Generation*, reels out studies comparing this generation of students with prior generations, finding that "they don't know any more history or civics, economics or science, literature or current events" despite all that available information.

Here is a third possibility: We may be developing a hybrid mind. The ultimate multitasking will be to live simultaneously in both the digital and the physical world, using computers to maximize our powers to process intellectual data and natural environments to ignite all of our senses and accelerate our ability to learn and to feel; in this way, we could combine the "primitive" powers of our ancestors with the digital speed of our teenagers.

Evolution may (or may not) be out of our hands, but as individuals we can accept and celebrate our technological skills at the same time that we seek the gifts of nature essential for the realization of our full intellectual and spiritual potential.

The best preparation for the twenty-first century may be a combination of natural and virtual experience. An instructor who trains young people to become the pilots of cruise ships describes "two kinds of students, those who are good at video games, who are terrific with the electronic steering; and those who grew up outside—they're far better at having a special sense of where the ship is. We tend to get one or the other kind." The ideal pilot, he says, is the person who has a balance of high-tech and natural knowledge: "We need people who have *both* ways of knowing the world." In other words, a hybrid mind.

New strategies of personal discipline will be required to integrate or toggle between these seemingly incompatible ways of being in the world. Perhaps a fifteen-year-old can begin to show us the way.

On his LinkedIn page, Spencer Schoeben describes himself as "Marketing Manager at Teens in Tech Networks; Founder, Chief Site Architect at Twitloc; Web Developer at Cassy Bay Area; Webmaster, Social Media Editor at Paly Voice; and Founder of Netspencer (Self-employed)." A full tech plate. He also does time as a student at Palo Alto High School. Schoeben expresses pride in his knowledge of the computer world, and he sees the plusses of living "a life of connectivity," as he puts it, on his Web site. "No matter where I am, no matter what I am doing, everything and everyone that I care about is at my fingertips." But he also describes the impact of two weeks of summer camp at Hidden Villa, a nonprofit educational organization with an organic farm and native vegetation in the foothills of the Santa Cruz Mountains south of San Francisco. He writes that he wasn't keen on going to Hidden Villa, at first. "I was thinking about how hard it would be for me to survive without an Internet connection." But off to camp he went, where he "made French fries from potatoes which we picked and I even walked a goat through the woods. It turned out okay. Actually, it turned out amazing. I couldn't believe that I had done it." And he learned that there are "thousands and thousands of species of trees and plants and animals that don't use an ounce of electricity."

When he got home, he went straight to his room and grabbed his laptop and paged through twelve days of e-mail and Facebook notifications. "But I just didn't care. What I really wanted to do was go outside and have fun in the real world." Perhaps the best way to live, he realized, "is in the middle." He can remain passionate about technology — "There is no use ditching it" — but the Internet is not the universe.

"It's hard to realize how isolated your life can be . . . until you experience what it's like to live on the other side."

Spencer has a new map for his life. At least for now, he intends to balance the technological world with experience in that world of natural connections. In pursuit of that hybrid experience, he quotes Carl Sagan: "Somewhere, something incredible is waiting to be known."

PART TWO

Vitamin N

Tapping the Power of the Natural World

for our Physical, Emotional, and Family Fitness

We need the tonic of wilderness.

—Henry David Thoreau

CHAPTER 3

The Garden

MEMORIES ARE SEEDS. When I was a boy, the good times in my family were, more often than not, associated with nature—with fishing trips, discovered snakes and captured frogs, with dark water touched by stars.

We lived at the edge of the suburbs, in Raytown, Missouri. At the end of our backyard, cornfields began, and then came the woods and then more farms that seemed to go on forever. Every summer I ran through the fields with my collie, elbowing the forest of whipping stalks and leaves, to dig my underground forts and climb into the arms of an oak that had outlived Jesse James. When the corn harvest was over, my father and I would walk through the stubble and search for the ground nests and speckled eggs of killdeer. Together, we watched with admiration as the parents attempted, with tragic cries and faked broken wings, to lead us away from their nests.

I recall my father's dark tanned neck, creased with lines of dust, as he tilled our garden. I ran ahead of him, pulling rocks and bones and toys from his path. My father, mother, little brother, and I planted strawberry starts and buried seeds for butternut squash and our own sweet corn. One year, my father read about the productivity of Swiss chard and, as was his way, became fully committed. That summer we bagged Swiss chard for weeks. Our kitchen and part of our basement overflowed with it. My mother canned it. I carried brown shopping bags full of chard to the neighbors. My mother loved to tell the story about the summer the Swiss Chard Ate the Neighborhood.

Controlled by no community association, our yard was humbled by locusts and heat and other natural covenants. With all my senses, I recall a late afternoon when my father and mother and my brother and I raced the weather to complete the construction of a retaining wall for sod and garden. We placed limestone slabs into a line to hold back erosion. We felt the wind quicken and the air change, and stood up together near the end; we wiped sweat from our foreheads and stared at the quilted pea-green sky, felt a queasy stillness and sudden burst of wind, and then we saw the hail advancing yard to yard like an invading army. We rushed to the basement door.

Such moments became part of the family lore, because our time in the garden and on the water and in the woods held our family together.

After a while, my father, who worked as a chemical engineer, earned more money and ventured out of the house less. The garden faded, replaced by Kentucky bluegrass sod. Neighbors erected chain-link fences. Our collie no longer ran free, and neither did we. Instead of Swiss chard and uneven bumps of earth for pumpkins and squash, the yard became ordered and lined with evenly spaced shrubs. Instead of planting vegetables we pulled dandelions, eliminated the variances, enforced order. The summer sun came to feel oppressive. My mother told the story of the Swiss chard on fewer occasions, and then not at all. The garden became a dim memory. We moved to a larger house.

While I was away at college, the job market for chemical engineers dried up. My father had always dreamt of retirement, of moving to the Ozarks. He believed that once there, he would fish all day and plant a large garden. So he and my mother and brother moved to the mountains of southern Missouri, to Table Rock Lake. By then, however, my father was spending most of his hours at the kitchen table, staring. He caught few fish. He planted no garden. He and my mother moved back to the suburbs.

A dozen years later, as I sat in the desk chair where he had taken his own life, I opened a drawer. There, I found a handwritten document titled "accounts due." It was a bitter ledger of his days, a reduction of our family into numbers, but tucked into those paragraphs was a sentence that mentioned a good period of his life — what he called his "one brief Eden."

I looked at the sentence for a while. I knew when that was.

I am now older than my father was when he died. My life and writing have been shaped by that time at the edge of the cornfields. Sometimes it seems to me that what happened to my father — the disappearance of nature in his life and his descent into illness — parallels the life of our culture, as children's freedom to roam has diminished, as families have pulled inward, as nature has become an abstraction. I understand that this equation is incomplete. Which came first, the illness or the withdrawal from nature? I honestly don't know the answer to that question. But I often wonder what my father's life would have been like if the vernacular of mental health therapy had extended beyond Thorazine and Quaaludes and into the realm of nature therapy.

As a boy, I must have sensed nature's power to heal. As I watched my father withdraw, I wished that he would quit his job as an engineer and become a forest ranger. Somehow I believed that if he were to do that, then he would be all right, and we would be all right. I realize now, of course, that nature alone would not have cured him, but I have no doubt it would have helped.

Perhaps these childhood experiences are why, as an adult, I am compelled to believe in the restorative power of nature, in a human/nature reunion. And that because of this reunion, life will be better.

CHAPTER 4

Fountains of Life

The Mind/Body/Nature Connection

TIME SPENT IN the natural world can help build our physical, emotional, and family fitness. The mind/body connection, of course, is a familiar concept, but research and common sense suggest a new container: the *mind/body/nature* connection.

Over two thousand years ago, Chinese Taoists created gardens and greenhouses to improve human health. In 1699, the book *English Gardener* advised the reader to spend "spare time in the garden, either digging, setting out, or weeding; there is no better way to preserve your health." And a century ago, John Muir observed that: "Thousands of tired, nerve-shaken, over-civilized people are beginning to find out that going to the mountains is going home; that wilderness is a necessity; and that mountain parks and reservations are useful not only as fountains of timber and irrigating rivers, but as fountains of life."[1]

Today, the long-held belief that nature has a direct positive impact on human health is making the transition from theory to evidence and from evidence to action. Certain findings have become so convincing that some mainstream health care providers and organizations have begun to promote nature therapy for an array of illnesses and for disease prevention. And many of us, without having a name for it, are using the nature tonic. We are, in essence, self-medicating with an inexpensive and unusually convenient drug substitute. Let's call it vitamin N—for Nature.[2]

New research supports the contention that nature therapy helps control pain and negative stress; and for people with heart disease,[3] dementia,[4] and other health issues, the nature prescription has benefits that may go beyond the predictable results of outdoor exercise.[5] The restorative power of the natural world can help us heal, even at a relative distance. On the surgical floors of a two-hundred-bed suburban Pennsylvania hospital, some rooms faced a stand of deciduous trees, while others faced a brown brick wall. Researchers found that, compared to patients with brick views, patients in rooms with tree views had shorter hospitalizations (on average, by almost one full day), less need for pain medications, and fewer negative comments in the nurses' notes.[6] In another study, patients undergoing bronchoscopy (a procedure that involves inserting a fiber-optic tube into the lungs) were randomly assigned to receive either sedation, or sedation plus nature contact—in this case, a mural of a mountain stream in a spring meadow and a continuous tape of complementary nature sounds (e.g., water in a stream or birds chirping). The patients with nature contact had substantially better pain control.[7]

Nearby nature can be an antidote to obesity. A 2008 study published in *American Journal of Preventive Medicine* found that the greener the neighborhood, the lower the Body Mass Index of children. "Our new study of over 3,800 inner city children revealed that living in areas with green space has a long term positive impact on children's weight and thus health," according to senior author Gilbert C. Liu, MD. While the investigation didn't prove a direct cause-and-effect, it did control for many variables, including the neighborhood's population density. The results support those who believe that changing the built environment for inner-city kids is just as important as attempts to change family behavior.[8]

While it's true that too much exposure to sunshine can lead to melanoma, too little time outside can also have a negative health impact. According to one study, as many as three-quarters of U.S. teens and adults are deficient in vitamin D, which is obtained naturally from sunshine and some foods, or supplements. African Americans are especially at risk, one researcher explains in *Scientific American*, because "they have more melanin or pigment in their skin that makes it harder for the body to absorb and use the sun's ultraviolet rays to synthesize vitamin D."[9] Some scientists question the percentage of people who may be at risk (which may be closer to half than three-quarters), but there is agreement that vitamin D blood levels are dropping and that deficiency is associated with a large number of health problems, including cancers, arterial stiffness in African American teens, type 2 diabetes, lower mood levels during winter, decreased physical strength in young people, and decreased lung function for children with asthma. Vitamin D also has been found beneficial in reducing risk for some infectious diseases, autoimmune diseases, fractures, and periodontal disease.

More research has been conducted on the impact of nature time on mental health than on physical health; the two arenas (along with mental acuity) are interrelated. The science isn't all in, and available evidence is not entirely consistent. Much of it is correlative, not causal. However, an honest reading of the science can yield cautious conclusions.

Several reports, including a thorough literature review by researchers at Deakin University in Melbourne, Australia, chart what is known.[10] According to the Deakin review, each of the following health benefits, among others, is supported by anecdotal, theoretical, and empirical research:

- Exposure to natural environments, such as parks, enhances the ability to cope with and recover from stress and recover from illness and injury.[11]

- Established methods of nature-based therapy (including wilderness, horticultural, and animal-assisted therapy) have success healing patients who previously had not responded to treatment of some emotional or physical ailments.[12]
- People have a more positive outlook on life and higher life satisfaction when in proximity to nature, particularly in urban areas.[13]

Outdoor Immunity

In 2007, naturalist Robby Astrove and I were driving through West Palm Beach, Florida, on our way to an event promoting the preservation of the Everglades. He told me: "As a kid, I was always glued to the car window, taking notice. I still do this and must sit in a window seat when flying. Looking back, it's no wonder I'm a naturalist, having trained my senses to detail, patterns, images, sounds, and feelings." In fifth grade, a school field trip to the Everglades led to his career choice. After college, he surveyed hundreds of miles of the Everglades. As an educator, he has taken thousands of students to the Everglades, to learn about the great river of grass, the threats to it, and its recovery. In 1979, when he was fifteen, Astrove was diagnosed with HIV and hepatitis C, which he contracted from three life-saving blood transfusions for a staph infection that had spread from a blister on his thumb. Following the blood test that revealed HIV, he was called into the doctor's office. He found his parents in tears. "The doc sat me down and shared the news. My first words were, 'What are we going to do now?'"

During the ensuing years, he found himself drawn, more and more, to the river of grass. "It's hard to explain, but acknowledging the cycles, patterns, and interconnectedness of the world has provided healing to me," he said. "Sometimes I awake in the middle of the night and find myself putting on boots, grabbing a raincoat and collection containers. I don't question actions like that. I'm excited to hike in the dark not knowing what I'll find. It might not be until I hear the call of a barred owl that I realize why I came. Or seeing a familiar tree that I've studied a million times during the day that reveals something new at night. I go because I trust my instincts, have patience, and allow for things to happen. Well, there's luck, too. But the same trust and instinct is required to manage a disease. When I haven't gotten enough nature time, my body tells me. I listen."

Astrove, who is attending Emory University to study international public health, finds HIV biologically fascinating. "It's able to reproduce rapidly and can mutate, always creating the demand for new medicines. In a weird way, HIV is elegant, beautiful. I understand what this monster is capable of, so I establish limits. Not staying out too late, eating healthy, not ever smoking." Avoiding these behaviors as a teenager was difficult for him, but respect for the virus trumped peer pressure. "Nature is always making adaptations, so why can't I do the same? I listen. When I hear 'rest,' I rest. When I see macroinvertebrates in a stream indicating clean water, that reminds me to pay attention to indicators for my own health. Stumbling upon a rare plant reminds me of the uniqueness of my situation. No two people are the same in their response to a virus."

In his role as an educator, he teaches his students that wetlands serve as "nature's liver" and relates to the system personally. "The wetlands purify water and trap pollutants." He explains that the rain forests and other natural places are the source of many of our medicines, that spending time in that world reduces stress. "We feel good from the endorphin release it stimulates, and it inspires us. Inspiration is another giver of health. I go to the woods knowing I will receive healing. And the benefits come in the form of physical, psychological, and spiritual gains. It's a natural high sometimes when I get the feeling of light, energy, and awe." He looked out the truck window at the passing landscape as he drove. "Now that I've been taking meds for some time, sensitive blood tests can't find the virus; I test 'undetectable.'"

Does research give weight to Astrove's experience? Possibly. A study of 260 people in twenty-four sites across Japan found that, among people who gazed on forest scenery for twenty minutes, the average concentration of salivary cortisol, a stress hormone, was 13.4 percent lower than that of people in urban settings.[14] "Humans . . . lived in nature for 5 million years. We were made to fit a natural environment. . . . When we are exposed to nature, our bodies go back to how they should be," explained Yoshifumi Miyazaki, who conducted the study that reported the salivary cortisol connection. Miyazaki is director of the Center for Environment Health and Field Sciences at Chiba University and Japan's leading scholar on "forest medicine," an accepted health care concept in Japan, where it is sometimes called "forest bathing." In other research, Li Qing, a senior assistant professor of forest medicine at Nippon Medical School in Tokyo, found green exercise—physical movement in a natural setting—can increase the activity of natural killer (NK) cells. This effect can be maintained for as long as thirty days.[15] "When NK activity increases, immune strength is enhanced, which boosts resistance against stress," according to Li, who attributes the increase in NK activity partly to inhaling air containing phytoncides, antimicrobial essential wood oils given off by plants. Studies of this sort deserve closer scrutiny. For example, in the study of natural killer cells, there was no control group, so it is hard to say if the change was due to time off work, exercise, nature contact, or some combination of influences.

Nonetheless, for Astrove, wilderness has helped create a context for healing—and *may* have strengthened his immune system and offered protective properties that he, and the rest of us, do not yet fully understand.

Ghosts of Nature Past

Terry Hartig, currently professor of applied psychology at Sweden's Uppsala University, offers a cautionary note. He sometimes gets the impression "that what the 'nature' people have in mind, when they talk about nature and health, is a 'pasteurized' nature—no teeth, claws, or stingers, offering no demands." He also points out that by far the largest amount of research on nature and health concerns topics like infectious illnesses and natural catastrophes. "It's important to bear in mind that people have been working hard over thousands of years to protect themselves from the forces of nature," he says.

An important point. But here's another view. From the backyard to the backcountry, nature comes in many forms. The negative impacts of the risks that do occur in wilderness (from large predators, for example) should be balanced by the positive psychological benefits of that risk (humility, for one). And, yes, most research on nature and human health has focused on pathology and natural disasters, but this preference by researchers has something to do with where the research funding comes from. Researchers looking at the health *benefits* of nature are, in fact, addressing a knowledge imbalance.

Relating to Hartig's concern, science does have a difficult time defining how we perceive nature. A few years ago, I worked with a council of neuroscientists, experts on the childhood development of brain architecture. When asked how the natural world itself affects brain development, they would usually draw a blank. "How do you define nature?" they asked, rhetorically. However, these same scientists simulate "natural conditions" in their labs, for control groups. A friend of mine likes to say that nature is anything molecular, "including a guy drinking beer in a trailer park and a debutante drinking highballs in Manhattan." Technically, he's right. For the most part, we've left the definition of nature up to philosophers and poets. Gary Snyder, one of our finest contemporary poets, has written that we attach two meanings to the word, which comes from the Latin roots *natura* and *nasci*, both of which suggest birth.

Here's my definition of nature: Human beings exist in nature anywhere they experience meaningful kinship with other species. By this description, a natural environment may be found in wilderness or in a city; while not required to be pristine, this nature is influenced at least as much by a modicum of wildness and weather as by developers, scientists, beer drinkers, or debutantes. We know this nature when we see it.

And centuries of human experience do suggest that the tonic is more than a placebo. How, then, when it comes to health does the nature prescription work?

The answers may be hidden in our mitochondria. As hypothesized by Harvard's E. O. Wilson, biophilia[16] is our "innately emotional affiliation to . . . other living organisms."[17] His interpreters extended that definition to include natural landscape. Several decades of research inspired by Wilson's theory suggests that, at a level we do not fully understand, the human organism needs direct experience with nature.

Gordon H. Orians, a renowned ornithologist, behavioral ecologist, and professor emeritus in the Department of Biology at the University of Washington, maintains that our attraction to the natural environment exists at the level of our DNA, and, in its many genetic forms, haunts us. He points out that, between the first appearance of agriculture and this morning's breakfast, only about ten thousand years have elapsed. "The biological world, like the mental world of Ebenezer Scrooge, is replete with ghosts," he says. "There are ghosts of habitats, predators, parasites, competitors, mutualists, and conspecifics past, as well as ghosts of meteors, volcanic eruptions, hurricanes, and droughts past."[18] These ghosts may reside in our genetic attic, but sometimes they speak to us, whispering *the past is prologue.*

This view, based on behavioral ecology or sociobiology, has its critics, who are suspicious that such thinking evokes genetic predeterminism. In recent years, though, the proponents of biophilia and its doubters appear to have come to something approaching agreement: long-term genetics may lay down a likely pathway for brain development, but the outcome is also determined by the more *current* environment—by attachment to nurturing human beings, for example. Orians argues that all adaptations are to past environments. "They tell us about the past, not the present or the future. . . . As Ebenezer Scrooge discovered, ghosts, no matter how inconvenient they may seem to be, can yield positive benefits." He adds: "People have clearly intuitively understood the restorative value of interactions with nature for a long time." Witness the gardens of ancient Egypt, the walled gardens of Mesopotamia, the gardens of merchants in medieval Chinese cities, the American parks of Frederick Law Olmsted, or even the choices we make when picking sites for our homes and our visual responsiveness to certain landscapes. Orians and Judith Heerwagen, a Seattle-based environmental psychologist, spent years surveying people around the world, testing their preference for different images. The researchers found that, regardless of culture, people gravitate to images of nature, especially the savanna, with its clusters of trees, horizontal canopies, distant views, flowers, water, and changing elevations.

Another explorer of human biophilic tendencies, Roger S. Ulrich, professor of landscape architecture and urban planning at Texas A&M University, proposed his psychophysiological stress recovery theory in 1983, suggesting that our responses to stress are located in the limbic system, which generates survival reflexes. Citing Ulrich, physician William Bird, an honorary professor at Oxford University and chief health adviser for Natural England, the British government's environmental arm, explains: "The fight or flight reflex is a normal response to stress caused by the release of catecholamines (including adrenaline) and results in muscle tension, raised blood pressure, faster pulse, diversion of blood away from the skin to muscle and sweating. All of these factors help the body to cope with a dangerous situation. However, without rapid recovery this stress response would cause damage and exhaustion with limited response to a repeat dangerous situation."[19] Evolution favored our distant ancestors who could recover from the stress of natural threats by using the restorative powers of nature.

One of the best explanations I have heard for this process came from the late Elaine Brooks, a California educator who worked for years as a biologist at the Scripps Institution of Oceanography. In *Last Child in the Woods*, I described how Brooks would often climb to the highest knoll in the last natural open space of La Jolla. She told me how, particularly in times of personal stress, she would imagine herself as her own distant ancestor, high in a tree, recovering from the threat of some predator. At those times, she would look out over the rooftops — which she would imagine to be the open plains of savanna — to the sea. She would feel her breath slow and her heart ease. "Once our ancestors climbed high in that tree, there was something about looking out over the land — something that healed us quickly. Resting in those high branches may have provided a rapid comedown from the adrenaline rush of being potential prey," she told me one day, as we walked that land. "We are still programmed to fight or flee large animals. Genetically, we are essentially the same creatures as we were at the beginning. Our ancestors couldn't outrun a lion, but we did have wits. We knew how to kill, yes, but we also knew how to run and climb — and how to use the environment to recover our wits." She went on to describe modern life: how today we find ourselves continually on the alert, chased, as she put it, by an unending stampede of two-thousand-pound automobiles and four-thousand-pound SUVs. Inside our workplaces and homes, the assault continues: threatening images charge through the television cable into our bedrooms. Probably, at the cellular level, we have inherited the efficient antidote to all of this: sitting on that knoll, as Brooks did.

It should be added here that there are many contexts in which nature can offset toxic stress that may entail no physical danger. Short, quiet encounters with natural elements can simply calm us and help us feel less alone.

CHAPTER 5

Re-naturing the Psyche

Applying the Nature Principle to Our Mental Health

A s DIRECTOR OF the Golden Gate Raptor Observatory, Allen Fish teaches raptor migration study and wildlife monitoring. Ninety percent of his work is with adults, the hundreds of volunteers who count, band, and track hawks.

"Many of our volunteers hang on for five or more years. Their raptor work becomes deeply therapeutic in their urban lives," he says. "I have heard stories of self-healing here that would make a therapist tear up: of manic depression, of abuse, of chemical dependency. The strength that these people bring to their resolve to connect with nature is utterly stirring. And I have heard this line dozens of times: 'I thought I had to give up nature to become an adult.'"

Nothing could be further from the truth. To find hope, meaning, and relief from emotional pain, our species embraces meditation, medication, merlot, and more. These methods work for a time, some longer than others, some quite well, and some to our detriment. But the restorative power of nature is there, always. "We gain life by looking at life." Those are the words of Dr. Mardie Townsend, an associate professor in the School of Health and Social Development at Deakin University in Victoria, Australia. "If we see living things, we don't feel as if we're living in a vacuum."[1] Spending time in natural settings is no panacea; it's not a total replacement for other forms of professional therapy or self-healing, but it can be a powerful tool in maintaining or improving mental health.

Nancy Herron, of Austin, Texas, has been married thirty-one years, and has two grown sons. She has worked as a volunteer director for a hospice and currently for Texas Parks and Wildlife. She describes herself as a type A overachiever. When her children were born, she took a break from full-time employment. When she returned to the workforce, she was eager to build her credibility and career. "But like any working mother, I still wanted to do the best for my children, my husband, my friends, family, and neighbors. I would work myself into a frenzy, not knowing how to stop. I lost sleep, worried way too much — we all know the drill."

That's when she started going camping again. As therapy, it worked. "You plan for just your most basic needs. You see wildlife taking care of its most basic needs. It reminded me that life asks very little of us. Eat, sleep, procreate — there really aren't too many actual demands on us. So what the heck was I doing? All those details that were worrying me, raising my blood pressure, choking the life out of me, had nothing to do with life, really. Being outside made it all crystal clear to me. Just live. When we're dead and gone, most of it really doesn't matter. We just made it up. Nature reminds me how simple and achievable life really is. When I start sweating the small stuff, I get back outdoors and remind myself about what really matters." And perfection, by the standard definition, does not matter.

As one father, who had been through a painful divorce, told me: "Sometimes I get out in nature to get a little exercise and loosen up the muscles, especially after having spent an inordinate amount of time in front of the computer or in meetings. But, more frequently, it is the need for psychological restoration that draws me to nature. It never fails, literally, to make me feel better — about myself, my life, my work, my family. It makes me a more creative and generous person."

The exercise itself helps ward off mental fatigue, of course. But he also recognizes that nature offers added value to his exercise. He turns to nature to heal the "emotional wounds that life can inflict." Shortly after moving to San Diego, he received a phone call from his first wife, "in which she told me she would probably not be following me back to California after all and, moreover, she wasn't really sure if she still loved me." Within minutes of hanging up the phone, he was in his car on the way to the nearest park, Torrey Pines State Park, which he had never visited. "After hiking through the coastal sage scrub in full spring bloom," he recalls, "I found myself at the edge of some impressive, storm-eroded cliffs overlooking the Pacific Ocean. I admit that at the moment I felt like hurtling myself off those cliffs, but the desire to keep returning to places like this was partly responsible for keeping my boots on terra firma." Nature always moves on, and life usually finds a way.

People who work in jobs associated with nature are, unsurprisingly, predisposed to appreciate nature's tonic, and also are more likely to make use of it, particularly during times of crisis. "Nature is the ultimate antidepressant," says Dianne Thomas, director of a county fitness program in North Carolina, who has seen the impact of nature on people in her outdoor programs. Some mental health organizations are beginning to agree—to a degree. Natural environments do seem to offer something extra for mental health, a tonic that goes beyond the benefits of physical exercise alone.

Nature's Tonic for Mental Health

As with general health issues, the application of nature to mental health takes three basic forms: self-applied or professionally prescribed therapy; the impact of environmental degradation on human psyche and spirit; and the restoration of nature where we live, work, and play.

"There is growing . . . empirical evidence to show that exposure to nature brings substantial mental health benefits," according to "Green

Exercise and Green Care," a 2009 report by researchers at the Centre for Environment and Society at the University of Essex. "Our findings suggest that priority should be given to developing the use of green exercise as a therapeutic intervention (green care)."[2] In a study of more than 1,850 participants, these researchers reported three broad health outcomes from green exercise: improvement of psychological well-being (by enhancing mood and self-esteem, while reducing feelings of anger, confusion, depression, and tension); generation of physical health benefits (by reducing blood pressure and burning calories); and (as we'll discuss in later chapters) the building of social networks.

The researchers also examined people who took part in two walks, one in a country park around woodlands, grasslands, and lakes, and one in an indoor shopping center; both groups walked for the same amount of time. "Improvements in self-esteem and mood were significantly greater following the green outdoor walk in comparison to the equivalent indoor walk, especially for feelings of anger, depression and tension. After the green outdoor walk, 92 percent of participants felt less depressed; 86 percent less tense; 81 percent less angry; 80 percent less fatigued; 79 percent less confused and 56 percent more vigorous." Meanwhile, "depression increased for 22 percent of people and 33 percent expressed no change in their level of depression following the indoor shopping center walk."[3]

Similarly, researchers in Sweden have found that joggers who exercise in a natural green setting with trees, foliage, and landscape views, feel more restored and less anxious, angry, or depressed than people who burn the same amount of calories jogging in a built urban setting.[4] In other words, the benefits to mood can be attributed to exercise, which generally helps, but also to vitamin N. And the lack of it may well contribute to our susceptibility to depression.

How much nature is enough to make a difference in mental health? One study suggests that the benefits are felt almost immediately. Recent results published by Jules Pretty and Jo Barton of the University of Essex in the journal *Environmental Science and Technology* suggest a proper minimum dosage of vitamin N. "For the first time in the scientific literature, we have been able to show dose-response relationships for the positive effects of nature on human mental health," Pretty wrote. Mood and self-esteem improved after a five-minute dose. Blue-green exercise is even better; the study found that a walk in a natural area adjacent to water offered people the most improvement. Which is not to say five minutes a day is all we need of nature. The analysis of 1,252 people of different ages, gender, and mental health status was drawn from ten existing studies in the UK, and it found that people of all ages and social background benefited, but the greatest health changes occurred in the young and the mentally ill. "Exposure to nature via green exercise can thus be conceived of as a readily available therapy with no obvious side effects," according to the report.[5]

Even exposure to dirt may boost mood, along with the immune system. The research noting the positive effect of *Mycobacterium vaccae* on the ability of mice to run a maze also noted a reduction in anxiety. A separate study, conducted at Bristol University and reported in the journal *Neuroscience*, found that mice exposed to *M. vaccae*, the "friendly" bacteria normally found in soil, produced more serotonin.[6] A lack of serotonin is linked to depression in people, and common antidepressants work by increasing the production of this brain chemical. While the influence of serotonin has been questioned by some scientists, studies on the impact of *M. vaccae* "help us understand how the body communicates with the brain and why a healthy immune system is important for maintaining mental health," according to lead researcher Chris Lowry. "They also leave us wondering if we shouldn't all spend more time playing in the dirt."[7]

Our fellow animals can help, too. The majority of research about the impact of animals on human mental health has been conducted on domestic pets. The results are positive. Scientists have found, for example, that levels of neurochemicals and hormones associated with social bonding are elevated during animal-human interactions. A study of institutionalized middle-aged schizophrenia patients found that the presence of animals helped during therapeutic sessions and everyday life. And a Purdue University School of Nursing study found that people with Alzheimer's disease who were exposed to brightly colored fish in aquariums had improved behavior and eating habits. This knowledge has been put to good use.[8] Therapists have long used animal visits as therapy for loneliness among the elderly, and, more recently, to reduce anxiety in psychiatric patients. The formal use of animals for mental health treatment even has its own acronym: animal assisted therapy (AAT).

In 2008, results were announced from the first randomized controlled study of the therapeutic benefits of farm animals. The study, by researchers at the University of Oslo, in Norway, found that farm animals may be able to assist with therapy for such mental disorders as schizophrenia, affective disorders, anxiety, and personality disorders.[9] But what about wild animals? A 2005 study suggests that direct interaction with at least one wild species—dolphins—can reduce symptoms of mild to moderate depression.[10] As reported in the *British Medical Journal*, swimming with dolphins "was effective in alleviating symptoms of depression after two weeks of treatment." The researchers suggested that patients with mild or moderate depression might be able to reduce their use of antidepressants or conventional psychotherapy. Dolphin-assisted therapy has its critics—including those who question some of the research and those who object to what they consider the exploitation of dolphins. But the research, if it holds up over time, does link our mental health to our relationship with members of other species.[11]

So, while much of the existing research is specific to exercise in nature, accumulating evidence indicates how simply living and working in a natural or re-natured environment—whether our houses, hospitals, neighborhoods, or cities—can have a profound impact on our mental health. I'll return to this theme in later chapters, and the news here is hopeful. However, we need to address another link to mental health: the negative, sometimes devastating impact that comes from how humans damage or deny the natural world.

The Ecological Unconscious

The idea of an "ecological unconscious" now hovers above the crossroads of science, philosophy, and theology — the notion that all of nature is connected in ways that we do not fully understand. In his 1841 essay "The Over-Soul," Ralph Waldo Emerson wrote of "that great nature in which we rest, as the earth lies in the soft arms of the atmosphere; that Unity, that Over-soul, within which every man's particular being is contained and made one with all other; that common heart." The theory of an ecological unconsciousness, with antecedents in Transcendentalism, Buddhism, and Romanticism, is a stretch for science and even offensive to some religious folks. However, most people sense a rupture, as indicated by the many thousands of us still feeling a profound sense of loss because of environmental damage from the BP oil spill along the Gulf Coast of the United States, a disaster that reached across state lines and across species boundaries.

The American Psychiatric Association lists more than three hundred mental diseases in its *Diagnostic and Statistical Manual.* "Psychotherapists have exhaustively analyzed every form of dysfunctional family and social relations, but 'dysfunctional environmental relations' does not exist even as a concept," says social critic and author Theodore Roszak. As he notes, the *Diagnostic and Statistical Manual* "defines 'separation anxiety disorder' as 'excessive anxiety concerning separation from home and from those to whom the individual is attached.' But no separation is more pervasive in this Age of Anxiety than our disconnection from the natural world." It's time, he says, "for an environmentally based definition of mental health."

In *Last Child in the Woods*, I offered the hypothesis of nature-deficit disorder, which describes the human costs of alienation from nature. Other observers have put forward other names. Australian professor Glenn Albrecht, director of the Institute of Sustainability and Technology Policy at Murdoch University in Perth, Australia, has coined a term specific to mental health: solastalgia.[12] He combined the Latin word *solacium* (comfort, as in solace) and the Greek root *algia* (pain) to form solastalgia, which he defines as "the pain experienced when there is recognition that the place where one resides and that one loves is under immediate assault." Albrecht formed his theory and invented his neologism as he worked with communities disrupted by strip mining in New South Wales's Upper Hunter Region and with farmers in eastern Australia suffering from a devastating six-year-long drought. During a visit to western Australia, I met Albrecht, a tall, kind, shambling man, who later sent me the words of Wendy Bowman, ninety-three, who resisted the stripping of her land, and who felt anguish, solastalgia, as the destruction moved closer. He described her clenching her fist and saying, "I lost a lot of weight. I'd wake up in the middle of the night with my stomach like that."

In one instance, man caused the environmental destruction. In the other, the long drought was a natural event—unless global warming is to blame. That possibility is very much on the minds of Australians now. Albrecht asks: Could people's mental health be harmed by an array of shifts, including subtle changes of climate?

By any name, we endure this loss at a primal level. Humans living in landscapes that lack trees or other natural features undergo patterns of social, psychological, and physical breakdown that are strikingly similar to those observed in animals that have been deprived of their natural habitat. "In animals, what you see is increased aggression, disrupted parenting patterns, and disrupted social hierarchies," says Frances Kuo, a professor at the University of Illinois, who, with her colleagues, has studied the negative impact of de-natured life on human health and well-being. Among them, they have noted decreased civility, more aggression, more property crime, more loitering, more graffiti, and more litter, as well as less supervision of children outdoors. "We might call some of that 'soiling the nest,' which is not healthy," she says. "No organisms do that when they're in good shape. . . . In our studies, people with less access to nature show relatively poor attention or cognitive function, poor management of major life issues, poor impulse control."[13]

If Albrecht is right, and if climate change occurs at the rate that some scientists believe it will, and if human beings continue to crowd into de-natured cities, then solastalgia will contribute to a quickening spiral of mental illness.

As with nature-deficit disorder, solastalgia remains a hypothesis, theoretical, not an official diagnosis. But anecdotally, these and other hypotheses offer a way to identify the dissonance, this psychological and even physical pain that so many of us feel as we see the natural landscapes that we love replaced by strip mines and strip malls. The heartsickness is real. That reality does not mean that urban life is, by itself, intrinsically bad for human health. But the *kind* of life many of us are living, even in rural areas, is not supportive of optimal health and well-being.

"Therapy as If Nature Mattered"

In Santa Barbara, California, psychotherapist Linda Buzzell-Saltzman asks her adult patients to keep a daily journal. She reports that some of her clients realize that, other than walking to and from their cars, they spend less than fifteen to thirty minutes a day outside, in any setting, natural or not. She tells them they need to get out more, and in her care, they do. But first they have to recognize that spending time outdoors, while fun, is serious business. Buzzell-Saltzman, founder of the International Association for Ecotherapy, offers perhaps the most succinct current description of nature-based therapy. She describes ecotherapy as "the reinvention of psychotherapy as if nature mattered."[14] By whatever name, nature-guided therapy is entering mainstream psychology as the combination of urban pressures and loss of natural habitat create psychological problems that other forms of treatment seem inadequate to fully address.

As with nature therapy for physical illness, the therapeutic use of the natural world for mental health began centuries ago. The American mental health pioneer Dr. Benjamin Rush, whose signature appears on the Declaration of Independence, believed that "digging in the soil has a curative effect on the mentally ill." Beginning in the 1870s, the Quakers' Friends Hospital in Pennsylvania treated mental illness, in part, by providing patients with a greenhouse and acres of natural landscape. During World War II, psychiatry pioneer Karl Menninger launched a horticulture therapy movement in the Veterans Administration Hospital System.[15]

Today, Mind, the leading mental health charity for England and Wales, describes ecotherapy "as an important part of the future for mental health," according to Paul Farmer, Mind's chief executive. "It's a credible, clinically valid treatment option and needs to be prescribed by GPs, especially when for many people access to treatments other than antidepressants is extremely limited." Mind is not claiming that ecotherapy can replace drugs, but does suggest that the range of treatment approaches must be broadened. If ecotherapy were part of mainstream practice, "it could potentially help the millions of people across the country who are affected by mental distress," he added.[16] In a major report, Mind recommended what it called a new agenda for mental health services: "With a mass of new and growing evidence, Mind calls for ecotherapy to be recognized as a clinically valid frontline treatment for mental health problems."

The approach is not universally endorsed. Alan Kazdin, a former president of the American Psychological Association and a Yale professor of psychology and child psychiatry, has said, "Modern psychology is about what can be studied scientifically and verified. . . . There's a real spiritual looseness to what I'm seeing here."[17]

Nonetheless, professionals who use nature therapy in their practices generally report good results.

Marnie Burkman, MD, board-certified in both psychiatry and holistic medicine, who works as an outpatient adult psychiatrist for the Department of Veterans Affairs in Colorado, treats veterans of all ages. She says she is "awed at the powerful effect that nature has to promote healing." She tells the story of one patient, Al (name changed), a Vietnam vet, and a very angry man—angry at the government, angry at life, angry with himself. Al struggles with how to cope on a daily basis. Burkman describes one session when Al was ranting and venting his anger at everything, sitting forward with clenched fists, practically yelling. "To redirect him, I asked him, 'How do you cope? What helps you relax?' He paused, then started sharing about how he loves to ride his motorcycle alone into the mountains, and go camping." Al told Burkman about sitting under the stars, no one around, outside a mountain cabin, and how he would love to spend the rest of his days in such a setting. "What was striking to me as I watched him, is that within *seconds* of starting to share about riding into the mountains to be in nature, a total bodily transformation occurred in front of my eyes, unconscious to him," says Burkman. "A posture of clenched fists and sitting angrily forward, waving his arms as he talked at loud volume, transformed to him leaning back in his seat, stretching his legs out, arms clasped behind his head, smiling face—a posture of ease and relaxation. I have not seen any antianxiety medication work this quickly! Within seconds, from simply *imagining* nature, this profound change was catalyzed in his nervous system."

Burkman has seen this effect in other patients as well, particularly in those who had established a tender relationship with nature earlier in life. And she has noticed a stark contrast with those who have not had a relationship with nature, usually her younger patients: "When I have asked young veterans [often vets of the Iraq and Afghanistan conflicts] how they cope, many say, 'I don't know.' Or, they cope through alcohol, or television, or sometimes by exercising at the gym. However, even in people who cope through exercise at a gym, when they share of these modalities, I have never witnessed the distinct healing bodily change that is obvious in people who share their deep connection with nature."

Yusuf Burgess (he prefers "Brother Yusuf," after his conversion to Islam) saw his first combat at age seventeen. Twenty years went by before he was diagnosed with posttraumatic stress disorder. "Two decades of isolation, separation, substance abuse, incarceration, and almost a mastery of avoidance techniques that left me very lonely and alienated even in a crowd and especially within a family," he says. "It was the combination of a 12-step program and being prescribed kayaking by a clinical psychologist that put me back on the road to recovery and back into the mainstream of life." Today, Brother Yusuf is known throughout the United States for his pioneering work taking young inner-city men into the Adirondacks for their own reformation. In that occupation, he finds restoration, and peace. Several initiatives, including the Sierra Club's Military Family Outdoor Initiative, provide returning veterans and their families with healing outdoor experiences.

Peter H. Khan Jr., associate professor of psychology at the University of Washington and a leading researcher on ecopsychology, and Patricia Hansen Hasbach, a psychologist in private practice who teaches ecotherapy at Lewis and Clark College, in Portland, Oregon, are currently working together to better define the connection between mental health and the natural world. Khan is focusing his work on the human relationship with the "greater than human world"; Hasbach is exploring nature as metaphor, what she calls "mapping the internal landscape." She views the emergence of ecotherapy as part of a natural progression of mental health care: psychological therapy began with the intrapsychic work of Sigmund Freud—the emphasis was on the individual's early experience—then broadened to the interpersonal, and then to the whole family. "In the 1970s, we took a huge leap into family systems and then in the late '80s, early '90s, we moved into social systems," Hasbach told me over coffee in a little café in Chautauqua, New York, where I had also met the sculptor David Eisenhour. "Ecopsychology or ecotherapy is taking us to the next round: the context in which we live our lives, the natural world," she added.

She explained how she uses nature as metaphor, to open patients up, and also as direct treatment. During the intake phase, she asks her patients questions about family, work, and other parts of their lives. She also asks them about their relationship to nature and how much time they spend outside. "Some will tell me, 'I haven't done it in years.'" She asks them if they had a special place as a child in nature. "And that is an icebreaker. It often gives me more information than when they tell me about their families." She also takes her patients outside.

"I was sitting in the park with a patient, when somebody went by on a bicycle. There was a cockatiel perched on the handlebars, and we both noticed it. Its wings were outspread, and it was clear that the bird's wings had been clipped, which is why it wasn't flying, and it was very moving to the woman. She broke into tears and talked about how she lived her life, with clipped wings." In another case, a woman was able to talk about the twists and turns of her life, "by observing the river from where we sat."

And Hasbach told the story of a seventeen-year-old patient. "This boy was doing serious self-damaging things. The parents were in the midst of a divorce and weren't really addressing him directly. He had been to two other therapists. Went once, didn't go back. But he and I made a connection when he started telling me about fishing. I said, 'I'm going to give you homework. I want you to go fishing three times this week.' He came back the next week and said 'sometimes I just go to the ponds and I just sit there.' He began telling me about the turtles—and how they draw into their shell. In our third session, he trusted me enough to say 'I thought of killing myself.' " Hasbach prescribed short-term medication, and more time outdoors. "I brought in his dad, with whom he was living, to reconnect that bond. This week they are in Alaska fishing together."

Later, as Hasbach and I walked outside, rain began to fall on Chautauqua's town square and the Victorian homes that surrounded it. The conversation paused.

I told her how I had seen my father disengage from nature, which had been an early source of his joy, as well as of the bonding that had occurred among my parents, my brother, and myself. This was long before the psychiatrists or the mental hospitals he frequented saw such illness as part of a whole family system. So his condition, probably bipolar disorder combined with the effects of alcoholism, was treated in isolation from his family, the society beyond, and the natural world.

I wondered if nature therapy could have helped my father. Surely, it would have helped our family.

Hasbach agreed. "So often when we have this kind of severe challenge, frightened family members lose hope," she said. "Through glimpses of a happier time, familiarity of place, a hope for the possibility of wholeness in a familiar shared activity, your father may have been able to connect with a deeper place of knowing and healing, one that is rooted in our biophilic connection to nature. The interior-mapping that we talked about might have been useful in touching that depth of experience," she said. "Nature therapy for your father might not have helped him turn the corner, but it might well have helped ease his pain, and given your family solace, and more good memories of him, and maybe it would have kept him with you a little longer."

CHAPTER 6

The Deep Green High

True Fitness Is Radical Amazement

J OHN MUIR ASSOCIATED wilderness with health and peak experiences: "One of the most beautiful and exhilarating storms I ever
enjoyed in the Sierra occurred in December, 1874, when I happened to be exploring one of the tributary valleys of the Yuba River."
He climbed to the top of a one-hundred-foot-tall Douglas spruce to experience a wild windstorm. The "brushy tops" of the chosen tree, and
the trees surrounding it, "were rocking and swirling in wild ecstasy."

He had climbed many trees for his botanical studies, so he reached
the top of this one easily. Then came the "exhilaration of motion." The
tops of the trees bent and swirled while Muir clung to the branches
"like a bobo-link on a reed." He kept his perch for hours. He frequently
closed his eyes "to enjoy the music by itself, or to feast quietly on the
delicious fragrance that was streaming past." When the storm began
to calm, he climbed down and walked through the woods. "The storm-
tones died away, and, turning toward the east, I beheld the countless
hosts of the forests hushed and tranquil, towering above one another
on the slopes of the hills like a devout audience. The setting sun filled
them with amber light, and seemed to say, while they listened, 'My
peace I give unto you.'"[1]

In Muir's world, the extreme animation of nature was contagious.

Health isn't just the absence of illness or pain, it's also physical, emotional, mental, intellectual, and spiritual *fitness*—in short, it's about the joy of being alive. Why fitness? Stephen Kellert, the Yale professor who helped refine and popularize E. O. Wilson's biophilia hypothesis, suggests that talking about fitness, in the broadest interpretation of that word, helps us move the discussion from pathology to potential.

Along this line, outdoor gyms make sense. The movements required for hiking, fishing, horseback riding, camping, and other outdoor activities strengthen the body, as do the lifting, reaching, and bending motions of gardening. Thus, we strengthen weak muscles and increase joint flexibility ranges, along with physical stamina, balance, and coordination. As the prior chapters described, nature-based exercise not only builds physical fitness but strengthens our senses, our intellectual capacity, and our mental health.

"I remember distinctly the moment that my approach to fitness was transformed," writes Tina Vindum, a former Alpine skier, competitive mountain biker, and author of *Outdoor Fitness,* a book that recommends stepping out of the gym and into the outdoors.[2] She had spent years of her life in gyms. "Over time, I had been growing increasingly frustrated with training in the static indoor environment," she wrote. "My muscles had grown so used to the repetitive exercises of standard gym equipment, I had reached a plateau that was taking away from my performance. One day I found myself staring out the window in the middle of yet another boring indoor workout, gazing at the majestic Sierra Nevadas, feeling stifled and frustrated. . . . Leaves covered the ground, and the wind was crisp and cold. Like a kid stuck in a classroom, I pined for the freedom that lay outside my window. That day, I rebelled." She headed outside and was soon running slalom on the more challenging, uneven terrain of the forest, doing strengthening exercises against tree trunks and boulders.

Like Vindum, Kelli Calabrese, a Texas-based trainer and coauthor of the book *Feminine, Firm & Fit,* writes about how outdoor terrain trumps indoor machines.[3] "Machines are created to make it easier on you, but the ground forces you to adjust to whatever the elements have done to it," she says. "Literally every section of a hill is different and will work your calves a little differently."

We don't need an exercise trainer to take us outside. But for some people, it helps. Then there's the group approach. In the UK, Green Gyms, as developed by the British Trust for Conservation Volunteers, gets people out of energy-consuming indoor gyms and in contact with nature, using their muscles to improve local landscapes.[4] The basic idea is that people can band together to organize their own nature gyms, meeting at local parks, gardens, and nature trails, where they can hike, garden, or do nature-reclamation work together. People can also do this on their own, of course. The bottom line: nature is full of gyms, if we look for them.

In addition to the benefits to physical and mental health, there's the added spiritual value of green exercise. The theologian Rabbi Abraham Joshua Heschel wrote, "Our goal should be to live life in radical amazement, to look at the world in a way that takes nothing for granted. Everything is phenomenal; everything is incredible; to be spiritual is to be constantly amazed."

Deep Green Exercise

That quote comes to mind every time I talk with Brook Shinsky, who lives in Oakland, California, and works for The North Face, an outdoor gear and apparel company. Shinsky lists a remarkable variety of exercise methods that she pursues outdoors: pedaling (mountain and road), snowboarding, rock climbing, running, and wingsuit flying (for that, she dons a special suit that shapes her body into an airfoil, creating lift). The wingsuit, sometimes known as a birdman suit or squirrel or Batman suit, allows Shinsky and other wingsuit fliers hair-raising advantages over typical skydiving, including reduced descent rates, longer free falls, and increased maneuverability. I asked Shinsky, who is in her early thirties, if she ever became so focused on the act of jump-ing, gliding, and landing that she stopped noticing the natural world. To the contrary, she replied. "I was always intrigued by birds as a kid, and now I know how it feels to fly—I become a bird. I see the world as a bird does, and it is in this time that I am truly present and fully aware," she said. As she described her experience, I came to a better understanding of the attraction of extreme outdoor sports, which are preferred by an increasing number of young people over more tradi-tional outdoor sports, such as fishing and hunting. This is a complete immersion in nature, with the added attraction of risk. Some men and women, in pursuit of outdoor sports, plug their ears with iPod earbuds; they're oblivious to the natural world—or, at least they obscure the experience of being there. But Shinsky clearly was seeking a different kind of communion.

A few years ago, I met Margot Page. She lives in a 160-year-old clapboard farmhouse on a rise that overlooks a village and a valley. Her house is white with green trim and is seemingly held to the hill by the deep-rooted maple trees circling it. Page is one of a handful of women who have made a name for themselves in the culture of fly-fishing. She and other women fly-fishers, and some men, too, she admits, are extending—subtly, imaginatively—their relationship with nature. They pursue "a different kind of fishing," she says. "They approach the water; they don't fish right away. They watch and listen and stand back and then they try to integrate themselves into the context of this environment. That is how you work with fishing, that's how you con-nect." I came to think of this kind of angling as "deep fishing."[5]

Page also described a different kind of fishing organization: Casting for Recovery, a nonprofit group that teaches fly-fishing to breast-cancer survivors. Though she has not had cancer, Page serves on the board of advisers. The idea of fishing as therapy is old; the creation of fishing therapy groups is relatively new. Most of the women who join Casting for Recovery, she explained, have never fly-fished. "When they return to that chemo room, to the hard time, they'll have a place to return to, in their minds, and it might give them a moment of peace." The doctors on Casting for Recovery's advisory board believe that the benefits are both physiological and psychological. "The casting helps muscles that have been frozen, nerves that have been severed. Some women get frozen shoulders after they have mastectomies. The physiological motion of casting helps to loosen them up. The instructors have been trained to help adapt the casting motion to whatever circumstance the patient finds herself in," Page explained. Beyond physical therapy, something else is at work here. Some of these women follow Page's lead and pursue a deeper healing immersion in nature.

Page's deep fishing concept is akin to Brook Shinsky's approach to wingsuiting. We might call what Shinsky does "deep flying." From her perch as an outreach employee for The North Face, Shinsky detects a change occurring among an increasing number of young people—the millennials, as the outdoor industry refers to them—who have tended to view the natural world as a stage for thrills: nature as a theme-park ride. "Many young people are realizing that these outdoor activities have more to offer than a simple adrenaline rush," she told me. "They're discovering the physical, psychological, and even spiritual benefits of exercising in nature, and are becoming more aware of their surroundings."

In a sense, surfers led the way in the late 1960s and early 1970s. Their films showed this deeper awareness, and now Shinsky can point to young filmmakers who prefer other extreme outdoor sports, whose films now express the same aesthetic and reverence for nature's gifts.

So "deep green exercise" may be the trend that comes after extreme sports, or at least makes them more interesting. One can imagine deep skiing, deep snowboarding, deep rock climbing. Conway Bowman, an ESPN fishing star, uses the term "ragged edge sports." He and I have considered what the parameters or precepts of this new genre might be. Among them: sensory immersion in nature rather than spectatorism;

doing outdoor sports in unusual ways and unexpected locales; doing more than one outdoor activity at the same time (fishing plus birding = bishing, or fishing plus wildlife photography = phishing); combining recreation with conservation (tagging sharks, counting mountain lions); eschewing the most expensive equipment, preferring handmade or restored equipment, and practicing minimalism; when fishing or hunting, killing to eat or not killing at all (some fly-fishers now use flies with no hooks, to feel just the thrill of the strike). And most of all, unplugging the iPod and opening one's senses to the full experience.

Walking the Genome Trail

We were born to walk. And run. And hike. We need to keep moving. Perhaps when we hike we do so by necessity, as we trace the invisible songlines of our genome.

One gratification that comes to some hikers—and perhaps especially to trail runners—is sometimes referred to as hiker's high, which can be defined as runner's high plus the sensory additives of being outdoors. Scott Dunlap took up trail running—runs in natural settings—in 2001, "to get off the work treadmill and see a bit more of the outdoors." In his blog, Dunlap describes the high, which occurs around eight or nine miles into a run, as a "mystical feeling that you can run forever, without borders—psychological or physical." His high, he says, "may be triggered by something as subtle as a sudden shift in temperature, or it may result from an epic moment such as traversing a razor's-edge ridge at 13,000 feet as storm clouds bubble on the horizon." Another hiker, Sage Ingham, of Rockville, Maryland, wrote on *National Geographic*'s online "Ask Adventure" feature: "It never fails that about three to four hours into a hike I get what I've come to call a 'hiker's high,' when I'm suddenly seized with a fit of the giggles. What's going on?" An explanation comes via research that shows that long-distance runners show an increase in the body's own opioids, resulting in feelings of euphoria and happiness.[6] In California, my nephew Kyle Louv is considered one of the best college runners. For years, beginning early in high school, Kyle practiced his running in the forests near his suburban home in Eureka. He is convinced the subtle and not-so-subtle influences (the occasional appearance of bears) of the terrain dramatically increased his speed, endurance, and euphoria. Perhaps he was tapping into his genetic past, the fight-or-flight response combined with the runner's high in nature.

Some of our society's hunger for drugs may be related to our yearning for this unified state of mind, body, and nature. Recreational drugs, or drugs used in a religious context, are present in nearly every society, including those of tribal peoples who live closer to nature. But the purpose and context is more often than not about transcendence, not escape. In Western society, drugs and alcohol are more likely to be used to blunt pain, to block the static and noise — the excess, often meaningless information that comes our way every day. By contrast, the high achieved through deep green exercise opens the senses; this high is about transcendence, about natural ecstasy. Australia's noted nature philosopher Glenn Albrecht has come up with a name for this spontaneous euphoria, this feeling of oneness with the earth and its life forces: "eutierria" (*eu* = good, *tierra* = earth).

When I was in my early twenties and working for Project Concern, a medical charity, I spent a few weeks in Guatemala. I had more time than work, so I hiked often. I walked for miles along the shore of Lake Atitlán, the deepest lake in Central America. That same year, an earthquake killed more than twenty-six thousand people in Guatemala; it was so massive that it cracked the lakebed, opened a subsurface drain, and within the month dropped the water level two meters. Nature, like people, can fill us for a lifetime, or empty us in a millisecond. Later, near Antigua, a larger town in the Central Highlands, I hiked up Volcán de Agua, or "Volcano of Water," known as Hunapú by the Cakchiquel Mayans. Beginning in tropical heat, I climbed the steep path up Hunapú into dense forest. By the time the mist began to close around me in the cloud forest, the temperature had plummeted and I was shivering. Unprepared for the extremes of the twelve-thousand-foot altitude, I reluctantly turned around and headed back down the volcano.

This is when I first experienced the hiking high. I had picked up a branch to use as a walking stick, and as I sped down the slick trail, at times jumping across deeply eroded fissures in the path, my strides became long and airy. The tragedies of the world, natural and man-made, disappeared. I felt as if I were flying through the clouds, and in those moments I wanted to—and felt I could—keep going forever, and leap across the world.

The only other time I have felt this particular euphoria was a few years later, after hiking up San Diego County's Stonewall Peak, which from a distance resembles the mountain above Atitlán. On the way back down Stonewall, with my future wife, Kathy, ahead of me—our pace was growing dangerously quick—I realized in a flash of intense clarity that I was happy, and that if I could keep walking with Kathy, this hike never needed to end.

CHAPTER 7

The Nature Prescription

Refill: Unlimited

Some of us think aging is bad policy. Having said that, here's some good news: spending more time in nature can make aging easier, perhaps even salutary. Think of it as nature-assisted aging. When I asked older adults how nature had or was assisting their own aging, their answers were revealing. One man said: "I don't feel old when I am in the natural world. My relationship with it allows me, or so it seems, to reconnect with an earlier time; it brings out the excitement and enthusiasm I had as a youngster, as though those days of fishing, searching for bugs and bird nests were just the other day. I know my body is getting old, but as long as I remain connected to nature, I don't feel old."

Others said that spending time in nature gave them needed perspective on time passing. "The time dimension of the natural world (billions of years) helps you cope with your mortality," said a scientist. Another woman wrote: "I don't quite have the ability to scramble up a tree like I once did, nor the inclination to build forts in the gathered cornstalks of the farmer's field behind my house, nor play in snow forts till our clothing froze solid and our skin hurt. When I think of those things, I can feel what I felt then, again, with fondness and some melancholy. The difference is I can consciously reflect on those experiences and place value on them because I see how defining they were in determining who I became. I appreciate things differently, with more intention."

Of course, as we move deeper into old age, our nature experiences change. "As I get older, I tend more toward the quiet and simple experiences in nature," writes a North Carolina woman. "Even with swimming in the ocean, I used to Scuba dive and spear fish. Now, I am very content, just swimming and sightseeing by swimming on my side or on my back. Don't need all the equipment, or maintenance, to see and feel and experience the richness of it all. I also savor the experiences more, really appreciating that they are there for the taking, and that I have the senses and abilities to access them."

Similarly, an artist who had moved to rural New England said: "Catching trout on the river is less important to me now. I'm thrilled and satisfied just seeing a fish rise, or seeing a great blue heron pass close overhead, seeing an annoyed beaver flap his tail at a fisherman or even having to stop fishing for a canoeist passing through." And a woman who plants urban forests said simply and optimistically, "I feel befriended and supported by the natural world, and the role it plays in my potential longevity."

Active engagement is not forever, unfortunately. An inability to take part physically in the outside world means indirect association with nature becomes even more important. More geriatric studies are needed, but existing research confirms that elderly residents in retirement apartments report greater satisfaction and stronger feelings of well-being if they have a garden view.[1] Other studies show benefits do increase if elders can get outside and into a garden. In 1994, a study divided eighty institutionalized seniors into two groups. One group received horticultural therapy — gardening time — and the other did not. They tested the groups three times over a six-month period and found predictable emotional and mental improvement at the midpoint, which dropped if therapy was withdrawn.[2]

Another perk of hands-on gardening is increased pinch and grip strength and improved dexterity. Kansas State University researchers Candice Shoemaker, Mark Haub, and Sin-Ae Park noted these benefits and others in a study published in 2009 in the journal *Hort-Science*.[3] In 2000, researchers reported that patients with Alzheimer's disease showed improved group interaction, reduced agitation, and less wandering if they could be outside in a garden at different times of the day and experience changing light levels. This apparently allowed their brains to provide structure in minds otherwise confused.[4] And a 2006 Australian study of 2,805 men and women aged sixty years and older, who were initially free of cognitive impairment and followed for sixteen years, found that daily gardening was associated with a 36 percent reduction in the risk of developing dementia.[5]

At the primal level, how we age depends on the health of mitochondria. "They were once small bacteria swimming in the sea. But about 1 billion years ago, they joined up with other bacteria for energy, and this created life as we see it all around us," explains the physician William Bird, one of the UK's leading voices for connecting people to nature.

Today, almost every plant and animal uses mitochondria to transform air and nutrients into energy. Every cell in our bodies contains some two hundred to three hundred mitochondria. These are our cellular power plants. They're also engaged in other processes, including cell differentiation, cell growth, and cell death. The mitochondria are happily employed until their lives are overwhelmed by free radicals—atoms or molecules that with a single unpaired electron in an outer shell are released as the mitochondria produce energy. According to the free-radical theory of aging, organisms age as cells accumulate free radicals, which can set off chain reactions that can lead to cancers and degenerative diseases, including cardiovascular disease, arthritis, diabetes, lung disease.

"All of these diseases are related to the aging process associated with mitochondrial dysfunction," says Bird. Toxins and obesity create more free radicals, as do stress and sedentary behavior. At the chemical level, antioxidants keep free radicals under control. Negative stress can tip the balance to the radicals. "Children who have been subjected to stress such as child abuse show premature aging later in life. Stress gives them a disadvantage by increasing the risk of chronic diseases such as diabetes later and also shortens their lives," he adds.

A minor industry now produces food and drink additives to increase antioxidants although research has suggested that some of these supplements may be toxic in high concentrations and not much is known about long-term impact. What does work then? "The more exercise someone does, the more the cell releases antioxidants to protect it," he says. "So a child who plays outside in a natural green space will reduce the chance of developing chronic diseases later in life." The balancing act continues throughout our lifetimes. Bird recommends exercise, as do most physicians. Also, considering the emerging literature on green exercise, he suggests that outdoor activity may have added antioxidant properties. If Bird is right, our personal and public policies about aging need some fresh air. So, it's time to take our mitochondria for a walk in the woods.

Or better yet, time for aging boomers to take children for a walk. Our generation still remembers a time when it was considered normal for children to get their hands muddy and their feet wet, to lie in the grass and watch the clouds move. There's no better form of green exercise than passing along to the next generation the gifts of nature that we received.

Toward a "Natural Health Care System"

Just as the nature experience's impact on intelligence holds implications for education—perhaps especially higher education, which will be discussed later—its role in shaping physical and mental health recommends a new approach to health care. How then might the Nature

Principle, which holds that a reconnection to the natural world is fundamental to human well-being, be applied to the health care system?

In 2009, Janet Ady of the U.S. Fish and Wildlife Service stood before a crowd of grassroots leaders working to connect people to nature and held up an outsized pharmacy bottle. Within the bottle was a physician's "prescription"—one that would be as appropriate for adults as it would be for children. It read: "Directions: Use daily, outdoors in nature. Go on a nature walk, watch birds, and observe trees. Practice respectful outdoor behavior in solitude or take with friends and family. Refill: Unlimited. Expires: Never."[6] Gimmicky? Sure. But effective— a direct illustration of how the medical industry's attitude, as well as our attitudes about exercise and wellness, could be reshaped to incorporate vitamin N.

Within the health professions, interest in the nature prescription is growing. Healing gardens on hospital grounds are already popular. The provision of these restorative nature spaces has become specialized, with ailment-specific gardens being designed by landscape architects for patients with cancer; patients requiring physical rehabilitation; those with Alzheimer's disease and other forms of dementia; and people suffering from depression and burnout.

Daphne Miller, a general practitioner in the Noe Valley neighborhood in San Francisco, California, envisions nature prescriptions as part of the burgeoning field of integrated medicine. In these medical practices, physicians offer the typical services, but also recommend to their patients other health modalities, including herbal medicine, biofeedback, homeopathy, acupuncture, and mindfulness. "Nature is another tool in our toolbox," says Miller, who, in addition to her medical practice, is associate clinical professor in the Department of Family and Community Medicine, University of California–San Francisco. She also believes that park rangers can, in effect, become health care providers. This epiphany, as she calls it, came to her at a conference held at Yosemite National Park, as she listened to a ranger preach the gospel of nature's impact on health and well-being—having witnessed its transformative effect on visitors to Yellowstone.

Miller recalls that, as he spoke, she realized "this guy is a health practitioner." She wondered: why not, with training, "anoint these rangers as health paraprofessionals—as paramedicals—to help people use nature as a conduit for health?"

In addition to park rangers, who else might be on a list of potential nature paramedicals? Farmers, ranchers, camp counselors, nature guides, park docents, clergy, teachers, nutritionists, architects, urban planners, builders. The list could go on. Why not establish a certificate in nature health, or continuing education credits? Individuals from a variety of professions and avocations might learn about practical applications appropriate to their discipline, plus receive more generalized training. In addition, health care professionals might earn such a certificate.

Colleges and universities could offer additional courses for certification in a variety of established arenas, under the watchful eye of state or national public health organizations. Businesses could offer this training, too. So could the National Wildlife Federation, the National Recreation and Park Association, the National Environmental Health Association, to name a few possibilities. Such nature paramedicals might be trained to teach about the general impact of the natural world on health; about practical applications of outdoor fitness, including exercise regimens specific to, say, nature trails; stress reduction; improving mental health through nature experience; how to make changes in the home or yard to encourage natural fitness; and so on. Potential nature therapies might also include adventure therapy for combating family disconnection, for improving body image in women and men, for the treatment of eating disorders, for aging. Other possibilities: special training in nature fitness for children, the elderly, or people with disabilities. Most of this could be done in concert with health care providers, but some of it could be offered independently.

This approach is attractive because there would be no need to wait for the great ship of mainstream medicine to turn, although physicians and other health care professionals may be more accepting of such ideas than one might expect. One reason is peak petroleum—that inevitable moment when the scarcity of oil becomes permanent. Filling our cars' gas tanks will be only part of the challenge. Howard Frumkin, dean of the University of Washington's School of Public Health, points out that the production of many of our most basic medications—aspirin, for example—is entirely dependent on petroleum-based molecules. While many synthetic alternatives will be available, FDA approval could lag behind need. Because of the impact of peak petroleum on supplies, packaging, transportation, and nearly every other aspect of health care, dramatic drop-offs could occur in the rates of cancer screening, renal dialysis, prenatal care, and physical therapy. Because of the recession and rising gas prices, that effect has probably already begun. After Frumkin published a paper on this topic in the *Journal of the American Medical Association*, he reported one oncologist's comment that "some of his patients were choosing to forgo appropriate chemotherapy in favor of surgery because they couldn't handle the cost of frequent fill-ups for numerous visits to the medical center." Also, like Australia's Glenn Albrecht, Frumkin worries about the indirect impact on mental health, as our petroleum-based way of life is disrupted.

Even without the peak petroleum issue, an aging population presents threats and opportunities to health care. "As the U.S. population ages, proportionately fewer medical practitioners, particularly in primary care, will be available," Miller contends. "That means our definition for a medical practitioner and where we obtain health care will change." Physicians are increasingly open to the other healing professions. "When you use that term, 'healing professions,' most people think of acupuncture, massage," she says. But the term could stretch. Miller also believes that patients are primed for the nature prescription. One of her patients told her, "I have a StairMaster right in my own basement, but honestly it's been there for years gathering dust and making me feel guilty. I started walking the three-mile trail in the park near my house, then I got serious about exercising. I do it now rain or shine. I love the fresh air. The best part is that I get a great workout and don't even mind sweating."

Miller has heard enough repetition of, and variations on, that patient's story that she has "started to make formal 'park prescriptions,'" she reported in a commentary for the *Washington Post*.[7] "The prescribing instructions are considerably more detailed than ones you might get with a medication or a typical exercise prescription (e.g., 'walk 40 minutes five times a week'). They include the location of a local green space, the name of a specific trail and, when possible, exact mileage." She is not the only health care professional handing out nature prescriptions. In 2010, the National Environmental Education Foundation (NEEF), working with the American Academy of Pediatrics, launched a training program for pediatricians, focused on prescribing outdoor activities. "I've begun hearing about doctors around the country who are medicating their patients with nature in order to prevent (or treat) health problems ranging from heart disease to attention-deficit disorder," says Miller. Among them is cardiologist Eleanor Kennedy, who worked with local funders and the National Park Service's Rivers, Trails, and Conservation Assistance Program to create a Medical Mile, a walking and running path along a downtown stretch of the Arkansas River. Nearby is a new, natural play space designed primarily by parents and children, which includes grassy hills for rolling down, tunnels for crawling, and wetlands. Kennedy told Miller, "If my patients feel that they can get outdoors, they are more likely to be consistent about exercise."

In 2009, the city of Santa Fe, New Mexico, in an effort to fight the high rate of diabetes there, launched its Prescription Trails program, which is partially funded by the Centers for Disease Control and Prevention. Besides trail time, physicians can refer their patients to a trail guide. "All these insurance companies focus on prevention, but no one thinks of the free public land resources that we have at our disposal," said Michael Suk, an orthopedic surgeon and former health adviser to the National Park Service (NPS). The Golden Gate National Recreation Area plans to create a prescription tool kit for doctors, "possibly in partnership with a large health organization such as Kaiser Permanente," Miller reports. She believes "it's not too much of a stretch to think of our national park system as an integral part of our health care system; the NPS is already offering wellness services that are free and accessible to all, regardless of preexisting conditions." In 2010, a similar pilot program in Portland, Oregon, began pairing physicians with park professionals, who will record whether the outdoor "prescriptions" are fulfilled; the park prescription program will be part of a longitudinal study to measure the effect on health.

"Woodland therapy" and "care farming," a partnership among farmers, health care providers, and health care consumers to care for people and land, are taking root in several countries. In Norway, general practitioners can prescribe their patients a stay in a care farm. In the Netherlands, six hundred health farms are integrated into the health service.[8] In 2006, a group called the Forest Therapy Executive Committee, made up of researchers and others, began to give forests across Japan the official designations of Forest Therapy Base or Forest Therapy Road. The designations are based on scientific evidence. As of 2008, thirty-one bases and four roads had been designated, and Chiba University's Yoshifumi Miyazaki hopes that over the next decade that number will reach one hundred. The forest therapy bases—typically a forest and walking path—are managed by local governments and independently observed by Japan's Forest Agency and the Health, Labor, and Welfare Ministry. People who visit the therapy bases and roads can take part in guided walks with experts in forest medicine; they can also enroll in other health classes, such as dietary management and hydrotherapy, and receive medical checkups. Some Japanese companies now send their employees to these forest therapy bases—presumably to increase their productivity. The therapy forests also bring tourists to local economies. And in the UK, a growing "green care" movement encourages therapeutic green exercise activities, therapeutic horticulture, animal-assisted therapies, ecotherapy, and care farming. "Nature's Capital," a 2008 report issued by the National Trust in Great Britain, calls for local funding for green exercise and "wellbeing prescriptions," adding: "There are potentially very significant cost savings for Primary Care Trusts in more widely recognizing green exercise as a clinically valid treatment option for mental and physical ill health. It has been estimated that a 10 percent increase in adult physical activity would benefit the UK by £500 million a year, saving 6,000 lives." The trust also cites a government report that anticipates an estimated 60 percent of the UK populace is likely to be obese by 2050.[9]

Do you see a pattern forming here? In England and Scotland, efforts are afoot to build a Natural Health Service as a supplement to the National Health Service (NHS). William Bird of Natural England explains: "This service will represent the green open spaces surrounding health centers and hospitals including parks, community gardens, allotments and trees in the street." Plans are also being made to create a National Health Service Forest, "in which 1.3 million trees will be planted, one for each NHS employee, to cool the urban heat of our island, provide shade, reduce stress, and increase activity."

The cumulative effect of such thinking could eventually lead to natural health care reform at the national level in the United States and around the world. Daphne Miller and other health care professionals are ready to quicken the pace. "Don't be surprised if, at your next visit to the doctor, you are handed a trail map and itinerary along with your lab slip," she says. "In fact, if you are not offered one, you should demand it."

To transform the health care system will require more than

institutional change. It will demand rigorous research and a philosoph-
ical evolution that goes beyond what we usually call preventive care.
That shift, toward natural fitness, can happen organizationally—as
well as at the level of the individual, in our social and family networks,
and in the living environments we create for the young and the old.

PART THREE

Near Is the New Far

Knowing Who You Are by Knowing

Where You Are

I do not know whether it is possible to love the planet or not,

but I do know that it is possible to love the places

we can see, touch, smell and experience.

—David Orr, *Earth in Mind*

CHAPTER 8

Searching for Your One True Place

Sustainable Happiness

EVERYONE HAS AT least one true place, a piece of land or water that calls to them—like that New Mexico farm with the swaying cottonwoods where I encountered the illusive *it*. Some of us search for such a place and call it home; and some of us finally come home.

Judging by the subject of his paintings, Adriano Manocchia was already predisposed to a more rural lifestyle when he and his wife decided they had to do something to reduce their nature-deficit disorder. Although he is an artist noted for his depictions of fly-fishing, Manocchia was born in New York City, lived half of his life there, and then married and moved to southern Westchester, to the suburbs. He commuted to work in Manhattan for eight years and spent another twenty years working from home. Once his son left for college, he and his wife began to question why they lived where they did. "I was unhappy there. The cost of living was outrageous. It smelled, was noisy, you had to live in fear most of the time. And worst of all I had to drive over an hour to get to a crowded stream to fish," he says. "So my dislike of where I was living began to fester like a sore." He found himself dreading simple chores, such as going to the post office or the bank. "Angry people were everywhere you went. Hostile, aggressive people."

He and his wife were spending more and more time driving north on the weekends looking for some space, fresh air, and what he called a "kinder environment." He adds, "The strange part is that it took us three more years of this unhappy living to finally make the decision to sell our home and look for a different lifestyle."

That, says Manocchia, is when fate intervened. One day, while on one of their excursions, he and his wife happened on a small community about 170 miles north of New York City. They found a small farm with a stream running through it, filled with native brook trout; a barn for a studio; an 1803 farmhouse and "two of the sweetest, kindest people one would ever want to meet," he recalls. "Bob and Irene were moving a few miles from where they had spent forty-five years and raised three great kids. After a total of ten minutes, we had agreed to buy the farm. Little did Bob and Irene Donally know they were adopting two more into their family. I suddenly found what I had been searching for perhaps my whole life."

The town, Manocchia says, was a community made up of artists, writers, musicians, farmers, retired people, poor people, rich people. All towns have scandals, depressed people, darkness in the corners. But he was surprised that so many of the people he met looked forward to the winter snow, that there were so many "who had the time to stop and say hello and really meant it, who made eye contact." And then there was the landscape: "Breathtaking rolling hills which rival any hills in Tuscany. And rivers to fish with more pools and more trout to catch than I could ever hope to in the time I have left. And stars. More stars than you ever imagined. There are people who actually look up around here and comment on how brilliant the stars were the night before. I was reborn ten minutes after the moving truck left us on the doorsteps of the Donally farm."

Almost four years later, Manocchia reports, he can still feel his senses reawakening with every passing day. He looks forward to the alarm at five a.m. so he can rush down to the river to fish, to inhale the early morning air, to listen to the silence, to the birds. He says he regrets not making the move sooner.

Like Manocchia, Gail Lindsey, who died in 2009, hungered for a home closer to nature. Lindsey, former chair of the American Institute of Architects Committee on the Environment, had also chaired initiatives to green the White House and the Pentagon. Her husband, Mike Cox, grew up in Midwest farm country and needed no convincing. Their goal was to find land with mature trees, no more than thirty minutes from the offices of her architecture firm.

"I remember the six-month search process with more humor than Mike does. He took the lead role in evaluating different properties," she said. "For a full six months, I said *no* to all of them, sometimes with definable reasons, other times just because they 'didn't feel right.' I know this reason frustrated my engineering husband but I truly believed that we would both know the right spot when we both *felt it* while we walked the land." Then a new property came on the market. To find it, they drove down a street that ended in a wall of trees, then walked. "Eventually we reached a spring surrounded by huge trees and chattering birds, including an enormous poplar that three people together couldn't put their arms around," Lindsey recalled. To their delight, they learned that the tree was indeed on their property. "And furthermore that it had at one time been an Indian camping area."

They bought the property. The next question was where to build, and not in that "magical area." They built their new home on the opposite side of the twelve-acre parcel: "As a girl, whenever I was stressed, depressed, or had received tough news as a young adult, including the deaths of my grandparents, I would find solace sitting under a tree. I would immediately feel connected. Now, as an adult, whether I am just sitting in our house looking out at all of the trees or taking a walk around the land with my husband to visit with the largest tree, I have a deep sense of being connected, of being at home."

Sustainable happiness

Where we choose to live can make a difference in our happiness and health. But it should be said that living in rural areas is no guarantee of it. In fact, the advantages can be outweighed by economic or social issues. Whether people live in cities or countryside, nature's benefits are diminished without a healthy social and economic platform.

While some demographers believe aging boomers will move to more concentrated, walkable urban neighborhoods (presenting the possibility of more demand for downtown nature), other urban observers, such as University of Arizona gerontologist Sandra Rosenbloom, believe that boomers are more likely to "age in place." This means they'll stick close to home, and if they decide to engage with nature, they'll become involved in greening their own neighborhoods, urban or suburban. Joel Kotkin, urban scholar and author of *The Next Hundred Million: America in 2050*, and demographer Mark Schill predict that, rather than moving downtown, downshifting boomers who do move will prefer "amenity-rich smaller towns and cities such as Douglas County, Colorado, and certain counties in Idaho, in the Berkshires of New England, and even in parts of Alaska."[1] At least before the recession, such counties were growing ten times faster than other rural counties. Another factor may be the increased number of adult children returning home to live with their parents; inexpensive, accessible nature activity may be just the ticket for economically stressed families.

In 2006, the Harvard School of Public Health reported that in terms of life expectancy, seven Colorado counties were the top-ranked counties in the nation. To be sure, many variables are involved. However, in all seven of the counties, life expectancy averaged 81.3 years.[2] These counties—Clear Creek, Eagle, Gilpin, Grand, Jackson, Park, and Summit—are on, adjoining, or near the Continental Divide and are noted for their natural beauty. Reporting the study, the *Rocky Mountain News* quoted Dr. Ned Calonge, chief medical officer of the

Colorado Department of Public Health and Environment, who opined that the longevity study's results could be attributed to Coloradans' active lifestyles, low smoking rates, and the lowest-in-the-nation numbers for obesity. But in an article for *Time* magazine,[3] writer Rita Healy offered another theory about Clear Creek County, where she lives, which ranked first in the United States for longevity. "One thing is certain," wrote Healy, "money doesn't buy old age." Jackson County, with a population of just 1,454, has a median household income of only $31,821—substantially less than the national average of $41,994. "Lots of freezers stocked with venison. Lots of pickups with rebuilt engines.... But among those who stay, there's at least one constant: even in their dotage, people remain full of life," she writes.

Something is at work here besides skiing, backpacking, and a diet of steamed vegetables; that indefinable something is *aliveness*. One factor is nature's occasional harshness. People at these altitudes stay lively "because it's too risky not to," Healy suggests. "Disregard the dark clouds coming over the Divide and you'll get slammed by bad weather." And that slight movement up on the ridge that you catch in peripheral vision? That could be a rock slide or an avalanche. "Your senses stay alert at these altitudes, and that alone must help prolong life."

I do have a couple of problems with Healy's analysis. First, it's a bit too easy to romanticize the hardship that comes with harsh weather, which does take a toll on health. Second, the people who move to places like Jackson County may be self-selecting hardy souls. The study does, however, suggest that, given the right combination of factors (including low smoking rates), rural life in beautiful places can be good for people. Lively people help other lively people stay lively. Perhaps your special place is in a small town, on a rural road, in a forest far from urban distractions. But not all of us need to live near the Continental Divide—or even in a small town surrounded by natural habitat—to receive these benefits.

Catherine O'Brien describes what she calls "sustainable happiness."

In 2005, O'Brien, with the support of the National Center for Bicycling and Walking, launched the Delightful Places Survey, distributed electronically around the world.[4] The survey was an effort to integrate urban planning with insights on happiness from positive psychology. "Happiness is not a topic that is generally discussed in transportation and planning meetings and yet it exists as the underlying motivation behind much of what we do, how we live, and the kinds of policies that are made," wrote O'Brien. She reported evidence that "genuinely happy people live longer, recover from illness more quickly, and are more likely to seek out and act on health information." She asked: What sorts of communities help provide their citizens opportunities for long-term happiness? Are current urban planning methods fostering sustainable happiness? "The new science of happiness indicates that authentic happiness, the enduring happiness that causes us to feel satisfied with our lives, is found through less materialistic pursuits," according to O'Brien. "It is grounded in intrinsic values. It is found in our relationships, meaningful work, and a sense of purpose." And sustainable happiness is also found in our relationship with *place*.

O'Brien's survey of residents of Seattle, Bogotá, Montreal, and Melbourne found that natural environments—trails, paths, and parks—were the sites of most delightful places: "The sounds that people associate with their delightful place most often were: water, the wind, silence, people talking, and birds. . . . The most common smells that were mentioned were: the earth, water, flowers, and food."[5] Despite her findings that urban places can be rich with delight, when it came to finding her own delightful place, O'Brien chose the country. She was determined to give her children a childhood steeped in nature.

"We moved to the Ottawa Valley nine years ago while I was writing my doctoral dissertation," she says. "My research had been in rural India, where we (my husband and two young children) lived for nearly a year. That year convinced us that we wanted a more rural life, and besides, buying an abandoned farm here was cheaper than renting an apartment in the city. Even though two hundred acres came with it."

As O'Brien and the others mentioned have learned, moving to the country can transform lives. But green flight can also exact a price.

Life above the Mason/Walmart Line

Three years ago, my wife and I spent a few days driving through New England. We stopped at the Briggs Carriage Bookstore, next to the eighteenth-century Brandon Inn. A fellow behind the counter snapped his finger on a map on the wall, demarking what might be called the Mason/Walmart Line. "The Industrial Revolution came to here," he declared.

His finger rested in the general vicinity of Manchester. "In Vermont, everything below Manchester is Massachusetts," he said. His tone was not complimentary. North of that line, the strip malls and quick-lube joints and coffee chains and big-box stores virtually disappear.

We drove north.

New Englanders can be strikingly honest about the benefits and drawbacks of living in rural America. One man I met had come north during the back-to-the-land exodus of the early seventies. He had lived alone in a cabin for a winter, using kerosene lanterns. He would walk a quarter-mile for water, carrying two buckets on a shoulder harness. Temperatures would dip to 40 below. "In April, the suicide rate is highest because you keep waiting for spring, and it doesn't come and doesn't come," he told me. "And then you hit a freak storm in April with eight inches of snow." An extreme view, of course. But who knows what freakish storms will come to humble the people who move here in search of some peace and respite?

Another New Englander, in his eighties, looked like a bemused Jimmy Stewart. He stood on his porch and looked across the misty fields and stone fences. His seventeenth-century ancestors had settled this land. "This is good land, healing land," he said. "There are bands of good land and bands of bad land. The Celts knew this. The Indians knew this. You have to be careful where you settle." He was amused by the people who come to rural New England expecting quiet but find the voices inside themselves amplified. He told me about an ex-urbanite who could not sleep because the apples kept falling. "She was always waiting for that next apple."

Still, like New Mexico, New England called us. On the other side of every rise, we saw a ridge of mountains, a valley, a farm; shapes and colors seemed to jar primal memory; even the architecture—Colonial, Victorian, rural—seemed built as much by nature as by human hands. The late fall colors may have blinded our eyes to the imperfections of this region: the lack of racial diversity and the rural poverty, burdens not displayed along the main streets. But during our road trip, we were impressed by the sense of psychological liberation. We longed for it.

Although growth in much of Vermont remains stable—what a concept!—the state is not immune to the forces shaping the rest of the country. For example, Rutland, a small city northeast of Manchester, offers a meticulously revived, brick-front downtown crossroads adjacent to a mall that could exist in any other burg in the nation. This was an unfortunate juxtaposition. Encountering it after nearly a week without seeing a single strip mall or big-box store was unnerving. In 1970, the state passed pioneering legislation to resist pressure from out-of-state developers, giving commissions composed of private citizens the power to approve or disapprove plans for subdivisions and commercial developments. However, the state struggles to keep its young people; as a job producer, nostalgia has its limits. This is the Hobson's choice that so many American communities believe they must make.

Surely we can find a better way, one that makes use of green technologies to resist the blizzard of strip-mall familiarity. Some towns and rural areas are, indeed, committed to preserving or restoring natural areas. Some are even *creating* them where they have never been.

In 2009, CBS's *The Early Show* featured the "twenty-five best cities in America for nature-deficit disorder" (as in how to *avoid* it). *Backpacker* magazine editor-in-chief Jonathan Dorn announced the top three cities: his editors selected Boulder, Colorado, as no. 1, followed by Jackson, Wyoming, and Durango, Colorado. All delightful places, for sure. Boulder was the magazine's first choice, Dorn said, because it offers easy access not only to wilderness, but also to hundreds of miles of networked bike and running trails. After snowstorms, the city plows its bike paths before plowing the roads.

Note that most of the top cities on this list are destination locations—small, scenic, and relatively wealthy. Moving to Boulder—or New England or New Mexico—may work out for those who can afford it (although there's still the pesky problem of people destroying what they seek, once they get there), but what about the rest of us, who either can't or aren't willing to pack up and migrate? How do we find—or create—our one true spot? One answer is to stay put, to discover and become fully immersed in our own bioregion, to encourage immediate changes and long-term policies that create nature *and* encourage higher human density where we live. And, wherever we end up, we can bring more nature to our homes and yards (no waiting required).

This is not an argument against following your heart to find your special place. But a suggestion that *it* may be closer than you think.

CHAPTER 9

The Incredible Experience of Being Where You Are

Overcoming Place Blindness

N EAR IS THE new far." That's the sly headline of an article in *Outside* magazine describing an alternative to long-distance, high-carbon ecotourism: getting to know your own neck of the woods. But here's the thing about travel. It helps us see more clearly where we live.

On a trip to Costa Rica, Kathy and I were on a bus headed into the rain forest. We passed through rugged farmland, bordered by undulating "live fences"—wire strung not to wood or metal posts, but to evenly spaced trees. We had never seen such a fence. With a little help from nature, farmers have probably been planting and stringing live fences for centuries. In England, hedgerows have been used since Roman times as field borders, but here the farmer deliberately plants the trees to hold wire, or birds drop seeds while perching on the original wood posts, and trees grow and become new posts that are integrated into the existing fence. Research in Costa Rica, Peru, Cuba, Nigeria, and Cameroon reveals how ingenious this ancient form of biophilic design can be. Living fences made of dense, thorny, and sometimes poisonous bushes are used by farmers who cannot afford barbed wire. Living fences provide mulch, erosion control, land stabilization, fuel, and food; in Cameroon, fences produce guava, citrus, bush plum, and other fruits, and they're a source of forage for cattle. They can also serve as seed banks.[1]

As the bus rose and fell along the dusty road, I was impressed by this ingenious partnership of life forms, human and plant. Like the stone fences of New England, and the windbreaks planted across the prairies of the United States, these fences seemed born to the earth.

That day, my wife and I were headed to a rain forest in a Costa Rican national park. In the country's Pacific coastal area, the California-like desert and dry forest turns suddenly into rain forest that stretches from this part of Costa Rica into South America.

Our guide, Max Vindas, had been raised "in the jungle," as he put it. He told us that a person cannot know the rain forest without meeting it personally. He found it humorous that North Americans so often consider the rain forest dangerous. It can be, of course, but Vindas had a different take. "When I visited California and went to the national parks, I learned that there were bears who would kill you, and that in Southern California, there were mountain lions that would attack you, but in this jungle we have sloths."

Dusk came on quickly during our visit and the forest seemed to become one being with a thousand voices, screams, and whispers, chatters and long calls. We heard feet or hooves racing through leaves and branches, and wings rising, and cicadas (we were told) that sounded like no earthly cicadas I had ever heard. I was stunned by the rising music—concurrently discordant, in tune, percussive, and smooth.

One thinks of our own habitats, our one-note yards, our three-chord city parks, our flat and tuneless soccer fields. What if, in our human habitats, we strove for biodiversity, for living fences and natural music?

We headed back the way we had come, on the roads lined with living fences, and then home to another landscape that, until recently, I barely knew.

Place Blindness

My wife, Kathy, was raised in San Diego. I moved here from Kansas in 1971, just out of college. She had spent little time exploring the natural habitats of this region, and I viewed it as a resort city, beautiful in its way, but I missed the green woods and plains of the Midwest. So when I looked for nature here, I saw less than met the eye. For years, we were restless. We bored our friends with all our talk of moving, of finding our one true place in, say, New Mexico, or maybe in New England. We even bored ourselves. One day Kathy said, "Our tombstones are going to say, 'We're moving.'" I may never bond to this region as I did to the woods behind my boyhood home, and who knows, we may yet move.

On the other hand, we both seem to be undergoing a vision shift.

The philosopher Ludwig Wittgenstein conceived the notion of "aspect-blindness" and "aspect-seeing" in imagery or language. Think of those strange drawings that appear as completely different images, depending on how, and on where, our eyes focus. The same adjustment can happen with our perception of place, and the nature within it.

A decade ago, my ignorance about this bioregion — San Diego County and northern Baja — became clear 153 miles south of the border, under the tutelage of the late Andy Meling. Andy was one of the elders of the family that founded the famous Meling Ranch, which had been established in the late 1800s by immigrants from Norway and Denmark. He looked a lot like the actor Robert Duvall in the *Lonesome Dove* TV series. I was there, with my oldest son, Jason, then a teenager, to research a chapter for a book. Andy had driven the two of us high into the Sierra San Pedro Mártir, one of the remnant sky islands of a strange archipelago called the Peninsular Range that extends from Southern California into Baja. We walked through tangled oaks in violet light and peered upward at the white granite of Picacho del Diablo, the highest peak in Baja California, which rises 10,157 feet through piñon pine and quaking aspen. I was stunned. I had had no idea that such a lush reality existed in Baja, which I had assumed was the shriveled lower limb of North America.

When I told Andy that, he pushed his cowboy hat back, squinted at me with a hint of disdain, and headed back to his cabin to make skillet stew over a wood fire.

Since then, I have learned a thing or two. I read in *Fremontia*, a journal of the California Native Plant Society, that this "true mountain island" is a lost world, a virtual relic of the Pleistocene epoch. Cut off by time and geography, life there is "ethereal . . . primeval," the journal reported. I now know that the trout of the Rio Santo Domingo in Baja, along with a closely related species in the mountains just to the north, in San Diego County, are as close as we can find to the progenitor rainbows that spread between fifty thousand and sixty thousand years ago from what would become northern Baja California and the southernmost county of Alta California, across the Kamchatka Peninsula between the Sea of Okhotsk and the Bering Sea, and then further dispersed—sometimes by the hands of trout worshipers— around the world. And I have learned that San Diego, though one of the most densely human-populated counties in the United States, contains more biodiversity than any other county in the country, with the exception of Riverside County just to the north.

Here, and south into Baja, is a land of sky islands, ring-tailed cats and mountain lions, whales, sea turtles, great white sharks, waterspouts and firestorms. In nearby Imperial and Riverside counties, there is a landlocked Salton Sea jammed with corvina. The Anza-Borrego Desert, a short drive east, holds badlands reminiscent of a small-scale Grand Canyon, and deep, palm-filled desert oases—mountain canyons so yawning that when camping in them in midsummer, one can awake in the morning shivering in frost. I had no clue how otherworldly my adopted corner of the world was, until, as a journalist, I made it my job to dig deeper into it. Until then, I had place blindness.

Perhaps I was afraid to attach to this area. In that, I was not alone. As a columnist for the *San Diego Union-Tribune* in the 1990s, I posed this question to readers: What are you attached to here in Southern California, other than good friends, good work, and the weather? The majority of responses were from people who said they felt, at best, a fragile sense of attachment to the region. Some blamed the crowding, the freeway traffic, the politics of the region—but often, they wrote about the threat to nature. "The haunting notion that this is only temporary has followed me to this day," wrote one reader. Another likened living here to standing on shifting sand: "One must constantly readjust one's position to stand in place or become lost. One has the sense that nothing is sacred here and that any place you bond to is likely to be bulldozed. Therefore we develop the strategy, which in attachment theory is called avoidance—pretending that our ties with someone or someplace are not important because it is too painful to show our feelings and risk being abandoned." I share that anxiety. But here's the problem: We cannot protect something we do not love, we cannot love what we do not know, and we cannot know what we do not see. Or hear. Or sense.

Fortunately, groups that help people really see where they live, that foster a sense of place, are growing in size and number. One of them, Exploring a Sense of Place (ESP), follows the model developed in 2002 by Karen Harwell and Joanna Reynolds in the San Francisco Bay Area. In their book, *Exploring a Sense of Place*, Harwell and Reynolds write: "As humans, we identify ourselves primarily through relationship—relationship with family, religion, ethnicity, community, town, state, nation."[2] They argue that our loss of connection to natural history represents a lost relationship, and that this connection is among the most important and least recognized needs of the human soul: "While most of us recognize where we live by its cities, buildings, places of business, even sport teams, how many of us identify with and understand the beauty, wonder and actual functioning of the natural ecosystem which supports us, and of which we are a part?"

Exploring a Sense of Place has developed a guidebook, leadership training workshops, and local courses, and has established additional regional programs. Harwell reports that requests for the guidebook have been received from over one hundred locations in the United States and from Canada, Australia, New Zealand, Switzerland, Germany, and France. In England, two pilot courses based on ESP are being established.

In 2009, an ESP-inspired San Diego group of twenty-five committed explorers spent one Saturday a month for seven months on day treks in my region. The explorers climbed to the top of Volcan Mountain near the headwaters of the San Dieguito River. At a Kumeyaay archeological site, they learned about the pre-European cultures of the river valley. They hiked a thousand feet up a winding trail through dense forest, which opened onto grasslands. Phil Pryde, professor emeritus, Department of Geography, San Diego State University, accompanied the hikers and described the bird life in the river valley. Two professional trackers taught the group to identify the footprints and scat of the wild animals. In the following months, as the group explored different geologies and microclimates of the region, the participants gained a deeper understanding of the whole territory.

Overcoming Plant Blindness

On an overcast April day, my wife and I joined the group to learn about native wildflowers on the plateaus and valleys south of Lake Hodges, a few miles from where we live. One reason I went on this hike was to overcome my plant blindness. For most of my life, I have looked past the flora to find the fauna, which means I have missed out on at least half of what I might have experienced outdoors.

The term *plant blindness* was coined by James Wandersee, of Louisiana State University, and Elisabeth E. Schussler of Southeastern Natural Sciences Academy. In an article for *Plant Science Bulletin* (published quarterly by the Botanical Society of America), they define plant blindness forthrightly, as "the inability to see or notice the plants in one's own environment."[3] Based on their review of a wide range of research, the botanists explore some of the complex reasons for plant blindness, including our "misguided, anthropocentric ranking of plants as inferior to animals, leading to the erroneous conclusion that they are unworthy of human consideration." One of the reasons may be the inherent constraints of our visual information processing systems. "It seems that visual consciousness is like a spotlight, not a floodlight," they write. "And if that is not shocking enough, we do not see events in real time. The computation time involved in processing the visual data we receive has been shown by experiment to take approximately .5 second, making the present a self-delusion." Plants simply live in a different dimension.

Whatever our limitations — cultural, physiological, or both — considering the acute plant *sightedness* of some cultures, and the neighbor with the green thumb, surely we can overcome some of our plant blindness. Schussler and Wandersee (the perfect name!) think so. They believe we're missing out on, and can come to see, another world. As part of their campaign against plant blindness, they encourage plant lovers to become "plant mentors" to help the rest of us develop a "botanical sense of place."

That morning, James Dillane, botanist and middle school teacher, was the leader of our group. Before we headed out on the trail, we gathered in a park building, where Dillane gave us a short course on the flora of this place — our place. He described our region's extraordinary biodiversity, how it is, above all, a land of chaparral and coastal sage and fire. The Spanish explorer Juan Cabrillo, who sailed to the area in the sixteenth century, called San Diego the Bay of Fire; in the 1880s, fire raged from the Mexican border to Los Angeles and burned everything in its path; and recently, firestorms threatened to do the same. My family has been evacuated twice.

Dillane then showed us a time-lapse video of the backcountry as one of those fires swept over; look closely and you can see chemise chaparral, its waxy cover bursting into flame even before the fire reaches it. The pace of the time-lapse video picks up, moving now much faster than real time—as in the movie *The Time Machine*. Birds of the Pacific Flyway flash by. The fire marches across the land, followed by charring like the sweeping dark shadow of a storm; then countless new plants appear, like camp followers chasing after the flames. I once thought that plants lacked the species-on-species violence of animals—although, is this true? Speeded up in the video, the plants fight for space and water; the natives beat back invaders or are overcome by them.

Watching these videos, I saw for the first time what the botanist sees: a story, a narrative of great families living, burning; and their resurrection—civilizations parallel to our own, but invisible to most of us.

We headed out to the ridges above the lake, steeped in cool afternoon mist. Dillane warmed to the task at hand as he spoke. This land, seemingly mild, lacking in drama, is, in fact, dynamic. Except during fire season, it alters at a pace as slow as an opening flower; we do not see the landscape shift, unless we look closely and know what we are looking for.

"This year the fire poppies, which show up *only* after fires, are spectacular," Dillane said. "A once in a lifetime event! Fire poppy seeds can sit for one hundred years waiting for another fire." What wakens them? "No one thing. Heat, a chemical in the smoke, a charcoal-caused chemical reaction." He pointed out desert broom, a chemise chaparral that the Spanish and Mexicans called *yerba de pasmo*, or herb of the spasm. They, like earlier residents, found it useful for convulsions, snakebites, lockjaw, syphilis, and inflammation. Sage and chaparral scrublands have ingenious survival techniques, he told us. Sage can produce different sizes of leaves depending on the amount of available water; and the leaves of one species of sage is covered with tiny hairs, "creating a kind of sunscreen."

In his book *Green Nature/Human Nature: The Meaning of Plants in Our Lives,* Charles A. Lewis, of the University of Illinois, counsels us to *look,* to see plants not as objects, but as interconnected strands in a larger design, in which we, also, are threads.[4] He writes that the two life forms, plants and humans, "are joined in ways that denote an even closer relationship than most people suspect." Lewis makes the case, as does writer Michael Pollan in *The Botany of Desire,* that we *Homo sapiens* should balance our sense of self-importance with the fact that we are a "plant-dependent species." The chlorophyll molecules of green plants "bear an intriguing similarity to hemoglobin, the prime constituent of mammalian blood," Lewis points out. Both consist of a single atom surrounded by a ring of carbon and nitrogen atoms. The difference is in the central atom: in chlorophyll, the atom is made of magnesium; in hemoglobin, it is made of iron. "The similarity of these two essential biological components suggests a common origin somewhere in the primordial soup where life began on earth," writes Lewis. "Although vegetation's role in sustaining physical mammalian life is fairly well understood, one aspect has remained unexplored. In what ways do plants in their myriad forms enter our mental and spiritual lives? What are the subtle meanings assigned to green nature by the human psyche?"[5]

Lewis is among those who propose that humans are participants in an environmental unconscious with evolutionary origins, that "we each harbor a hidden self that reacts without thinking to signals embedded within our bodies and in the outside world." He adds, "Every subconscious response reveals threads that comprise the fabric of our lives, a protective cloak that has been woven about us for millennia to ensure our survival. Today, in a world largely shaped by intellect, those ancient intuitive threads are frequently pulled. We must learn to read them, for they provide insights into our basic humanity."

Beneath the placid surface of the shrub forest, fungi connect the chaparral roots into vast communities; through this grid, the roots and fungi exchange water and nutrients. This system is comparable to a battery that holds energy until part of the community of chaparral and fungi needs it. Aboveground, lichen—a complex organism consisting of fungi and algae—bonds to chaparral, but some age-discriminating lichens refuse to grow on any chaparral younger than fifty years old.

Now our group stopped in a small canyon that was tucked down tight, with a slender, twenty-foot waterfall. The rock walls of the canyon were illustrated with designs of concentric circles and squares some five hundred to fifteen hundred years ago by Kumeyaay Indians, with paint made from wild cucumber seeds and red ochre and stinkbugs. A member of our party peered at a plant, possibly a willow dock: "I believe I ate that plant as a child. Slightly different." He popped a leaf in his mouth and survived.

As we walked higher, Dillane gestured to a rocky point on a hill above the ridge. "Up there is a shaman's cave. Some guy wanted to build a trail to it, but fortunately that didn't happen."

The air grew cooler as we climbed. We met other dwellers of this shadow world. Chinese houses, toad flats, sun cup poppies. And filaree, a ground cover, one of the first plants introduced to North America by Europeans. "Filaree can 'walk' until it finds a good crack," said Dillane. He introduced us to the "fire followers," including golden earth drop, adder's-tongue fern, the parasitic witches' hair lichen, "the vampire of the plant world." And a towering yucca, a species that can grow two inches a day and, dependent on a single species of moth for pollination, flowers only once every fifteen years.

For a while, Dillane and the members of the group walked in silence. As we hiked to another ridge, he said: "Your eyes don't know what to look at, so you don't see." He stopped suddenly. "Oh, fire poppies! We got fire poppies!"

We stood together on an outcropping of dark, lichen-licked rock. The lake, slate gray in the gathering fog, was below us. "We're seeing one snapshot of one day of the year," he said. "Not like any other. A day when it's a whole different world."

A world that suddenly seemed as exotic as a rain forest.

CHAPTER 10

Welcome to the Neighborhood

Human/Nature Social Capital

SOME PEOPLE DIDN'T believe in the white deer of Mission Hills until they saw it, usually at dusk, slipping through the canyon chaparral. For a decade, the little deer haunted an old urban neighborhood in San Diego, and the people who saw it came to love it. They named it Lucy. After an animal control officer, in a misguided effort to protect it, shot the deer with a tranquilizer gun and it died, over two hundred men, women, and children came to Lucy's funeral at a nearby park. In these hard-edged years, such sentiment may seem strange; to some, even silly. As it turned out, the deer wasn't even truly wild, but an escapee from one of the last urban farms. Even when that information was made public, people in surrounding neighborhoods, including my own, continued to talk about the deer for years, almost as if it were still alive.

To me, the tale illustrates the deep yearning that many urban dwellers feel, a desire to be part of a community that extends beyond human neighbors to the fellow creatures among us. That yearning, acted upon, can improve our lives in countless ways by surrounding us with a larger sense of belonging. In 1995, Harvard sociologist Robert Putnam, in his seminal book, *Bowling Alone*, described the increasing isolation of life, how the associations that once held us together have fallen away.

He pointed to plummeting membership in PTAs, Boy Scouts, and yes, bowling leagues. He used a variety of methods to measure "social capital," a term that describes how well people in a community look out for one another.

Since the publication of his book, Putnam's methodologies have been challenged. Some social psychologists point to the rise of other forms of community, such as book clubs and Internet-based social networking. Nonetheless, Putnam's phrase has entered the language and serves as a useful concept. Now it's time to broaden the social capital hypothesis to *human/nature social capital,* whereby we are made stronger, richer, through our experiences not only with humans but with our other neighbors—animals and plants, and the wilder and more native, the better.

Human Kindness in the Natural Community

Until recently, researchers seldom, if ever, considered exposure to nature a factor in avoiding social alienation or as an important ingredient in the formation of social capital. Building on studies suggesting that wilderness adventures increase participants' capacity to cooperate and trust others, a newer body of research reveals an even broader impact.

Scientists at the University of Sheffield in the UK have found that the more species that live in a park, the greater the psychological benefits to human beings. "Our research shows that maintaining biodiversity levels is important . . . not only for conservation, but also to enhance the quality of life for city residents," said Richard Fuller of the Department of Animal and Plant Science at Sheffield. In related work, researchers at the University of Rochester, in New York, report that exposure to the natural environment leads people to nurture close relationships with fellow human beings, to value community, and to be more generous with money. By contrast, the more intensely people in the study focused on "artificial elements," the higher they rated wealth and fame. Participants were exposed to natural or man-made settings by looking at images on computer screens or by working in a lab with or without plants. "Previous studies have shown the health benefits of nature range from more rapid healing to stress reduction to improved mental performance and vitality," one of the researchers, Richard M. Ryan, noted. "Now we've found nature brings out more social feelings, more value for community and close relationships. People are more caring when they're around nature."[1]

Andrew Przybylski, a coauthor of the Rochester study, offered one explanation: the natural world connects people to their authentic selves.[2] Humans evolved in hunter-and-gatherer societies that depended on mutuality for survival, Przybylski said, thus the evolution of our "authentic selves" is connected to our biophilia. ("Right now, I feel like I can be myself," said one participant in the study, when focused on nature.) Natural environments may also encourage introspection and may provide a psychological safe haven from the man-made pressures of society. "Nature in a way strips away the artifices of society that alienate us from one another," said Przybylski. The authors said the findings have implications for urban planning and architecture. Netta Weinstein, the study's lead author, suggested that people can also take advantage of the hidden benefits of nature by surrounding themselves with indoor plants, natural objects, and images of the natural world.[3]

More contact with nature within cities can also, in some settings, reduce violence. Research conducted in a Chicago public housing development compared the lives of women living in apartment buildings with no greenery outside to those who lived in identical buildings—but with trees and greenery immediately outside. Those living near the trees exhibited fewer aggressive and violent acts against their partners. The researchers linked violence to low scores on tests of concentration, which can be caused by high levels of mental fatigue. This study demonstrated that women living in housing with no greenery outside were both more fatigued and more aggressive.[4] The same researchers, at the University of Illinois, have also shown that play areas in urban neighborhoods with more trees have fewer incidences of violence, possibly because the trees draw a higher proportion of responsible adults.[5]

Human/nature social capital is boosted by the botanical, but animals, like the deer in Mission Hills, also do their part.

Lucy Hollembeak was in her seventies when I first met her. I was eighteen then, and working on a small-town newspaper. Sometimes I would walk to her little house in Arkansas City, Kansas, at dusk, and we would talk far into the night. She was a woman of the prairie who had lived through her share of tragedies; after her husband died, she lived alone for three decades, by choice. She was in her nineties the last time I saw her.

Nearing the end of her life, she was amazed and awed and touched by the smallest things. "My sons say I can get more out of watching a butterfly than anybody they know," she told me. As long as she could maintain her kinship with other species, she did not feel alone.

"Simply getting people together, outside, working in a caring capacity with nature, perhaps even intergenerationally, may be as important as the healing of nature itself," suggests Rick Kool, a professor in the School of Environment and Sustainability at Royal Roads University in Victoria, British Columbia. "Perhaps, in trying to 'heal the world' through restoration, we end up healing ourselves."

Indeed, anecdotal evidence suggests that social capital is increased when people get together to improve or protect the environment in their communities. According to a 2008 comprehensive review of scientific literature conducted by researchers at Australia's Deakin University, when young families were engaged in such activities, "significant social benefits were found to flow from that involvement, including the widening of their social networks." Volunteers working together to care for land "experienced and contributed to higher levels of social capital" and noted "the 'symbiotic' relationship between social and natural capital."[6]

The Western definition of civilization is simply too narrow. At the center of an ancient Chinese view of civilization is the notion of *wen*, which at its root means patterns or markings, like patterns formed by a tangle of branches or the patterns of bird feathers and tree bark. (*Wen* also means cultural or literary values, and was a much-discussed term that was especially important in Chinese governance from 960 to about 1279 CE, during the Song dynasty.) Nature explains itself through these patterns. From *wen* comes:

> *wen-ren* — the civil and literate person
> *wen-xue* — literature
> *wen-ya* — refinement
> *wen-hua* — culture
> *wen-ming* — civilization

Our current concept of civilization, which stems from the words *citizen* and *city*, is bound to the human-made environment; Chinese tradition has it coming from nature. (The existence of this older philosophy does not suggest that China's modern cities are more nature-friendly than anywhere else. There, and in other modern cultures, the work of civilizing our urban life through nature is beginning anew.) As we'll see, building human/nature social capital offers multiple benefits, among them: productive work for people of all ages; new or deepened relationships with neighbors or networks of people who share an interest in urban wildlife or urban agriculture; a social relationship with other species that enriches daily life. Through the restoration of species other than our own comes the restoration of our community — and our families. A caveat: nature *alone* does not civilize us. Adding more nature to our lives improves our civilization only in the context of personal, social, and economic justice.

We Are Not Alone

One of the advantages of living in most cities is human cultural diversity; by applying the Nature Principle, our homes, our neighborhoods, our cities can become more biodiverse, more interesting places to live.

Species diversity, like cultural diversity, enriches our lives and gives us hope.

Building human/nature social capital in our cities can restore optimism among even the most discouraged conservationists. Suzanna Kruger, a seventh-grade life science teacher at a small public middle school in Seaside, a town on the north coast of Oregon, tells how, in the summer of 2002, a connection to another species gave her a sense of hope. She was attending graduate school at Portland State University, at the time, and working as a field assistant for a study of the diversity and abundance of small mammals in remnant urban green spaces within the Urban Growth Boundary in the Portland Metro area. Twice a day she and her colleague checked 156 live traps, tagged the ears of any creatures they caught, and released them. Mostly, they caught deer mice, and sometimes voles and shrews.

"One day we were having a very gloomy conversation about the destruction of the Earth's environment, the type that biologists and biology students frequently fall into," she recalls. The conversation had lasted most of the day. They were working at Marshall Park in southwest Portland. Midway through the collection, she picked up a trap and felt a creature inside. By its movement, she could tell it was not a mouse. She poked open the top door and a little head, like a snake's, popped up and stared into her face. She quickly closed the door. It was a short-tailed weasel. "Our gloom-and-doom conversation stopped immediately and we celebrated finding such a tiny predator not two miles from downtown Portland. Later that summer we caught northern flying squirrels. Everyone I tell—'Hey, did you know that you are living with flying squirrels and weasels in your backyard?'—is astounded. No one knows this. They know about coyotes and deer and raccoons, sure, but not these small nocturnal creatures that are either up in the canopy or under the litter layer.

"I came to question the idea that to have a 'wilderness experience' one must be separated entirely from other human beings in a non-human-impacted environment," she adds. Though she has led numerous wilderness treks for young people, and likes being able to "leave the city behind and get up into the craggy places above timberline," she values her summers as a field assistant in the Portland Metro area just as much.

Mike Houck, executive director of the Urban Greenspaces Institute in Portland, has helped revive or create green spaces there, and has published several editions of his book *Wild in the City*, which is about the wildlife within the Portland city limits. "When I started working as an urban naturalist at the Audubon Society of Portland, I was told by local and regional planners that there was no room for nature in the city, that nature was 'out there,'" he says. Portland Parks and Recreation was preparing to bulldoze what later became a regional prize, Oaks Bottom Wildlife Refuge, "a 160-acre wetland in the heart of the city, where I've seen over one hundred species of birds over the year, and last year witnessed five immature bald eagles in one tree." In 1980, conservation groups ridiculed Houck for wasting time and resources on what he was told was a "totally trashed" environment. The older conservation theories, he believes, were too attached to Henry David Thoreau's aphorism: "In wildness is the preservation of the world." Conservation was focused almost exclusively on wilderness areas, agricultural lands, old-growth forests, and the marine environment.

Today, Houck represents a sea change in thinking. He recommends a twenty-first-century complement to the protection of wild lands. "In livable cities is preservation of the wild, he says." Building human/nature social capital is at the heart of his work—and could be applied to urban regions everywhere, bringing cities to life by bringing more life into cities.

As an extension of his advocacy, Houck leads field trips for Portlanders who want to meet their local urban wildlife. When I spoke with him, he had just returned from escorting twenty people to a local wildlife refuge. "All of them were waxing eloquent about the experience they'd just had," he said. "They watched an immature Cooper's hawk preen for fifteen minutes. They were blown away to see critters that they couldn't imagine live in the heart of the city." Since the 1970s, the Audubon Society of Portland has grown from about one thousand members to over eleven thousand members, "mostly due to the fact that we started doing conservation work in their neighborhoods."

Houck has witnessed firsthand the impact of urban wildlife on the social fabric of the city. "People feel that they are part of a new family. Some of the members of that family are people, some are critters. People develop elaborate walking paths through the city, and they come to have a relationship with the animals they see. They come to know the kingfisher who they see every morning." Houck added, "I had a wonderful feeling this morning, as I walked. I saw the Anna's hummingbird that I've seen almost every day for the last three years. I saw him when I stepped out of my car. Anyone who had a camera would have caught me with this huge smile on my face—because *there was my buddy.*"

The bird was not a buddy to have a beer with, as Houck might say, nor a friend in the human sense, but a neighbor at once familiar and alien, known but mysterious. "With their parallel lives, animals offer man a companionship which is different from any offered by human exchange," wrote the British critic and writer John Berger. "Different because it is a companionship offered to the loneliness of man as a species."[7]

Loving the Land You're With

Researchers have yet to determine just how deeply the nature, meaning both animals and plants, of a new place can seep into a person's consciousness—if it can find a residence as deep in the soul as the first landscape experienced. But surely we can grow closer to a place, and the life that inhabits it, by deciding to do so. To paraphrase the old song: If you can't be with the land you love, love the land you're with.

La Jolla, California, lost a tree one day, but perhaps only Elaine Brooks noticed. She had moved west from Michigan in 1962, but had never quite adjusted to California. Still, in her spare time, Brooks, a marine biologist and community college teacher, studied and cared for the last piece of open natural land in that seaside California town. The patch of canyon and grassland and woods, forgotten in time, nourished her, even after construction began on multimillion-dollar homes crammed into the 1.7 acres along West Muirlands Drive, chewing away the elbow of the patch. In three days, a single bulldozer "removed just about everything that had taken fifty or more years to grow there," Brooks told me that week. For some reason, a camphor tree survived, like one of those freakish points of light—a school, an intact chimney—that remains after a tornado has rummaged across the plains.

In the three years that followed, Brooks often walked past the stunted little camphor tree, stopping to photograph it and all the changes taking place around it. But one Sunday, on her walk along Muirlands to the grocery, she realized that something had changed. "The tree was gone, not gone really, but it was splintered into a crumpled heap at the curb mixed with mounds of dirt and slabs of concrete, wrested into a pile."

A cynic might say that a camphor tree is relatively insignificant; it does not contribute to the economy or the high-tech future, and is replaceable, like the rest of us.

People can become deeply attached to trees, even ones like Brooks's camphor tree, neither native nor particularly special. And some trees *are* magnificent: consider the giant Moreton Bay fig tree of Spring Valley, south of here, the object of a community drive to protect it from the axeman: or, to the north, the Tasmanian blue gum eucalyptus of Escondido, which stands more than ten stories high, the focus of a fifteen-year community effort to protect it—a campaign that survived even the death of a homeless man who fell from the blue gum's highest branches one December morning; or, to the east, the colonnade of Ramona's red gum eucalyptus trees, planted by the children of pioneers in 1910, which, like soldiers in a slow-motion battle, are falling to an invading insect known as the lerp psyllid. The town hopes to replant the row with strong young trees, but the future takes a long time to grow.

Brooks believed that the vegetation that surrounds us "for any length of time completes a kind of transkingdom emotional graft." That graft is easily severed. "It used to take a man with a shovel and an ax or crosscut saw and a team of horses a day or so to cut down a sizable tree, and with the longer time it took, there was also time for reflection about whether or not it was a good thing to do," she said. Yet, standing over what was left of the camphor tree of La Jolla, Brooks told me, she felt a stirring. "What was remarkable to me was that there was this lingering cloud of camphor odor, a rich old scent that just hung in the air over the exposed roots and the wilting leaves, released from the root tissue in the destruction of the bulldozers. Although the carcass was hauled away days earlier, you could still get a whiff of it as you walked by." Just before the camphor tree was removed, she took a few cuttings and carried them home.

CHAPTER 11

The Purposeful Place

You can't know who you are until you know where you are.
—Wendell Berry

THERE WAS A time when developing a spiritual, psychological, physical attachment to place came naturally; today, awareness of our surroundings and our role in this larger life must be developed purposefully, not only by each of us, but by government and business.

One day, I found myself riding through Las Vegas with a Nevada State Parks ranger. We drove through the casino district, commercial strips, and into the land of interchangeable stucco homes and shopping centers—the same cityscape that dominates our urban regions and, increasingly, our mood, in so much of the United States. I looked up and saw the ring of white, blue, and gold that surrounds the city. To the northwest, there is Charleston Peak, which the local residents call Mount Charleston (when they think of it at all). With Joshua trees at its base, and ancient bristlecone pines at its heights, the mountain reaches nearly twelve thousand feet. There are the Spring Mountains and all those distant ridges and peaks that circle the city, and beyond them the Valley of Fire, a vast, beautiful expanse of red sandstone formations that look like beached whales or human hands.

I had been out there just a few weeks before, hiking with my photography buddies, Howard Rosen and Alberto Lau. We had been stunned by the little-known landscape within an hour or so of the Strip. The three of us stood on a rock to photograph petroglyphs. Our shadows from the low sun were cast on the red wall. We instinctively raised our arms. Our silhouettes, arms and legs elongated, seemed to dance on the smooth curves and undulations of the rock wall and matched the depictions of human beings on the rock, with their elongated torsos, arms, and legs. Perhaps the earliest people in the Valley of Fire had stood right here, considered their shadows, then made their mark.

"All that beauty, so close to the Strip. Does Las Vegas promote that as part of what defines Vegas?" I asked the ranger as we drove through the city.

"Some. Not much." She shrugged. "Not enough."

"Wouldn't it be in the region's interest to do that?"

She looked over at me with a bemused expression. "Would seem that way, wouldn't it?"

As it turned out, this was a sore point. She explained: The big casinos decide the reality of Las Vegas, and the last thing that the owners of the casinos want is for tourists to go outside. They want them gaming. "The little casinos, out on the edges, they might want to do that, but not the big ones." It seemed to me that in an economic downturn, and as Indian casinos across the country siphon off some of the gambling business, diversification in tourist incentives should be attractive.

I looked up again at the ring of white, blue, and gold surrounding the city.

"You could call it the Golden Ring," I said.

When I asked the ranger if Las Vegas promoted that ring, I didn't just mean as a tourist attraction (though diversifying this region's economy wouldn't hurt); I was thinking more about a richness of identity, of purpose.

As our lives grow more technological, media-dominated, and abstract, our hunger for a more authentic sense of personal and community identity will grow. As the parts of modern existence become more interchangeable, two outcomes are possible. The value we place on authenticity will fade, or our yearning for it will become so painfully felt, so clear, that we will be drawn irresistibly to whatever remains authentic and real. If the latter, the value of the natural world will grow in our eyes and in all our senses. We will come to view natural history to be as important to our personal and regional identities as human history, particularly in those places where human history has been interrupted or forgotten.

Just as individuals can develop a natural sense of place for their own well-being, the leaders of a region—a city, a town, or a bioregion that crosses man-made borders—can become more *purposeful* by identifying the unique natural qualities of their bioregion.

As defined by the Planet Drum Foundation, a bioregion is "a whole 'life-place . . . a distinct area with coherent and interconnected plant and animal communities, and natural systems," often marked by a watershed. Raymond Dasmann, a professor emeritus of ecology at the University of California–Santa Cruz, as well as a founder of international environmentalism, and Peter Berg, an activist who founded Planet Drum, are cited for bringing the bioregion concept into the public conversation in the 1970s. (Poet Gary Snyder's writings, a decade earlier, also explored this theme.) Planet Drum sponsors publications, speakers, and workshops to help start new bioregional groups and encourages local organizations and individuals to find ways to live within the natural confines of bioregions. Dasmann and Berg call their approach reinhabitation—or "living-in-place. . . . Simply stated it involves becoming fully alive in and with a place."[1] Fully alive. That, to me, is the most active phrase. We can reinhabit our bioregions, according to Dasmann and Berg, through exploring, mapping, naming, and promoting their special natural qualities, and then incorporating them into a bioregional identity, creating a new story for a region. Or an old story, newly realized.[2]

We already have early-stage examples of such communities. Branded "Ecotopia" by Ernest Callenbach, the Northwest is known for its (not always consistent) commitment to environmental values. Salmon, for instance, has historically shaped Seattle's daily culture and its ever-present iconography. In the late 1990s, I attended a conference about a conflict between Canada, the United States, and several Indian tribes—or First Nations, as Canadians call them—over salmon fishing rights and the threat of Pacific salmon extinction. "Soon we're going to be arguing about the last fish!" said Billy Frank, the man who forced the U.S. government to honor its fishing treaties with the Northwest tribes. To Frank and others, the debate was not only about economic resources, but also about personal, tribal, and regional identity. Then-Rep. Elizabeth Furse, from Washington County, Oregon, agreed. She spoke about salmon as an icon of health and identity. "Their presence is what tells us that we are or are not healthy. On a personal level the reason the salmon mean so much to me is that they have such a sense of home. The salmon know how to get home. They know where they came from."

Adirondacks Park in upstate New York is an example in the United States of a purposeful place that has been both reinhabited *and* rewilded—brought back to a natural condition that had been lost for a century. No land-planning model is perfect, in execution, and none are applicable everywhere. But Adirondacks Park suggests one approach to restoring environmentally damaged bioregions, by seeding them with people.

Howard Fish, director of communications for the newly opened Wild Center at Tupper Lake, a natural history museum dedicated to the region, explained why this could serve as a model for other regions around the world.

"Outside of the state, and even most places in the state, people really don't know how remarkable this park is," he said, as he drove me north to the Wild Center. Here, the word *park* has a special meaning. Unlike most mountain ranges that run north, offering migration paths, this massive dome of rock and forest—visible from space—was a cold barrier to human transportation, for American Indians and early European settlers alike. That is, until the loggers arrived. "Centuries-old white pines fell for their timber; other trees destined for pulp mills and steel furnaces jammed Adirondack rivers," according to Fish. Photographs of the region from a century ago show wide swaths of devastated landscape largely denuded by loggers, a fit habitat for skeletal stumps and mud. Remarkably, the region is wilder today than it was in the late nineteenth century. "There may be nowhere else on Earth where the same claim can be made for a space of this great scale," said Fish. "The mountains are again blanketed in wild forests. Moose bugle here; beavers smack their tails and it's possible that mountain lions growl."

Driving through this region, one sees seemingly endless lakes and streams and marshes and mountains, fertile forests inhabited by bears and people. How did this happen?

First, in 1894, a group of scientists, everyday citizens, sportsmen, and conservationists persuaded New York voters to amend the state constitution and designate some five hundred thousand acres "forever wild." Over time, through land trusts and other methods, the original five hundred thousand acres grew to three million. This is the largest publicly protected area in the contiguous United States, larger today than Yellowstone, Great Smoky Mountains, Yosemite, Glacier, and Grand Canyon national parks combined.

The second characteristic is that the region was designed for people, the prescient idea being to achieve human/nature restoration, a return of wildness and human habitation, as one piece. The entire park boundary encompasses some six million acres, nearly half belonging to private landowners. From the outset, the preserve resembled a series of islands more than a protected park. They exist inside a park boundary that is like a lasso that loops often random parcels into a single entity. Inside that loop there are Forest Preserve lands, and private holdings, including towns and hamlets, some no more than a store at a crossroads, along with farms, timberlands, businesses, recreational camps, and homes. The Adirondack Park Agency sets hamlet boundaries "well beyond established settlements" to allow for expansion. The Nature Conservancy is currently engaged in major transactions that, when complete, will add another one hundred thousand acres to the protected area of the Adirondacks. "The lands they are securing include Follensby Pond, where Emerson and others gathered in 1858 to reflect on the value of wilderness to the human spirit," said Fish. "This is one of the places in the United States where a human population and wildlife live together in relative harmony. If 20 percent of New York State can be wild, then we can have Adirondacks-like preserves—for humans and other animals—all over the world," albeit not as large.

As Fish and I traveled across this wild land and through occasional settlements, I wondered if a U.S. map had ever been drawn identifying those areas of the country where such a model could be applied: ecologically damaged regions that could be restored in a new way, as, essentially, human/nature reservations. No, he said, but there should be such a map, and not only for the United States. "What has happened here is that the natural landscape of a region the size of Vermont has been brought back to life. *People* have made this restoration happen." And in the process, people have been restored. And when they move away, like those salmon of the Northwest, they often come home.[3]

A Human/Nature Report Card

The creation of the purposeful place on a large scale requires a sophisticated toolbox that includes individual effort or programs that encourage individuals to find their sense of place; regional planning; rewilding; a method to measure the complete economic value of a region's natural history; and news media and policymakers who consciously value a bioregion not only for its extractive or recreational value, but also for something deeper.

Let's consider one of those tools, the need to define the *full* economic value of a bioregion by measuring a number of indictors, including nature's impact on human health. Translating the natural world into economic worth is a controversial subject; many people resist reducing nature to dollars and cents. Doing so, they say, commodifies and devalues spiritual life enriched by the world, as well as nature's intrinsic and immeasurable worth. Indeed, if we go down the road of economic measurement *without* an accompanying moral argument, we risk applying the same reductionism that shaped education reform in the recent decade: *Only that which can be counted counts.* (It's apropos that the sign on Albert Einstein's office door at Princeton said, "*Not everything* that counts can be counted, and *not everything* that can be counted counts.")

Still, if a community fails to make the economic argument for a bioregion's worth based on values involving the health of the humans and other creatures who live in that zone, then the community rolls out a red carpet for corporations or governments that wish to strip nature of what *they* define as its economic worth. These interests know exactly how to define their interpretation of value; through the economics of extraction and, ultimately, destruction. Those of us who place more value on nature's intrinsic worth and its impact on human health and well-being need a more convincing set of metrics. Ideally, every urban region in every bioregion should establish the economic importance of nature experiences for children and adults. Today, many cities and states produce Kids Count report cards, which compare the conditions of children over time. Similarly, cities, counties, states, and economic development agencies could produce report cards on economic health — again, with the purpose of comparing progress or decline over time. Policymakers are inclined to rely heavily on such reports.

A Human/Nature Report Card would include but go beyond traditional measures of profit and revenue from outdoor recreation (fishing, boating, hiking, and so on), or concerns about the negative results of environmental toxins; it would consider the positive economic impact on public mental and physical health, education, and jobs. Measures of the influence of the natural world on child and adult obesity and depression, for example, could be translated into direct and indirect costs of health care and lost productivity. The positive impact of parks, open space, and nearby nature on property values could also be measured, year to year, going beyond the spot studies that already show a higher resale value of homes on the edge of natural places. The economic benefits of outdoor classrooms and place-based education might be estimated.

Such an ongoing, comprehensive regional study—linking human health and economic well-being to the health of the bioregion—would help policymakers who do care about the environment make a convincing argument for its protection.

In 2009, the New Economics Foundation announced its first Happy Planet Index (HPI). Caerphilly County Borough in South Wales, which scored well, pursues the goal of regional vitality. In 2008, the borough "became the first local authority in the UK to truly build well-being into its understanding of sustainable development," according to the HPI. "Living better, using less," is the borough's motto. Caerphilly already had one of the lowest ecological footprints in the UK, but saw room for improvement. "A key aim of the new strategy is to enable [members of] the communities of the county borough to live longer, healthier, more fulfilled lives, in a sustainable way that breaks the link between wealth and resource consumption, and between resource consumption and fulfilled lives," according to the HPI report. Caerphilly adopted HPI's equation as a key element when explaining its definition of sustainability, with a goal of achieving the three main objectives of the strategy. Their target date is 2030, when the world is expected to hold eight billion people. Among other actions, Caerphilly has started work on developing community gardens, "which get people doing mild exercise, meeting others in their community, eating healthily, and reducing their reliance on imported food."

HPI offers an intriguing formula for achieving its interpretation of sustainable development; it reaches beyond the traditional definitions of sustainability and economic and human health—combining them into one measure.[4]

Or consider Costa Rica, which in 2009 was at the top of a list of 143 countries measured by the Happy Planet Index 2.0.[5] In addition, the World Database of Happiness gave Costa Rica 8.5 points out of 10; runner-up Denmark scored 8.3 points.[6] The fact that Costa Rica hasn't funded a national military for decades helps; that money goes to social services, education, and protecting their natural areas. The government there also raises revenue through a carbon tax, introduced in 1997, and it ranked third in the world, behind Iceland and Switzerland, in the 2010 Environmental Performance Index published by Yale and Columbia universities. (The United States held sixty-first place, just behind Paraguay.)[7] In a 2010 article headlined "The Happiest People," *New York Times* columnist Nicholas Kristof wrote, "Costa Rica has done an unusually good job preserving nature." Which is not to say Costa Rica has entirely transcended the troubles of the rest of the planet; for example, drug and related crime problems continue in that country. ("It's surely easier to be happy while basking in sunshine and greenery than while shivering up north and suffering 'nature-deficit disorder,'" he added.)

The search for personal happiness is one impetus for moving toward a living-in-place philosophy. Another related motivation is the surging need for energy efficiency, including the local production and distribution of food, and the creation of localized electricity sources through solar and wind-driven generators, ocean wave turbines, and other methods. Architect Sergio Palleroni, a professor and Fellow of the Center for Sustainable Practices and Processes, Portland State University, Oregon, predicts: "Housing will get more regionalized. Too much of housing is driven by prototypes that are supposed to apply nationwide. Increasingly, sustainability is driving us to understand local issues and opportunities, both in how buildings perform and with changing economics."[8] In other words, think globally, build and plant locally.

This brings us to the Transition Town movement. At this writing, there are 266 communities (towns, cities, regions), mainly in the UK (a few exist in the United States, Australia, and New Zealand) that have identified themselves as transition towns, cities, villages, or regions. By *transition*, proponents mean a shift to the postpetroleum age. Rob Hopkins, a British teacher and permaculturalist, hatched the idea in 2006. Permaculture is the practice of designing human communities and food systems that mimic sustainable ecologies. In essence, permaculture is permanent agriculture. The transition philosophy holds that, in the era of peak oil, we can't wait for our governments to make the necessary changes, and individuals can't create a new society entirely on their own. But communities can move relatively quickly to plan a fifteen- to twenty-year transition to locally grown food, restorative transportation (more walking and biking paths and alternative fuel vehicles), the use of local building materials, and other approaches.

Communities considering becoming transition towns are called "mullers"—as in, they're mulling it over. One of the most advanced transition towns is Totnes, in the southwestern corner of England. When I visited Totnes and surrounding countryside, I was impressed by the foundation already in place: a medieval pattern of small cities and villages, circled by land that had remained in agricultural use or forested for centuries. Good place to start.

Hopkins remains determined to win people over with upbeat ideas. Far from doing with less, the creators of transition towns believe they're part of a twenty-first century renaissance. "It's about unleashing that potential," says Hopkins, "and you don't do that by trying to depress everyone into action. It's about feeling part of something historic, something timely. . . . I often liken where we are now to 1939. It's like a wartime mobilization. Scale of response is what we need to get through this process."

In 1939, though, government led the mobilization. So government will be required to reach the scale Hopkins believes is necessary. Still, one can imagine a coalescing of place-based movements: energy- and food-focused Transition Towns, Sense of Place explorers, experiential educators, Citizen Naturalists (to be described later in these pages), and a host of other nature-oriented campaigns. One shared characteristic of the leaders of these campaigns is that they're not waiting for the usual authorities. They're taking Buckminster Fuller's advice: "You never change things by fighting the existing reality. To change something, build a new model that makes the existing model obsolete."

Living in Place

Today, I no longer have quite the same reaction when people ask me where I am from. In the past, I might have said Kansas or Missouri. But now, increasingly, when people ask me about my roots, I might mention Kansas, but then I say that California is my home. Given a chance, I will also begin to tell them about the richness of my region, the strangeness of it, and that this strangeness and beauty comes from the biodiversity. And I would describe my region's nascent sense of purpose that comes from efforts to create natural corridors for animal migration, protect endangered species, produce more local food, and at least begin to think about building nature-focused neighborhoods and greening older neighborhoods.

Not long ago, Mike Hager, president and CEO of the San Diego Natural History Museum, asked me to do some brainstorming with him about the future of the museum. I was eager to meet with him, to share some of my thoughts.

What if the museum, working with the zoo, the universities, media, businesses, and others, were to rethink how we describe our region and how we market it? What if we took deep pride in our diverse and fascinating bioregion?

Without that pride and that sense of regional identity, there will be no protection of the miraculous. Even as I spoke with Hager, a coalition of groups was busy designing what it calls a "conservation vision" for a 2.5-million-acre area of Southern California and northern Baja. One of the initiative's goals is establishment of an extensive binational park system connecting wilderness, forests, and parkland. Several years ago, California's Condor Recovery Team, led by a long-time researcher with the San Diego Zoo, released three condors in the Baja's isolated Sierra San Pedro Mártir. The researchers hoped that the condors would someday fly north to Ventura, to Sespe Condor Sanctuary or the wilderness near Big Sur, and join their U.S. relatives. Prior to this, the last condor seen in the Sierra San Pedro Mártir was in the 1930s—by a young rancher named Andy Meling, whom Jason and I had met so many decades later. I can imagine him then, hat set back on his head, squinting into the fading light, watching creatures with nine-foot wingspans circle the lost world.

Perhaps, I suggested to Hager, we should name our region, with its great natural attributes, including sea and mountains and micro-climates, something romantic and mysterious that would identify this region for people from all over the world, a name that would place nature first. Perhaps an ancient Kumeyaay Indian word. Or Cuyabaja? Pandora? By any name, this would be our found world, our purposeful place.

The Citizen Naturalist

In every bioregion, one of the most urgent tasks is to rebuild the community of naturalists, so radically depleted in recent years, as young people have spent less time in nature, and higher education has placed less value on such disciplines as zoology.

The word *amateur* has fallen on hard times, as in, "Oh, she's such an amateur." It's become something of a pejorative. The original use of the word probably came from the French form of the Latin root, *amātor:* lover, or lover of, or devotee. In Thomas Jefferson's time, when society was agrarian, few people made their living as scientists; most were amateurs, as was Jefferson. He was an amateur naturalist who tutored Meriwether Lewis in the White House before sending him off to record the flora and fauna of the West. The times are right for the return of the amateur, a twenty-first-century version—the citizen naturalist. (A form of that concept that already exists is the "citizen scientist," but I prefer the word *naturalist* because it is more specific to nature and, well, sounds like a lot more fun.) To be a citizen naturalist is to take personal action, to both protect and participate in nature.

Citizen naturalists are especially valuable in a region like San Diego, a biodiversity hot zone. Here, fortuitously, four hundred volunteers helped compile the landmark *San Diego County Bird Atlas* before massive firestorms burned 20 percent of the county's land surface, possibly wiping out entire bird populations. The volunteers expanded our knowledge of the nearly five hundred species of birds that live, vacation, or loiter here, from geographically confused parrots to a bushtit that builds its nest from spiderwebs. These volunteers detected changes in bird ranges and discovered a few avian species not previously known to live in the county. The atlas's chief compiler and author, Philip Unitt, calls these citizen naturalists the book's backbone, its spine.

This approach offers equal billing to catastrophe and fulfillment. "Our focus isn't only on endangered species, but on all the other birds that live around us," says Unitt. In short, he wants to keep common birds common—iridescent in late afternoon light, and alive.

If Unitt's success with volunteers is any indication, a nascent citizen naturalist movement is already beginning to expand. In my region, citizen naturalists are young and old; they're teachers, journalists, and plumbers. They sit on mountaintops for weeks in the Anza-Borrego Desert to record the ghostly presence of bighorn sheep and help track mountain lions; they trek through backcountry in search of the genetic Adam or Eve of rainbow trout, which may still live in nearly inaccessible creeks. Students, working with a marine biologist, tag and track threatened shark species. Around the world, in Africa and Europe, Asia and the Middle East, other amateurs do similar work, sometimes losing or saving their lives in the pleasure of the pursuit. These are passionate, dedicated people, Jefferson's spiritual heirs.

In response to concern about the shortage of professional naturalists and taxonomists, the BBC launched an unprecedented project called Springwatch, inviting viewers and listeners to help map climate changes in the British Isles. Focusing on six key signs that spring has arrived, the BBC collects data sent in by the public and uses it to create a televised seasonal event. Participants are encouraged to record their findings online. Meanwhile, a Springwatch partner, the Woodland Trust, the UK's leading woodland conservation charity, is expanding its network of over eleven thousand registered nature "recorders."[9]

Some U.S. conservation and nature-education organizations are moving in a similar direction. For example, the California Academy of Sciences organized the Bay Area Ant Survey, recruiting citizen naturalists to help document more than one hundred distinct types of ant species in the eleven-county Bay Area.[10] On a larger scale, the National Wildlife Federation (NWF), with over four million members, is expanding its efforts to train young people to become NWF-certified citizen naturalists. And Cornell University's Project FeederWatch has for many years enlisted the interest and sharp eyes of amateur birders across North America to help scientists understand movements of winter bird populations.[11] With these amateurs' help, researchers track trends in bird numbers and distribution over the United States and Canada. Volunteers pay a small fee, are issued a participant kit, and follow clear guidelines to ensure accuracy. They report their counts, by species, to Cornell University for data analysis. The annual survey extends for twenty-one weeks, from November through the first part of April. Results are published in scientific journals and shared online.

In some communities, citizen naturalists are taking up "plant rescue." In King County, Washington, the Native Plant Salvage Program organizes hundreds of volunteers to save plants threatened by development. As James McCommons writes in *Audubon* magazine, these salvage operations "draw up to 300 people, who literally run into the woods to stake out hard-to-find species—trilliums, sedges, and mosses." The plants are transferred to ecological restoration projects, demonstration gardens, and wildlife habitats created in backyards. Ambivalence comes with the turf. Some may see plant rescue as another form of mitigation, green-washing the destruction of habitat by developers. More accurately, it's a creative response to development and a way to publicize the threats to the natural habitat. In Tucson, Arizona, the Tucson Cactus and Succulent Society organizes volunteers to rescue cacti. "Wherever lands are being developed there are opportunities to do plant salvages," McCommons writes. "Even small parcels, such as a lot for a single-family home, can yield a treasure trove of native flora."[12]

Another citizen naturalist role is "work-camper." During the Great Recession, some park managers felt the economic pinch so acutely they closed the gates, but others relied on volunteers in their motor homes to keep trails clear and trash picked up until funds become available to hire regular staff. "Work-campers come together in one place—leading nature walks or staffing visitor centers, typically working 20 hours to 30 hours a week—then take off to their next assignments," reported the *New York Times*.[13]

At Seattle's Woodland Park Zoo, Deborah Jensen, the zoo's president and CEO, would like to see more community involvement. Typically, zoos offer education programs, but Woodland Park, with a more regional focus than most, is planning a particularly ambitious outreach program. Rather than just taking animals to local schools, the zoo will become the focal point for a growing network of the state's environmental education programs. Jensen told a story that illustrated the potential role zoos could play. A few years ago, a gyrfalcon escaped from the zoo. "This was a large bird with an attached transmitter, but we couldn't find it, so we put out a press release to the media," she says. People all over the region, young and old, were looking for the bird, and someone found it. "Later, we received a letter from a boy who had been one of the searchers. The experience changed him. He said he had never realized how many birds lived in Seattle, how much nature was in his own neighborhood."

So let's increase the number of front-line citizen naturalists, who count, chart, map, collect, protect, tag, track, heal, and generally get to know countless species of plants and animals in the wild, in the elfin forests of their own backyards, or the woods, or the great national parks, or at the end of the alley in an inner-city neighborhood.

A Tree Grows in South Central

With human/nature social capital in mind, we must create or retrofit whole communities in which humans, wild animals, domesticated animals, along with native vegetation, live in kinship. This can be done in a way that strengths the diversity of human settlements and the planet. The question of human/nature kinship is one of the great architectural, urban planning, and social challenges of the twenty-first century.

Let me introduce you to a hero and friend of mine. I sat down with him recently, at a conference focused on connecting the next generation to the outdoors.

Juan Martinez, twenty-six, was wearing his customary flat-brim ball cap and baggy chinos. Juan was raised in South Central Los Angeles, and he grew up angry. "I was the poor of the poor. People would make fun of me, people would tease me about my clothes. So it was my defense mechanism to pretty much kick their ass," he recalled. At the time, he seemed to be a prime candidate for a short, unremarkable gang life. When he was fifteen, a teacher at Dorsey High School in South Central offered an ultimatum: Juan could flunk the class and likely be held back a grade, or he could join the school's Eco Club.

Begrudgingly, he chose the latter. "The first couple weeks I didn't talk to people. I focused on growing my little jalapeño plant," he said.

"Why a jalapeño?" I asked.

He described how his mother had broken through a piece of concrete behind the family's house, exposing soil for a small garden. There, she grew jalapeños and medicinal plants, including aloe vera for cuts and burns. "She would make teas out of these plants whenever we were sick," said Juan. "So I wanted to show my mom that I could do that, too, that I could grow something, that I could give her something in return."

A trip to Wyoming's Grand Teton National Park, organized by the Eco Club and Teton Science Clubs, changed his life forever—and at first, not entirely for the better.

"I saw bison. I saw more stars than I could count. I was where there was no concrete, no gunshots, no helicopters over my head," he recalls. When he came home, he found he couldn't get enough nature. "It became like an addiction." He joined the Sierra Club's Building Bridges to the Outdoors program, and participated in every program he could that would transport him back to wilderness, becoming an outdoor leader. "Every time I came back from a trip, I was more depressed with where I lived. I would lock myself in my room. I just hated being home."

His growing distaste for what he considered "the dreaded dead-end road" of South Central showed and, he says, limited his effectiveness as a leader. Fortunately, his outdoor mentors noticed his depression, and understood its source. "They sat me down and talked to me. Then they took me to community gardens and local green spaces, places not so far away, places that I could get to on a bus." And he continued to organize wilderness expeditions.

As we spoke, Juan told me about taking twenty kids from Watts on a backpacking course into the Eastern Sierra. Many of them were heavily medicated for behavior problems. "The first day of the fourteen-day trip was a rough one, with threats of violence, crying, fighting," he said, but halfway through the trip the young people began to settle into a more natural rhythm. "Our nightly fires were filled with laughter. All they wanted was to be listened to, to be heard, to be recognized. They talked about the songbird that had captivated them that day or why people got hooked on drugs back home."

Around that fire, he found himself thinking of his own community, which was hundreds of miles away. And he came to a realization: "I love nature because I love people," he said. Juan concluded that he had to stop thinking mainly about what nature did for him personally. "It was never just about me! It was always about the love I have for my family, for my culture, for my community, for the mentors that have stood by my side through thick and thin," he said. "I became a better person when I stopped caring about only my smile, my sanity, my therapy in nature and I found one of my greatest joys came from the laugh of a kid (whose mother had beat her with a bat and abandoned her in an alley), helping them make s'mores for the first time, making a wish on a star."

He returned from that backpacking trip with a purpose: Instead of leaving South Central, he would commit to it. "I would do all I could to share with my community the joy of nature, even by building a place in the middle of the 'hood for songbirds, by sharing the crops of our small garden at home and teaching others how to do their own raised-bed gardens."

Since then, Juan's work has expanded. He serves as National Youth Volunteer Coordinator for the Sierra Club and leads the Natural Leaders Network of the Children and Nature Network, a group of several hundred young people, many of them, like Juan, from inner cities. He also advises U.S. Interior Secretary Ken Salazar on his department's emerging plan to create a youth conservation corps. And Juan has been invited to the White House twice.

But he always comes home to South Central.

Natural Capacity

As Juan talked about his mother's garden of jalapeños and medicinal plants, I was reminded that it's a mistake to focus only on the cultural or geographic barriers that stand between nature and people. We need to consider the strong cultural links to nature that already exist and can be built on. This requires thinking outside the tent, not only beyond ethnic and racial stereotypes, but about what qualifies as outdoor recreation. For example, national and state park officials describe, with respect and appreciation, the many Hispanic families who use the outdoors for family picnics and reunions—social activities now seemingly rare among people who look like me. That's natural capacity.

"Portland was once a lily-white city. With more Hispanic and Asian immigration, we're changing rapidly," says Mike Houck, Portland's wildscaper. These populations are often overlooked in the effort to protect or expand wildlife in a city. When Houck asked a local Spanish-language radio station to help out with an effort to save urban wetlands, 450 Hispanic residents showed up for a rally. In California, where 37 percent of the state's citizens are Hispanic or Latino, that population voted disproportionately in favor of an open-space initiative. "It all depends on your approach," he says.

African Americans bring their own heritage to the outdoors. "Stereotypes persist that African Americans are physically and spiritually detached from the environment," writes Dianne D. Glave, in *Rooted in the Earth: Reclaiming the African American Environmental Heritage.* "This wrongheaded notion is so ingrained in our culture that many of us have begun to believe it ourselves."[14] The history is complicated but rich. Forests and farms existed in the shadows of slavery. Nature, therefore, could be a forbidding place. Despite that, according to Glave, "African Americans actively sought healing, kinship, resources, escape, refuge and salvation in the land. . . . These positive and negative forces made the wild theirs, for better or worse." That, too, is natural capacity.

In the age of climate change and nature-deficit disorder, such experiences underscore this truth: Our relationship with nature is not only about preserving land and water, but about preserving and growing the bonds between us.

CHAPTER 12

The Bonding

How the Nature Principle Can Strengthen
Our Relationships with Family and Friends

OREDOM HAS ITS benefits. So does solitude, that lost art in
the age of wall-to-wall media. To occasionally be alone—not
lonely, but alone—is an important part of parenting and of
marriage. One time my wife, Kathy, rented a room at the beach, and
spent a weekend with no electronic interruptions, no demands for time
or attention, just the sound of the waves and gulls. She came home
looking even younger than she usually does.

Several years ago, facing a writing deadline, I drove to the Cuyamaca
Mountains. My friends Jim and Anne Hubbell had invited me to house-
sit a magical little hobbit house on their property there, and I planned
to spend a whole week there, alone.

I had done this once before, on another deadline. I had spent a week
in a bunkhouse made from an abandoned railroad car in the hills of
Mesa Grande, just west of the Cuyamacas. There, I had worked during
the heat of the day and then wandered at dusk through mountain lion
country. I had always felt watched, and had carried a dried yucca walking stick. Each evening, when the stars began to appear, I would stop
at an open watering tank to wash up. I'd float for a while, looking at the
stars. Then I'd head back to the boxcar.

This time, the accommodations were better, a charming little house with windows of stained glass—I even had electricity, and a comfortable bed to sleep in. In the gray dawn on my first morning there, I opened my eyes to see a coyote standing next to a window. It stared at me.

I got up, made coffee, and went to work.

During these days of solitude, moving clouds and lifting wind would begin to bring forth voices: of a father and a mother, now gone, and of my wife and children. On the fourth day, Kathy and the boys, Jason and Matthew, arrived in the flesh for a visit. In solitude, even for a few days, a person changes subtly; the customary phrases and patterns seem odd, somehow. So our first minutes together felt a little awkward. But this is why taking a retreat, as a husband or wife or parent, is a good thing. Familiar patterns can shield us from true familiarity.

At the end of their visit, Kathy took me aside and said that Jason had commitments at home, but Matthew would like to stay with me for my remaining three days. He was terribly bored at home and needed a break from his brother (and his brother needed a break from him). "Of course," I said, "as long as he understands that I need to work, and he'll have to entertain himself."

At eleven, Matthew was in the between time, in the gap between childhood and adolescence. This is a particularly magical stage in a boy's life, a time when it's good to take a break from routine, to spend some time in silence.

My wife and older son drove off, and Matthew and I went through the house to look for books for him to read. There was no TV and no radio. Not a single electronic game, either. He picked out a J. R. R. Tolkien novel and another book about a boy who adopts a wolf cub. He sat on an old couch behind me and, respecting my need for quiet, began to read.

Three hours later I realized he had not said a word. I turned around. He was asleep, holding Tolkien like a stuffed bear.

That evening, we walked up the hill and swam together in a round, tiled pool under a quarter moon, and later, we listened to the wind come up and the coyotes jabber in fits and starts. For the next three days, we talked only occasionally, usually in the pool or at dinner. He was a voluble boy, so I was surprised that silence came so easily to him.

The absence of electronics (except for my laptop computer) helped. So did the wildness of the land around us. So did the fact that his father was there, but quieter than usual. I asked him to take charge of feeding the cats and dog. He gave names to the cats, who followed him around the property, scrambling up the oaks to show off for him. In the evenings we swam or walked, and he took his camera, and snuck up on the deer that wandered through an orchard at dusk.

Matthew and I moved into a new rhythm. I got to know him better during those days, and perhaps he came to know me better, not because we talked, but because we didn't. As a parent, you capture such quiet moments when you can, in the loudness of time.

The Bond

Just as the re-naturing of everyday life can be an important component of strengthening physical, psychological, and intellectual fitness, a sense of purpose in a bioregion can also strengthen relationships between parents, children, and grandparents; and between extended families, couples without children, and just plain friends.

When life opens new doors for Ron Swaisgood, they usually lead him outside. Swaisgood is director of Applied Animal Ecology for the San Diego Zoo Institute for Conservation Research. He and his wife, Janice, shared their first date on the Dyar Springs and Juaquapin Loop, a trail east of the city that climbs gently through the Cuyamaca Mountains. They stopped at a rocky outcropping, and Ron set out strawberries, cheese, and sparkling grape juice. It was then that Janice first realized it was a date. "It's where I should have kissed her, had I not been so nervous," says Ron. "We spent the day together and got to know each other well, far beyond what would have ever been possible on a more traditional date."

A month later, Janice and Ron went on their first trip together. They traveled to Michoacán, Mexico, to witness the spectacle of the monarch butterflies overwintering in the mountains. Millions of monarchs congregated on the pines, so dense that you could not even see the green needles. The ground was covered by "a sad carpet of dead monarchs," he recalls. "And the air was so filled with butterflies that if we paused for even a moment, the monarchs would begin to land on us. My new girlfriend, gazing deep into my eyes, covered with butterflies — that's an image to remember." A year and a half later, Ron took Janice back to the rocky outcropping in the Cuyamacas, where he had failed to kiss her. "I summoned up my courage and was going to propose to her at the outcropping, but it was summer and hot, and there was an unusual outbreak of biting flies on the trail. We turned back before we got to the rock, bug-bitten, hot, and sweaty. I didn't want my proposal met with a slap across my face — meant to kill a fly." They never lost their love for that place, though. Years later, they named their firstborn after the trail: Owen Dyar Swaisgood.

Since then, Ron tells me, he has discovered a whole new world. "The past six years since arriving at fatherhood have provided more vivid and meaningful experiences in nature than my first forty years without children," he says. "My children have reconnected me to nature on a more profound level than ever before. They have opened my eyes — the eyes of a trained animal ecologist! — to nature as I've never seen it before, or can no longer remember from my own childhood."

Such a statement may seem surprising, coming from a man with one of the best pedigrees in the nature business. Quiet-spoken, at once easygoing and intense, he describes some of his past adventures: how, in Africa, he almost "became part of the food chain for the first time" when a rhino charged him and stopped just a few feet away, and when a buffalo chased him into the trees; how in a Peruvian rain forest, he sat spellbound as animals passed by "like animate waves," including white-lipped peccaries "that snort and root and clack their tusks," and brown capuchin monkeys, "leaping from one palm frond to another." But now, he says, "I spend a lot more time looking down at the creepy crawlies. I move a lot slower through nature and, thus, spend more time *in* nature."

Nature relaxes and opens the channels of communication, he explains. "Nature can be coexperienced by parent and child in ways that Chuck E. Cheese's just can't."

Special People and Special Places: Attachment Theory and Nature

Families can be bound, over generations, by a shared love of baseball, by a family business, by other shared interests—but nature has its own power. What better way to escape the constant, interrupting beeping of modern life and actually have a chance to spend concentrated time with one another than a walk in the woods?

"Research has not looked specifically at a link between outdoor experience and quality of parent-child attachment, and certainly parents can be sensitive and responsive to their babies and young children indoors or out, but, in many ways, the natural world seems to invite and facilitate parent-child connection and sensitive interactions," according to Martha Farrell Erickson, a developmental psychologist, founding director of the University of Minnesota's Children, Youth, and Family Consortium, and expert on attachment theory in child psychology. In a 2009 paper for the Children and Nature Network, she wrote, "Building gradually and slowly over the first year of a child's life, parent-infant attachment is a child's first close relationship and, to a large extent, a model for all relationships that follow."[1]

Research into the importance of the quality of the attachment between a child and primary caretaker, and how that relates to a person's development throughout life, has been accumulating since the 1960s. While child care providers and other adults can offer children a sense of security, most of the responsibility for building attachment falls to the primary caregiver—the parent, grandparent, or guardian. Approximately 70 percent of babies in the United States develop "secure" attachments but about 30 percent experience "insecure" or "anxious" attachments.[2] According to developmental psychologists, positive early attachment is linked to whether children (and these children later, as adults) perceive the world as a safe place, learn to trust and affect the people around them, have the power to ask for what they need, and feel confident and enthusiastic.

Unplugging from electronics and taking a baby "into the backyard, a park, or a nature trail," Erickson writes, can eliminate distractions "and create an opportunity for what is called 'affective sharing'—oohing and aahing together over the sun shining through the leaves of a big tree, feeling the rough bark and the soft moss on the tree's trunk, listening to the sounds of birds or squirrels, feeling a soft spring rain or a light winter snowfall on your face."

Time in nature helps both the child and the parent by building their shared sense of attachment and by reducing stress. "By following a prescription for more nature experience *together*, families will discover a win/win situation in which both children and adults benefit as individuals, even as they are strengthening those important family bonds that all children (and adults) need," she says. "Because most of us as adults still have much to learn about nature, these outdoor experiences can be times to learn with our children and *from* our children. The reciprocity and mutual respect such interactions engender are important elements of close parent-child relationships as children move toward adulthood." As children grow older, "the possibilities to share both adventures and quiet times in the outdoors multiply rapidly."

At the very least, such times offer family members the gift of shared memories. Michael Eaton, a father in Springfield, Missouri, recalls such a moment: "One time, after a Christmas dinner in the country with the in-laws, at their farm, my son and I went for a walk in the falling snow." In the woods, they lay on their backs, "listened to the falling snow, and fell asleep for probably five minutes." Seven years later he still recounts that time. "Best five minutes I ever spent with him."

For a parent, particularly if one of the many adults who missed out on nature experiences when they were growing up, taking the first step outdoors may feel awkward. Fortunately, there are lots of places to go for assistance or advice, including guidebooks, Web sites, and outdoors-oriented organizations. Your family can go for a walk when the moon is full, tell stories about past adventures outdoors, spot birds or other wildlife on country drives, learn to track together. And, you even can hike, fish, tent camp, and go on digital wildlife photo expeditions together. You can make the Green Hour (National Wildlife Federation's recommended goal of one hour outside a day) a family tradition.

Working together in nature works, too. Families that garden together can help feed themselves, and perhaps share with neighbors or donate to a food bank. In urban neighborhoods, they can create a garden on a landing, deck, terrace, or flat roof. Families can also pick berries and other fruit or vegetables on farms or orchards open to the public. (Though the family farm all but disappeared in recent decades, organic gardening and the Slow Food movement hold the promise of an eventual resurgence in family farming and ranching. Linking to that movement is another route to bonding through nature.)

Louise Chawla, one of the leading experts on nature's impact on human development, whom we met earlier, describes the need for both "special places and special people," referring to Rachel Carson's thinking on how to help young people develop a positive relationship with nature. Grandparents can be a great resource. They often have more free time, or at least more flexible schedules, than parents do. Most grandparents can remember when playing outside in nature was considered normal and expected of children. They'll want to pass along that tradition—and will be enriched in the process. Martha Erickson agrees, from a professional and personal perspective. "I have found over the years that even very short 'nature breaks' allow me to calm down and focus when I'm having a particularly challenging day," she writes. "I carry a couple of collapsible canvas chairs in the back of my car so, in the midst of a busy day, I can seek out a grassy spot (or even a snowy spot during our cold winters) and sit in my chair for a few minutes to breathe deeply and be soothed by my natural surroundings. The reason I have 'a couple of' those chairs is that my oldest grandchild has taken up the idea of nature breaks, too, and likes to join me when we're out and about together."

Wileta Burch, who lives in northern California and is active in the nature-connection group Hooked on Nature, created a more elaborate grandparenting nature ritual. For five years, she and her husband spent one week a year with their children and grandchildren in a rented cabin at Bear Valley in California. Their three grandkids spent much of their time playing at the nearby lake; the fathers took the children rock climbing, lizard hunting, hiking, fishing. Each year, when it was time to leave for home, she took the three grandkids into the woods "to visit the grandfather and grandmother redwood trees that I had scouted. We sat beneath these magnificent trees in a ceremony of thanksgiving for such beautiful times together," she recalls. "The children brought with them stones, leaves, or anything they found that was special to them. They participated in the ceremony with great seriousness. I know that the times we had in this place of natural beauty and our ceremonial expression of gratitude have made a lasting impression on them."

Burch adds this personal note, which lends extra dimension to the idea of family bonding through nature. Once, while sitting quietly in her garden, Burch experienced "a distinct feeling of being with family"— the fruit trees, the flowers, bushes, and grass were all parts of an

extended family "whose energies were available if I would open to receive their supportive presence." Her husband has recently been diagnosed with Parkinson's disease. "He will often sit outside to receive
the sun's warm rays and the healing gifts from his garden 'family.' He
doesn't expect to be healed of Parkinson's, but he does calmly accept
this to be but another stage of his life's journey."

The Family Nature Club

Families can also bond with nature by banding together with other
families. In 2008, I received an e-mail from Chip Donahue, a father of
three and a second-grade teacher in Roanoke, Virginia. After reading
Last Child in the Woods, Chip and his wife, Ashley, contacted me and
told me how they had begun to spend most weekends on family hikes
and other outdoor adventures. One day, their five-year-old son asked,
"Why are we the only family having this much fun?"

Over Christmas break, the Donahues sat down and mapped out a
monthly adventure schedule for the coming year, and they decided
to invite their neighbors to join the first adventure. To his surprise,
five families that he had never met showed up for the first event. The
weather was so cold that day that the gathered parents decided to do an
indoor craft project and read nature stories to the kids. Once again, a
youngster—a four-year-old girl—had a better idea. She walked up to
Chip and said, "Hey, mister, when are we going outside?" The families
bundled up and went on a hike. Now they go outside, rain or shine.
"After word of mouth and two local newspaper articles, our membership has grown to over six hundred families," Donahue reports.

Families on the list contact each other by e-mail, Web site, or phone
to set up what are essentially family outdoor playdates. Some adventures are devoted to just having fun outside, others to volunteering
for nature restoration projects. Chip and Ashley formalized their club,
calling it Kids in the Valley, Adventuring! (KIVA). "We send out a

monthly e-mail newsletter that lists recommendations for places for families to play and books to check out," he says. The nature outings and newsletter are free. For safety and family bonding, he emphasizes one absolute requirement: parents or guardians must stay with their children at all times. "We say, 'Stay and make a memory with your child.'" There are many other reasons—that work for adults as well as kids—for participating in a family nature club:

- The club approach can break down key barriers, including fear, since there is perceived safety in numbers.
- The clubs can be created in any neighborhood, whether inner city, suburban, or rural; they build community and a sense of place.
- The clubs can be joined or created by any kind of family.
- There is the motivation factor—it's much more likely that you and your family are going to show up at a park on a Saturday morning if you know there's another family waiting for you.
- Shared knowledge: Many parents want to give their kids the gifts of nature, but they don't feel they know enough about nature.
- And, importantly, there is no need to wait for funding. Families can do this themselves and do it now.

The Roanoke venture, which received national attention on NBC's *Today* show, isn't unique. Nearly one hundred such clubs now exist in the United States. One, in Rhode Island, has created a smartphone app to make it easier for families to connect. Parent volunteers from the Orange County, New York, Audubon Society, concerned about how empty local trails had become, initiated a free family nature-study club called Nature Strollers. Lorin Keel, a participant in Nature Strollers, describes the experience, one that can be contagious: "When I am showing my children the footprints in the snow and asking them who they belong to, I am teaching them awareness. . . . Traversing streams takes courage and good planning. Offering seeds to the birds when everything is covered in ice is an act of kindness. Observing a wasp fill underground cells with food for its young exemplifies devotion. Digging the deepest hole requires strategy and strength . . . knowing how to start fires without matches is security, as is being able to safely identify wild edibles."

Debra Scott, a longtime member of a parent-and-child nature club called the Active Kids Club, in Toronto, Canada, was once skeptical that nature time was all that valuable. "When I first learned about the importance of being outdoors my first reaction was to dismiss the idea. If it wasn't in all my 'good parenting' books and research, it couldn't possibly be that important." She joined Active Kids Club with her daughter, who had befriended the club founder's child, and Scott wanted to encourage the relationship. "So we went outdoors. It wasn't bad for us, so why not? We went outside in all kinds of weather once a week. And I noticed on those days my daughter slept better and had a better appetite. I noticed I slept better as well and was in a better mood." Especially in the winter months, stressful things seemed less important, to both Scott and her daughter, after being outside. "Being outside is now a priority for us. My daughter has gained confidence in herself and her abilities. I only wish we had started earlier."

Most organizers of family nature clubs emphasize that the primary focus should be on independent play—on experience, not on information. But doesn't the very concept of a "club" work against independent play? Chip and Ashley Donahue don't think so. When they first started taking their kids out for nature adventures—before they started the club—the kids would often whine and cling to them. But once other families began to join them, the children disengaged from the adults, quit whining, and started having serious fun on their own.

Bethe Almeras, another parent who has balanced the need to protect with her children's need for independent play, considers herself a "hummingbird parent" rather than a more controlling "helicopter parent." "I tend to stay physically distant to let them explore and problem solve, but zoom in at moments when safety is an issue (which isn't very often)."

In San Diego, Janice and Ron Swaisgood, inspired by the family nature club trend, created their own club: Family Adventures in Nature (FAN). Since then, FAN has spawned subclubs throughout the city. Ron describes a scene when several families first met at a eucalyptus-filled canyon near their suburban homes. Within minutes of leaving their cars, the families left the trail. "We were by the creek, visiting the chaos created by a recent storm—downed trees, upturned roots (creating wonderful little muddy caves underneath), and piles of debris left behind by the rushing waters," Ron recalls. The Swaisgoods' oldest son "took great pains to ensure that there was no patch of clothing clinging to him that wasn't caked in mud." The kids built dams and used sticks to excavate dirt. "What struck me was the sense of community, communication, and common purpose that quickly emerged. Parents stepped in to help or coexperience nature with all the kids, with little regard to whether they shared DNA with the child."

One of the most attractive features of nature, he adds, "is the social glue it provides"—the way it brings adults together in a way that may not often happen at a typical gathering.

During the family nature club outings, he is impressed by the quality of adult conversation. In other settings, when families get together socially, "either parents talk grown-ups' talk the whole time and virtually ignore the kids, or they just focus on the kids and don't get to have some good adult conversation." Adults converse differently during the family nature club outings. "What struck me was how the conversation, standing under the eucalyptus, moved easily back and forth between kid-focused enjoyment of their experience and 'intelligent' adult conversation. I have found time and time again that I get to know people better in the woods than at a cocktail party."

The Trekker's Guide to Life and Romance

Children are not required in order to experience the relationship-bonding power of nature. Like the Swaisgoods, Jonathan Stahl and Amanda Tyson have strengthened their relationship with each other, with friends, and with their community—one step at a time.

Before meeting Amanda, Jonathan was already acquainted with the bonding properties of nature. "As a nervous first-year student from New Jersey who had never been backpacking, I took my first steps with a group of strangers who had several things in common," says Stahl. "Mainly, we all wanted to make new friends before starting college and we all generally liked being outdoors. At the time, I didn't realize the profound and lasting impact that the University of Vermont's Wilderness TREK program would have on me, not to mention its influence on my career path."

Precollege outdoor orientation programs are intended to ease the transition from high school to college for new students, Stahl explains. "About ten of us, including our two student leaders, hiked, camped, and worked as a team for five days while exploring the northernmost section of Vermont's Long Trail." Later, at the University of Massachusetts–Amherst, he coordinated the school's SUMMIT wilderness orientation program, which fashioned outdoor adventures to help students acquire "the skills they'd need to successfully navigate their way through the wilderness *and* a large public university."

Along the way, he met his fiancée, Amanda. As "our engagement adventure, or 'wilderness orientation to marriage,'" as Jonathan puts it, he and Amanda decided to hike the Pacific Crest Trail. While on that trail, they took time to reflect on what they had learned—particularly about their relationship—and posted their thoughts on their travel blog. Among other lessons, they learned that meticulously thought-out plans will constantly change. They learned "to tune in to our bodies and know when to say when (water, rest, food, pain, etc)." They learned to "share . . . everything!" They learned that "many foods that are meant to be eaten hot are actually not that bad cold . . . with Amanda's exception being freeze-dried eggs." Amanda learned to keep track of her possessions and not "lose them in the moonshadow." And while they searched for a new place to lay their plastic tarp each night, they learned that wherever they are, "as long as we're together, we feel like we are home."

Trekking two thousand miles isn't every couple's idea of a great date. Room service offers its own romantic charms. But the gain that came from the long journey, the strength it gave to their new marriage, was worth the discomfort. Whether or not they have children one day, they look forward to the trail ahead, says Jonathan, and to learning more "about ourselves, each other, and the earth."

PART FOUR

Creating Everyday Eden

High-Tech/High-Nature Design Where

We Live, Work, and Play

A habitation marvellously planned,

For life to occupy in love and rest;

All that we see — is dome, or vault, or nest,

Or fortress, reared at Nature's sage command.

—William Wordsworth

CHAPTER 13

The Nature Principle at Home

Way beyond Feng Shui

Nature is not a place to visit, it is home.
—Gary Snyder

THE YARD SURROUNDING Karen Harwell's home is only six hundred square feet, yet it harbors ducks, a beehive, eighteen semidwarf fruit trees, an organic vegetable garden, calming places to sit and read and think, and neighborhood teenagers. The teens visit Summer, the dog, and sit in the rabbit hutch, hold the baby rabbits, and conduct that archaic form of social networking: talk.

"I wake up in the morning and I throw on my vest over my nightgown, and then Summer and I head out the front door and we just walk around the garden *noticing* things. It's just a wonderful way to start the day," Harwell said, as she escorted me around her minifarm. Somehow, she has arranged all this so there is a feeling of openness.

Harwell, who is in her sixties, is well-known in the San Francisco Bay Area for her leadership of Exploring a Sense of Place, the now-international organization that takes groups of people on treks deep into their local ecosystem, thereby enriching their lives. But, she reminds me, you can also experience nature at home. "Come around here and I'll introduce you to the ducks," she said. She named her garden the Dana Meadows Organic Children's Garden after a hero of hers, the late Donella (Dana) Meadows, who wrote the book *Limits to Growth*, founded the Sustainability Institute, and helped build an ecovillage and farm in Vermont.

Three ducks waddled along in front of us. Harwell originally intended to buy chickens, but ducks lay eggs, too—and she believes they have more personality. In the evening, she leads them like a Pied Piper around the side of the house to a wire shelter where they spend the night, safe from raccoon raids.

Here and there, I stepped over yellow duck poop. "We call it gold fertilizer. Why do you think we have such great fruit trees?" At the base of one tree, I saw a basket filled with colorful plastic clogs. "Duck shoes. When kids come over, they put these on. We don't want kids going home and getting poop on the carpet."

The richness of vegetation and the variety of food produced on such a small piece of property is impressive: Bartlett pears, black mission figs, nectarines, three kinds of corn, cucumbers, eggplant, lima beans, melons, squash, radishes, carrots, sunflowers, raspberries, blueberries, oranges, avocados, herbs, lettuces, spinach, potatoes, broccoli, cauliflower, cabbage, and strawberries. In what she calls the forest garden, there are native plants, including wood roses, California poppies, and Pacific dogwood. The single beehive produced an impressive 440 pounds of honey this year. The garden pretty much sustains her; supplements come from a nearby farmer's market. "I'm mostly eating food in season," she said.

Harwell believes in raising as much of her own food as possible, in conserving energy at home, and in using recycled material. "All the benches, and the patio, are made out of salvaged wood from Wholehouse Lumber."

We were sitting in the California sun on a recycled redwood bench. A solar shingle roof and two solar panels provide electricity and heat her water. "Wouldn't have any electric bill at all, except for the pond pump, which means my bill is horrible. About nine dollars a month."

Energy efficiency is part of what constitutes a restorative home, but here's what Harwell is really proud of: the impact on her neighborhood, especially the kids, starting with Margot, who is now fourteen. "She and her brother Bowen were the first kids to start coming here. They taught the ducks to swim. When I built the pond, I'd put the ducks in and they'd go, 'Help, help, what do you think we are, *ducks?*' And so Bowen took Webbers, the little male, and he'd hold him gently so his feet could start to feel the water and then eventually he started swimming, and the other ducks were on the ledge thinking, 'Webber seems to like that.'"

When seedlings are started for the winter crop, Harwell explains to the neighborhood kids, "seedlings are like babies, you've got to take care of them." In the mornings, she wheels a seedling cart out in front of her garage door for the sunlight and sets out watering cans. On the way to school and on the way home, the kids stop and water the seedlings.

The neighborhood children know that the Dana Meadows Organic Children's Garden is their garden. When Harwell puts out a call for help with the spinach harvest, they come, sometimes with their parents. "If you want to come around the side here," Harwell said, "I'll show you what my neighbors are doing. See up their walkway? They've got lemons. Over here they planted tomatoes." Harwell's philosophy is spreading through the neighborhood, just like those squash vines in her not-so-secret garden. As you can see, the restorative home isn't just another pretty edifice. The real gift here is human/nature social capital.

Harwell also brings the outside in. Inside her house, she surrounds herself with biophilic low-hanging fruit: a collection of stuffed ducks, bird posters, potted plants. The practitioners of biophilic or restorative design suggest that such touches, though small, do create a sense of psychological comfort.

Restorative Homes and Gardens

She could get a bit fancier. In Connecticut, one interior designer moved eight dead birch trees into the high-ceiling living room of his ranch-style house.[1] Tom Mansell, a thirty-one-year-old video editor and producer in Ann Arbor, Michigan, fills his house with nature sounds that he has recorded.

Current interest in the re-natured home can be linked, in part, to the popularization of feng shui, an ancient Chinese discipline, rooted in Taoism, that some designers refer to as they rearrange a living (or burial) space for good qi, the circulating life energy considered present in all things, according to Chinese philosophy. A "perfect spot" is a location and an axis in time, in which the orientation of a structure and its interior maximizes the good energy emanating from the surrounding environment, including the slope of the land, vegetation, soil quality, and microclimate.

Now comes a resurgence of a similar early discipline, an Indian philosophy called Vastu Shastra or simply Vastu, a Sanskrit word that translates roughly as "energy," with its own rules of design. (Don't place your bedroom in the southwest corner of your home; that's where the agitating fire element resides. You'll have trouble sleeping.)

Like a lot of folks, I'm skeptical of any proposition that sounds like it requires a sacred decoder ring. But devotion to Vastu is not required for the restorative home. Nor is the purchase of hi-def wall panels depicting the mountains of Tibet.

The home nature-restoration market is growing. Sales of ecosensitive "natural" decorations are flourishing. A catalog company called Viva Terra, for example, offers twig furniture, a "vintage fir dresser" made of reclaimed wood, robes made of sustainable bamboo fabric, rustic stools individually carved from Chinese fir root balls. One of the most intriguing and increasingly popular techniques for home nature restoration is the indoor or outdoor vertical garden, with automatic drip-irrigation systems and grids and panels for planting. A Canadian company called Nedlaw Living Walls, produces indoor "living walls" of ficus, hibiscus, orchids, and other plants. The method, first developed to sustain human life and improve air quality during long space missions, is said to remove up to 80 percent of formaldehyde, as well as other toxic substances, from indoor air. At first, the company specialized in building living walls in commercial buildings, but now the residential market is booming. One reason may be increased public awareness of the poor quality of most indoor air. The living walls have their downside, including bugs that must be controlled by organic means, as well as increased indoor humidity and corresponding mold growth. Not every air-quality scientist believes that indoor plants are effective air filters. Still, many people are saying that the positive impact on mood and the sense of well-being overrides the negatives, which can be controlled.

For individuals and a few developers, an emerging high-tech/high-nature housing design philosophy includes conserving energy, using earth-friendly materials, and also applying biophilic design principles to promote health, human energy, and beauty.

A hybrid house may have pond rainwater collectors, a superinsulated green roof that can last eighty years, perhaps straw-bale walls that will stand for a century. Add to that list of possibilities recycled beams, cordwood masonry (lumber set in earthen mortar), cement mixed with recycled-paper pulp, and aerated concrete. These homes are so energy efficient that they typically need no air-conditioning. At the same time, high-tech features of a hybrid home can include a geothermal heating system that takes advantage of constant temperatures deep beneath the home, solar panels that produce electricity for lighting and computing, fluorescent lights that adjust throughout the day via light sensors at the windows, bird-warning elements built into the glass, motion-sensitive light switches, sensor-regulated water taps and soap dispensers, waterless urinals and water-saving toilets, and solar panels incorporated into skylights or mounted over water features, perhaps a natural wastewater treatment system, including a water garden. The Bonner Springs, Kansas, company, Total Habitat, is one of many firms that create chlorine-free "natural swimming ponds," as Europeans started calling them two decades ago. The swimming ponds, which can be lined with rubber or polyethylene, are cleaned by regeneration zones: aquatic plants, rocks, loose gravel, and friendly bacteria that act as water filters. Natural swimming ponds can look modern or rustic, but when boulders and native plants surround the pools, in addition to using nonchlorinated water, you get the added health benefit of human restoratioin.

Virtual Vastu
In some cities, zoning laws prohibit skylights larger than two feet square, so Sky Factory, a company in Fairfield, Iowa, sells sky-simulating ceiling panels that replicate full-spectrum natural light; computer programming changes luminosity, creating the illusion of a sky changing from sunrise to sunset. The company offers a line of virtual views designed to promote health and well-being in homes, hospitals, casinos—you name it. Sky Factory describes its trademarked SkyCeilings as "authentic illusions of real skies," including displays of changing cloud patterns and seasons, the light and color of sunrises and sunsets, even the activity of birds flying overhead. Such virtual Vastu does raise a few questions.

Researcher Peter Kahn and his colleagues at the University of Washington compared how people responded to working in three different indoor settings: a workspace with a real window offering a view of real nature; a workspace with an HDTV screen showing a "live" nature scene; and a workspace with blank walls. People with the real view reported the highest rate of physiological restoration, but the rooms with the HDTV view proved to be more restorative than the room with the blank walls. In Kahn's book *Technological Nature*, one participant commented about the HDTV "nature" experience: "This window will take me anywhere in the world, but it won't let me smell anywhere in the world. . . . So the image is still an image. It's not actually being there, but it is very close."[2] Another participant pined for the HDTV "window" when it was removed. "I miss having the ability to take time to just look at what's going on outside . . . to just watch the world outside and kind of shift your thinking a little bit. That to me was probably the greatest asset."

Kahn's real-time, high-def window did not, however, "solve the parallax problem, meaning that the view did not shift as one moved around the screen." Decades may pass before the parallax bug is eliminated. But even without that design leap, such windows could become standard issue in homes and offices in the future. Creating such "windows" into nature isn't exactly efficient or practical—yet. Some European countries have laws prohibiting offices with no windows. Virtual windows could be a work-around. And as the supply of *real* nature diminishes (to think of this in business terms), the demand for technological nature will increase. Not long after the publication of *Last Child in the Woods*, a company began selling what it claimed was "the cure for nature-deficit disorder"—computer screen-saver images of nature. If humans continue to destroy nature, designers of the built environment will "increasingly shunt out what remains of nature from our urban lives," according to Kahn, and the advantages of real nature will "drift from our purview. We should not let that happen."

The main goal should be to erase the wall between the inside and the outside. Environmental psychologist Judith Heerwagen advises: "Most landscapes are designed to look good from the curb, but what you really want to do is create good views from inside."[3] The view can be of woods or other natural landscape: a creek, a lake, a river. Chinese and Japanese garden-makers mastered this design principle long ago. For space-restricted urban dwellers, miniature bonsai trees or dwarf varieties can transform small balconies and windowsills. Even there, roof gardens, or a green roof, can create a living zone to link indoors and outdoors.

When the well-known biophilic-oriented architect Gail Lindsey and her husband designed and built their own home, they were concerned about energy efficiency, but their primary goal was to create a place that rested their hearts and offered health, happiness, and beauty. I asked Lindsey what she suggested to people building a new home or remodeling their current residence, and she offered this inventory: Place the house in sync with the sun's movements, so that sleeping and waking are in accord with available light. Use local materials, wherever possible, to bring the nature of the region inside. Place large windows on the south-facing wall for passive solar heating, but also for a view of nature. Use natural ventilation, with appropriately placed windows and high ceiling fans. "In our house, the windows usually stay open; my husband can enjoy the wall of sounds that the frogs and insects by the stream make at night," she said. "As spring approaches, he's out on the deck at dusk, listening. When it warms up, our indoor plants explode out onto the decks, which serve as our outdoor 'rooms,' shared with birds and other wild neighbors."

Backyard Revolution

As much as I admired Karen Harwell's yard, I missed a sense of wildness. How might suburban or urban yards (paradoxically) contain more of that?

The Morrison-Knudsen Nature Center, located in an urban neighborhood of Boise, Idaho, suggests some imaginative possibilities. Boise is one of those cities where nature is extraordinarily accessible. There are major trout streams and elk herds within a twenty-minute drive of downtown. The nature center was built on a 4.6-acre site along the Boise River Greenbelt near downtown that includes a stream walk and a minipark adjacent to the river. A visitors' building has a special room with a glass wall through which you can look out at a slice of Idaho nature.

Standing there one day, I was transported into another world. I watched native trout through an underwater viewing window. Above and below were muskrats and local birds, and I was told that deer and even an occasional elk wander into the viewing area. I was struck by a thought and a question: first, this room and its living view beats TV; and second, what if a neighborhood were structured around a rehabilitated wildlife habitat? Developers of middle-class neighborhoods might orient homes in a sensitive way near nature corridors, with the natural theater visible from windows, glass walls, and porches. Was there a way to do this, I wondered, in new or existing neighborhoods, without adversely affecting wildlife?

In Seattle, my friends Karen Landen and Dean Stahl enjoy a miniature version of that. Karen first became truly conscious of birds in the 1970s, while visiting her grandparents in the Florida Keys, where brown pelicans swam in the canal right behind the house and a Wurdemann's heron came to the door begging for fish. On a visit to the Everglades, she was photographing a great egret, and the transformation became complete. "I had a feeling I can only describe as falling in love. In that instant, I became a birder. Years later, walking in our garden one night in Seattle, in the dark mist, I suddenly felt a presence. Then it hit me. Birds were sleeping in the hedges and trees, unseen. It occurred to me that they live all around us, yet not really with us—almost in a parallel universe—unless you look. Birds are so beautifully made, so mysterious and so full of life, I can't help but look."

Their backyard is like many other suburban parcels, except that Dean has planted bird-attracting plants, and the trees and bushes are left mostly natural, untrimmed.

For decades, this neighborhood with its vacant lots of blackberry patches and scrubby native salal supported twenty or so California quail in a single covey. They would roam, breed, produce chicks, and occasionally fall prey to cats and hawks, but their numbers remained stable. Then, one March, the covey was reduced to two hens. "One called for two months from the rooftops, in search of a mate, then disappeared," Karen said. "In May, just when we had given up, a hen arrived with a cock, walking up the road from the north, and they had a brood nearby. The cock was soon killed. The hen raised her chicks alone. Several of us knew this was the last chance for quail and tried to figure out what to do." Karen and a friend appealed to 144 of their human neighbors with a letter that began: "For many of us, quail are the symbol of this neighborhood." The campaign led to a neighborhood "quail watch," which helped protect the covey for two more years. The birds are gone now, but their presence gave a number of neighbors a reason to learn more about the wildlife that lives on the other side of the glass, and to receive their company.

Some will dismiss such thinking as misplaced compassion or romanticizing nature. But we live on common earth. In his book *About Looking*, the art critic John Berger writes, "Animals first entered the imagination as messengers and promises." Until the nineteenth century, "anthropomorphism was integral to the relation between man and animal and was an expression of their proximity." Today, separating ourselves so starkly from other animals empties them, in our eyes, of "experience and secrets."[4] And empties us, as well.

Doug Tallamy would never be accused of engaging in anthropomorphism, but sees messages from a natural environment in trouble. Habitat fragmentation and degradation are disrupting bird and butterfly migration routes and diminishing biodiversity, but Tallamy believes that we can do something about these trends, from our backyards. Tallamy, a professor and chair of the Department of Entomology and Wildlife Ecology at the University of Delaware, is a self-effacing man who offers this radical idea: the promise of North America's resurgent biodiversity is in your home garden. "My central message is that unless we restore native plants to our suburban ecosystems, the future of biodiversity in the United States is dim." He tempers this gloomy prediction with two points of optimism: "First and foremost, it is not yet too late to save most of the plants and animals that sustain the ecosystems on which we ourselves depend. Second, restoring native plants to most human-dominated landscapes is relatively easy to do." For the first time in history, he argues, "Gardening has taken on a role that transcends the needs of the gardener. Like it or not, gardeners have become important layers in the management of our nation's wildlife. It is now in the power of individual gardeners to do something that we all dream of doing: to 'make a difference.' In this case, the 'difference' will be to the future of biodiversity, to the native plants and animals of North America and the ecosystems that sustain them."

Tallamy's efforts bring to mind the work of Michael L. Rosenzweig, an ecologist who founded and developed the Department of Ecology and Evolutionary Biology at University of Arizona, Tucson. In his book *Win-Win Ecology*, he popularized the term *reconciliation ecology*, which he defines as "the science of inventing, establishing, and maintaining new habitats to conserve species diversity in places where people live, work, or play." Analyzing data from all over the world, Rosenzweig found a one-to-one relationship between species loss and loss of native habitat.[5]

Usually, when landscapers recommend the use of native plant species, the goal is either to conserve water, to save native plants, or to replace the ordinary with the novel. Tallamy suggests a new motivation: to save insects and, in doing so, the wildlife that depends upon them as a food source. His urgings follow a personal story of discovery.

In 2000, Tallamy and his wife moved from the city to ten acres in southeastern Pennsylvania, an area that had been farmed for centuries before being subdivided. "We got our rural setting, sort of, but it was anything but the slice of nature we were seeking," he recalls. "Like many 'open spaces' in this country, at least 35 percent of the vegetation on our property (yes, I measured it) consisted of aggressive plant species from other continents that were rapidly replacing what native plants we did have." He and his family decided to make it their goal to remove alien plants and replace them with the species of the eastern deciduous forests, the ones that had evolved there over millions of years. As they began to remove the autumn olives, Japanese honeysuckles, and "the mile-a-minute weeds," he noticed something peculiar. All had little or no leaf damage from insects, while the native flora—the red maples, pin oaks, black cherries, and others—had obviously been a food supply for many insects.

One might think that translates into a minus for the natives. But Tallamy saw a different reality. "This was alarming because it suggested a consequence of the alien invasion occurring all over North America that neither I—nor anyone else, I discovered, after checking the scientific literature—had considered. If our native insect fauna cannot, or will not, use alien plants for food, then insect populations in areas with many alien plants will be smaller than insect populations in areas with all natives." Because so many animals depend on insect protein, "a land without insects is a land without most forms of higher life." In other words, eventual sterility. Tallamy points out that "the terrestrial ecosystems on which we humans all depend for our own continued existence would cease to function without our six-legged friends."

E. O. Wilson calls insects "the little things that run the world."

Unless we change the places where we live, work, and play "to meet not only our own needs but the needs of other species as well," says Tallamy, "nearly all species of wildlife native to the United States will disappear forever." This is not speculation, he insists, but a prediction backed by decades of ecological research on the necessity of biodiversity. What the predictions do not take into account, however, is the potential for *increased* multispecies cohabitation with human beings. Countless species, he says, "could live sustainably with us if we would just design our living spaces to accommodate them." Tallamy and his colleagues have begun the large, controlled research projects required to nail down his case, and preliminary data are beginning to accumulate. "So far, the results provide exciting support

or gardeners who have already switched to natives or who are enthu-
iastic about doing so."

If Tallamy's hypothesis turns out to be right, he says, "these garden-
rs can and will 'change the world' by changing what food is available
or their local wildlife." His work underscores one of the fundamentals
of the Nature Principle: conserving wilderness is not enough; we must
conserve and *create* nature, in the form of native habitat, wherever pos-
ible, on roofs and in gardens in our cities and suburbs. This is the
oad leading to natural communities. Tallamy's book *Bringing Nature
Home: How Native Plants Sustain Wildlife in Our Gardens*, is among the
best sources on this topic and useful reading for those who want to
naturalize their property.[6] When I asked him for some specific sugges-
ions, he offered the following:[7]

- *Rebuild local food webs.* Nothing lives in isolation. Every species
  exists within complexes of interacting species that ecologists call
  food webs. For a species to thrive in your yard, you must provide
  the fundamental parts of that species' food web.
- *It all starts with plants.* Food webs start with plants, because plants
  are the only organisms (with the exception of some bacteria) that
  can capture the sun's energy, which fuels life on earth. All animals get the energy they need either by eating plants directly or
  by eating other animals that eat plants. The amount of vegetation in your yard will determine the amount of nature in your
  yard.
- *All plants are not the same.* Unfortunately, all plants are not equal in
  their ability to support food webs. Food webs develop locally over
  thousands of generations, with each member of the web adapting
  to the particular traits of the other members of the web. A plant
  that evolved outside of a particular food web is usually unable to
  pass on its energy to the animals within that food web because
  those animals find it unpalatable.

- *Natives support nature best.* Typically, when we build a development, we bulldoze all of the native plant communities and then landscape with ornamental plants. You can be sure that an ornamental plant from Asia or Europe did not evolve within your local food web and therefore will provide little or no food for the creatures you are trying to encourage. Look for plants that are native to your area because they support nature best in your yard.

- *Insects are key.* Most of us have been taught from childhood that the only good insect is a dead insect. To the joy of many, we have created sterile, lifeless landscapes, but that is precisely why our children do not have nature in their yards any longer. Insects are the primary way most animals get their energy from plants. Birds are an excellent example. Ninety-six percent of the terrestrial birds in North America rear their young on insects. Bottom line: if you want birds, or toads, or salamanders, or countless other species in your yard, you must also have plants that support local insects.

- *Reduce your lawn.* Lawns are now the largest irrigated crop in the United States, which has 45.6 million acres of lawns (including residential and commercial sites, golf courses, etc.), or 23 percent of urbanized land, and that figure is increasing. When it comes to supporting food webs, lawns are nearly as bad as pavement. Consider replacing the parts of your lawn that are not regularly used for walking with densely planted gardens of native plants. The life in those gardens will draw your kids out of the house.

- *Plant a butterfly garden.* Butterflies need two kinds of plants: (1) plants that produce nectar for the adult butterflies, and (2) plants that serve as food for larval development. Avoid planting butterfly bush (*Buddleia*). Although it is a good nectar plant, it does not support the larval development of a single butterfly species in the United States, and it has joined the long list of invasive ornamental plants despoiling our natural areas.

- *Woody plants support more animals.* Trees and shrubs are hosts for more species of moths and butterflies than herbaceous plants and thus provide more types of food for birds and other insect-eaters. Supplying birds with the caterpillars they need while nesting will bring just as many birds to your yard during spring and summer as a bird feeder does during winter.

If such gardens grew everywhere, wouldn't unwanted insects soon inundate us? Tallamy says that an ecologically balanced garden may show a bit more damage from insects, but true to its biome, such a garden also attracts a diversity of natural predators such as ladybird beetles, fireflies, praying mantis, and thousands of tiny parasitic wasps too small to notice, along with a richer array of birds, toads, and salamanders. These keep plant-eating insects under control.

An online search for "native plant nurseries" by region can get you started. Short of replacing gardens and yards with native species, planting native shrubs and trees around the edges of your lot, or fitting them into existing landscaping, can also produce biodiversity. The payoff: a more interesting and potentially beautiful landscape, at least to the trained eye, and psychic rewards, as well. In addition to promoting biodiversity, a native landscape offers physical benefits (no pesticides) and may well boost the health of the gardener and the gardener's family.

At one point, my local natural history museum considered (but did not act on) a plan to hand out packets of seeds to schoolchildren, so that they might plant their own yards with species to help restore bird and butterfly migration routes. The notion remains enchanting. Here is a way to enter into intimate participation in the life currents of the world through the modest doorway of a suburban garden or a window box in an inner-city neighborhood.

We exist in a matrix of electronic currents and beeping cell phones. What if we were equally aware of the swirling currents of, say, monarch butterflies, whose progeny each year migrate over a thousand miles to spend the winter in a small patch of Mexico? Or of the neotropical birds—the wood thrushes, cerulean warblers, scarlet tanagers, indigo buntings, and Baltimore orioles on the wing from Kentucky to the Andes? Or those birds that cross seas and mountain peaks to migrate from Europe to Africa? What if we were to take part in these migrations by nurturing the plants their food sources require? Those yards would then be connected to a very different kind of network, one that is immense, mysterious, and magnificent.

Just Do It

About now you may be wondering, who has the time to do all this? My wife and I don't see ourselves as master gardeners or cutting-edge biophilic interior designers. Or as any kind of interior designers, for that matter. In the 1990s, we bought a house in the stucco wastelands. The living room, as I recall, came with gold-flecked, semipsychedelic wallpaper. We were baffled and blinded by the decor. Trying to decide what to do led to one of our few real fights. So we scraped together dollars we didn't have and hired a pro to help us. She replaced the semipsychedelic stripes with Victorian Vertigo. Since then, when newcomers arrive at our home, I point to the backyard and say: "See that mound? Interior decorator's buried there." We have, however, replaced that wallpaper and made some progress indoors, mainly by introducing as much natural material and as many images and icons of nature as possible. We've partially re-natured the garden (not a hard task, given our predisposition against yard work). We've reduced watering, made a none-too-successful effort to do some square-foot gardening, hung two bird feeders, and we've amped up our general awareness of who lives in or passes through our yard. Skunks, raccoons, coyotes, possums, and rabbits. And that alligator lizard that keeps showing up in our living room.

I asked Karen Harwell what she would say to people like us.

"The way we do just about everything in the United States is: 'I've got to go get a degree in this and then I'll start this process.' And we constantly put off the doing of anything because we think we must learn more, go to another workshop." She talked about Alan Chadwick, an English master gardener prominent in the development of organic farming. "He came to America and created the gardens at UC–Santa Cruz," she said. "A quote of his is carved in wood at the garden center there. 'The garden creates the gardener.' Chadwick would ask people: 'What do you like to eat? Plant that.' He'd say: 'If you plant seeds in the wrong place, the plants will tell you right away that something is wrong. Just learn as you go, but start now.'"

Harwell smiled. "When I first heard that, every cell in my body relaxed." In other words, don't worry, plant happy; and don't sweat the small watts. She advised that the goal should be to create a home, with a little help from nature, "that just *makes you feel good*."

For my family, the restorative home and garden remains a work in progress. But we're moving in the right direction.

CHAPTER 14

Stop, Look Up, and Listen

Fighting Global Blaring and Sky Blindness

KAREN HARWELL'S OPTIMISM is infectious, and she's shown that one yard can seed the next. But if we're going to create truly restorative human/nature habitats, we'll be facing some formidable foes.

Global warming? Welcome to global blaring.

Gina Pera, a northern California writer and former magazine editor, describes her struggle to cope with urban noise. "Right now, I am sitting in my home office. I have a stunning view of the East Bay and Mt. Diablo," she wrote in an e-mail. "My backyard is starting to bloom with hyacinths and peach blossoms. Rather than be out partaking of this beauty, I am blasting Puccini on my computer speakers. Why? Because it is the only way to drown out the omnipresent cacophony of chain saws, wood-chippers, blowers, and other thermonuclear lawn implements cluttering our airspace." She said she's stopped walking in her beautiful neighborhood because she is "shell-shocked."

Noise, like fear of crime, keeps people indoors, or outdoors with iPods plugged into their ears. A nature-loving friend in Seattle is so disheartened by the noise of car alarms and leaf blowers in her neighborhood that she wears noise-canceling earphones when she's gardening.

Appropriately, the word *noise* is derived from the Latin word *nausea*, which translates as seasickness. Excessive noise in neonatal intensive care units may disrupt the growth and development of premature infants, according to the American Academy of Pediatrics. Noise is linked to elevated blood pressure, myocardial infarction, loss of sleep, and changes in brain chemistry. The World Health Organization warns that such noise-induced problems "can lead to social handicap, reduced productivity, decreased performance in learning, absenteeism in the workplace and school, increased drug use, and accidents."

Excessive noise can also affect animal physiology and behavior, including the reproductive success and long-term survival of sound-dependent sea life. It's even changing the sounds of nature. Bernie Krause, a bioacoustician and author of the book *Wild Soundscapes*, has sold over 1.5 million CDs and tapes of nature sounds. He reports that the places where he can record such sounds uninterrupted by human noise are disappearing. The task is even difficult at the North Pole, in Antarctica, and in the Amazon Basin.

Everywhere he goes, he hears aircraft, chain saws, and other aural intrusions. In the 1970s, it took Krause about twenty hours of tape to record fifteen minutes of usable natural soundscape. By 1995, it took him two hundred hours. As a musician, who once played the Moog synthesizer with the Rolling Stones, he's particularly sensitive to the musical chorus of wild creatures. He calls it a biophony. "The songbirds living around us today have had to adapt their songs to their new neighbors—us. To some extent, a few birds, like American robins, sparrows, and wrens, are able to change their voices so that they can be heard even when it's noisy nearby. . . . Almost certainly, birdsong would be different than it would normally be in a forest."

In the past, noise was like the weather. Everybody complained about it, but nobody did much about it. That's changing. Antinoise groups are calling for new regulations and new technology. Some cities have banned leaf blowers, with ordinances mainly limited to residential neighborhoods and targeting gas-powered blowers. Enforcement is generally lax. An additional, and probably more effective, approach is to do the math. The typical gasoline-powered leaf blower lasts about seven years. In a short-lived program in Southern California, the South Coast Air Quality Management District launched the state's first public incentive program to exchange noisy, smelly backpack leaf blowers with quieter, cleaner models. The trade-ins were crushed at a recycling center. Another program offered residents a good one-day deal: trade old gasoline-powered lawnmowers for new electric mowers.

"There is a tremendous opportunity over the coming years to dramatically reshape our neighborhood soundscapes by reshaping the lawn and garden marketplace," reports the nonprofit Noise Pollution Clearinghouse (NPC). Coming soon: affordable hybrid gas-and-electric riding mowers. "If everyone in your neighborhood was mowing at the same time with a quiet electric mower, it would probably be quieter than if just one person in your neighborhood was using a typical gas-powered mower," according to the NPC.

Similarly, road noise could be reduced through wider use of hybrid-engine autos, which represent the first significant reduction in car noise in decades. Jets are already quieter, at least the larger commercial variety. Now researchers at Ohio State University have developed an even better silencer technology using electrical arcs to control turbulence in engine airflow, the main producer of engine noise. Urban designers are paying increasing attention to soundscaping and planting green areas around buildings; the plants absorb sound.

So change can occur. The trouble is, brains will be more difficult to retool; technological advances are seldom matched with political action. We'll see more demand for quieter technology and living soundscapes only when a sufficient number of us want to be outdoors.

Given the seriousness of the health risks, noise shouldn't be an afterthought, and trade-in programs shouldn't be a novelty. Nor should antinoise campaigns stop at the city line. They should, in fact, target hose places in or near cities that offer natural refuge, including lakes. The NPC has, in fact, launched a "quiet lake" campaign, pointing out hat boat noise limits are less stringent than federal limits for tractor-railer trucks (eighty decibels at fifty feet) across the country.

We already have wildlife refuges. Now it's time to create silence anctuaries. One day, I was talking with a man who lives near Barrett Lake, an isolated backcountry reservoir east of my home. This is one f the most unpopulated areas of our region. Ridges stretch toward the horizon, and mountain lions are more at home here than are people. The man said he was retiring soon and planned to move to a distant orner of Arizona. "It's too noisy here," he explained.

Noisy? *Here?*

"Helicopters and airplanes. Too many of 'em. I'm out of here."

Later that day, I heard what he was talking about. I was out on the water, which is usually protected by the immense dome of solitude hat covers this special lake, where the number of boats and size of engine are strictly limited. Hawks circled above. I could hear their wings move the air. Then a black helicopter popped over one of the idges and dipped toward the water, its engine noise reverberating off he walls of rock.

Sky Blindness

n addition to noise, there are other barriers to human/nature habita-ion. Electronic competition, of course. Poor urban design. Work pres-ures. And fear of strangers and nature itself (the root causes of which re valid, though hyped beyond reality by incessant media attention).

Then there's the sky blindness. In everyday—and every-night—life, ooking up is part of the cure for nature-deficit disorder. But if you ook up at night in most cities, you'll just see a dome of artificial light. Stealing starlight" is what Jack Troeger calls it. Troeger, who lives in Ames, Iowa, retired from teaching astronomy and earth sciences in 999, when the Milky Way was no longer visible in nighttime Ames.

But he didn't quit caring. He initiated the Dark Sky Initiative, arguing that the overuse of artificial light wastes energy, disrupts the sleeping or migration patterns of wildlife, and contributes to climate change "The stars you see tonight are the same stars your ancestors saw thousands of years ago," Troeger writes. "Stargazing . . . bonds you, links you, fuses you to all the people who have ever lived on this planet. . . You are the stuff of stars. The atoms that shape you were once the dust and gas of ancient stars."[1] The concern here isn't only about seeing stars, but about the opportunity for humans to experience the absence of artificial light. Natural darkness itself has value; for one reason, our biological clock counts on it.[2]

Those who have done it know that long-term night work wreaks havoc with circadian rhythm, but there are greater risks than interrupted sleep. To cite one example, researchers in Israel looked at light at night (LAN) in 147 communities using nighttime satellite images and compared that data to breast cancer rates. The conclusion: "The analysis yielded an estimated 73 percent higher breast cancer incidence in the highest LAN exposed communities compared to the lowest LAN exposed communities."[3] Other studies have investigated links between serum melatonin levels (melatonin is normally produced at night) and different forms of cancer. By the end of 2007, the International Agency for Research on Cancer, a branch of the World Health Organization, had listed overnight shift work as a possible carcinogen The American Cancer Society lists shift work as a "suspected carcinogen." Some estimates show 15 percent of the U.S. population does shift work.

The most damaging contributors to sky blindness are air pollution and artificial light in cities and countryside. The poet, journalist, and fiction writer Jack Greer describes a year-round, twenty-four-hour-a-day security light outside a cabin in an otherwise bucolic lakeside atmosphere as something comparable to "a stuck car horn that never stops." The Native American word *Shenandoah*, he writes, "means 'daughter of the stars' and now we must wonder whether we'll have to change that to 'daughter of the security lights.'"[4]

In a remote area of my county, a band of Kumeyaay Indians operates the Golden Acorn Casino. Built on the highest point on a great, empty plateau, the casino boasts a multistory, high-voltage sign—a midnight sun visible for twenty miles on clear nights. (This is one example of what I call the Trojan Horse Effect: the influence of a relatively small development whose noise, light, or visibility far exceeds the project's size. Because the next time someone objects to a proposed backcountry development and more lights, the logical response will be a shrug: See all that light out there already?)

One researcher, Terry Daniel of the University of Arizona–Tucson, offers a different sky-blindness theory. He suggests that the human eye is less sensitive to stimulation from the upper region of the visual field and is most sensitive directly in front of the eye and below the horizontal plane. Why? Because we evolved upright, with eyes necessarily on the front of our heads—where food and enemies are most likely to be. "To see the sky clearly the human must tilt his head back and look up—or lie on his back to place the sky in the most sensitive part of the visual field," according to Daniel.[5] If this is true, skywatchers are defying not only urban barriers to seeing what's above us, but also evolution. Still, it's hard to believe that humans are wired for sky blindness, especially considering the millennia of human navigation by stars.

Even if Daniel is right, then sky consciousness is a bonus experience, an expansion of our awareness. At a dinner party not long ago, I mentioned that, as a former Midwesterner, I remain fascinated by tornadoes, and feel admiration and even envy for the stormchasers who hurtle across the prairie in pursuit of twisters. A professor at the dinner, one who spends his days in a lab, couldn't understand the appeal. *Why?* he wanted to know. *It's just wind.* The best explanation I could muster was that they're not chasing wind; they're chasing dragons, each with a distinct personality. Even more than Alaskan brown bears, they stimulate awe. The scientist shook his head and shrugged. Not all of us see the same sky.

In recent years, urged on by astronomers whose work has been disrupted by those domes of artificial light, cities in the United States have begun to require low-pressure sodium streetlights and other light-pollution controls. In addition to stricter regulation, we can expand human appreciation for the gifts of the sky. This can be accomplished through sky-watcher groups, amateur meteorologists, and other citizen naturalists. Star charts—some of which you hold up against the night sky to locate constellations—are now available for smartphones and computer tablets. So the case could be made that technology can increase the odds that we'll see the details and subtleties of the sky. Telescope manufacturers would certainly agree. We do have necks that bend, and the sky above us remains an immense theater, art museum, symphony hall. And we have four-season tickets, even if the view is only from a window.

A couple of years ago, I visited a friend and his family outside Washington DC, in a neighborhood with broad yards, gnarled old trees, and Colonial-style homes. The two children, a girl and a boy, were filled with opinions, spirit, and energy. They loved nature. The boy spoke impressively about his interest in science. Later, their father said that his little girl spent a lot of time outdoors, but his boy seldom ventured past the front door. He explained that this child suffered from several learning difficulties and a condition that caused him to be overwhelmed when he went outside. So he spent most of his time in his room.

On my way home, in an airport bookstore, I thumbed through an intriguing book called *The Cloudspotter's Guide*, by the Britisher Gavin Pretor-Pinney, who encourages people to look up. He launched the Cloud Appreciation Society in 2004. Build a garden weather station, he advises—all you need is a view of the sky. Cirrus, cumulonimbus, and altostratus "come to remind us that the clouds are Nature's poetry, spoken in a whisper in the rarefied air between crest and crag." Clouds can be specific to place as well; the sky as seen over Melbourne, Amsterdam, Santa Fe, and one's own home exhibits subtle, and sometimes dramatic, distinctions. Who knew that clouds are used as tools to predict earthquakes? Or that glider pilots in Australia have learned to surf a cloud like a wave? The society's manifesto proclaims: "We seek to remind people that clouds are expressions of the atmosphere's moods, and can be read like those of a person's countenance. . . . Indeed, all who consider the shapes they see in them will save on psychoanalysis bills. And so we say to all who'll listen: *Look up, marvel at the ephemeral beauty, and live life with your head in the clouds!*"[6]

I bought the book and sent it to my friend's son. He might not be able to step outside the front door comfortably, but he could still exercise his curiosity about nature—he could still see the sky from his bedroom window. Then I bought a copy for myself.

Some of the barriers separating people from the rest of nature are self-imposed, others created by media or the commercial world. That will continue, but we can resist; we *can* tune down the decibels, turn down the lights, and turn on the senses. A few businesses may even join the resistance.

CHAPTER 15

Nature Neurons Go to Work

The Nature Principle in Business

M ARK TWAIN FAMOUSLY said that golf is a good walk spoiled. But maybe business golfers have been onto something all along. Think of all those deals arranged on the greens. Politicians and other movers and shakers have long been known to gather at confabs under trees and stars to exchange ideas and plan campaigns. Camp David, the retreat of presidents, comes to mind. Writers and artists retreats allow people time away from the familiar, time to breathe and think. The same is true for business retreats.

The company Airbus now uses wilderness retreats as a reflective catalyst for leadership training, while other companies sponsor weekend hiking excursions, scheduling time for discussion about new business opportunities or for brainstorming about products. Nature-smart retreats don't have to take place in remote, immersive locations. A hike in a nearby park for a product development team can be stress-reducing and brain-stimulating.

The green architect Gail Lindsey, whom we met previously, saw an opportunity at the intersection between business, personal growth, and the outdoors. She and three colleagues created Adult Summer Camp as an antidote to nature-deficit disorder. "We set up an early September week in the Adirondacks," Lindsey told me. "We brainstormed during the mornings and enjoyed time in nature in the afternoon. We found that the canoeing, hiking, just being with nature was magical. New ideas bubbled up each morning and by the end of the week we knew that several breakthroughs were the direct result of the outdoor experience that allowed our childlike awe, openness, and creativity to flourish."

Today, these weeklong Adult Summer Camps are held at locations around the United States. Lindsey's idea not only represented a nature-smart business venture, but has applications *for* the business world.

Taking businesspeople outdoors can produce more than new marketing ideas. Mark Boulet and Anna Clabburn, in a report for Monash University, Melbourne, Australia, make the case that nature retreats also can help companies ask such questions as: "How can meaningful concern for environmental and social sustainability be embodied?" The authors examine the outdoor experiences of Romantic period painters and Australian Aboriginal nature retreats, and conclude that "the act of placing oneself in the wild and of tuning into the intricate texture and dynamism of the natural environment is a vital step towards awakening a sense of 'ecological' self." The nature retreat "is perhaps one of the most effective ways of alerting human beings to their intimate relationship with (and co-dependence on) the rest of the organic world."[1]

Okay, use such language around most businesspeople and they'll start looking at their watches. Still, there's opportunity here, in the workplace and beyond. New markets will emerge, and some of the early customers will be corporate.

The High-Performance Workplace

One of the most direct applications of the Nature Principle for business is through the creation of the "high-performance" workplace, as some architects and designers call office buildings that go beyond traditional green design to incorporate the benefits of more natural environments, including views of nature.

Today, most office buildings or workplaces are far from restorative. Stephen Kellert, a social ecology professor at Yale University and one of the leading authorities on biophilic design and environmental conservation, has served as an adviser on the development of such projects as the Bank of America's office tower at One Bryant Park in New York. As Kellert points out: "Some of our most alienating work environments, in the sense of separating us from nature, are often in the modern office building, where people are in these very bland, hostile environments with no access to windows or any experience of the outside or natural environments. Ironically, if you tried to do that to a caged animal in a zoo, you would violate legal statute, and would be prevented from doing so. . . . We don't see ourselves like that tiger in the cage, that we're just as much dependent upon those experiential connections as the tiger is."[2]

Many cubicle-bound workers would beg to differ; they do see themselves caged. Naturalizing the workplace may be part of the solution. Vivian Loftness, a professor at Carnegie Mellon University School of Architecture, refers to restorative buildings and points to potential reductions in lost work time, absenteeism, and turnover rate. "Retention of workers is the real sleeper," she says. "It costs an employer about $25,000 every time a valued employee leaves."[3]

Of course, that amount depends on the employee's position and the job market's condition, but the point is taken. For the millions of employees who work in cubicles, their productivity, health, and happiness could be dramatically improved by incorporating natural elements, according to psychologist Judith Heerwagen, whose clients include the U.S. Department of Energy and Boeing. The new rules of the restorative workplace parallel the rules for the restorative home. Employees who sit next to windows are more productive and exhibit consistently fewer symptoms of "sick building syndrome" than other workers; at one organization, absenteeism quadrupled after a move from a building with natural ventilation to one with sealed windows and central air.[4] Studies of such restorative workplaces show improved product quality, customer satisfaction, and innovation. Successful models are emerging, including the 295,000-square-foot Herman Miller headquarters building in Zeeland, Michigan, designed for abundant natural light, indoor plants, and outdoor views, including views of a restored wetlands and prairie on company grounds. After moving into the building, 75 percent of day-shift office workers said they considered the building healthier and 38 percent said their job satisfaction had improved. Another positive example is the fifty-three-story Commerzbank Tower in Frankfurt, Germany, which contains indoor gardens on every thirteenth floor. The conservation of energy and the production of human energy can go hand in hand. In San Bruno, California, the new Gap Inc. office has a green roof of native grasses and wildflowers, which reduces sound transmission by up to fifty decibels and provides an acoustic barrier to nearby air traffic—and the stress associated with that noise. The remodeled California Academy of Sciences in San Francisco offers a glass pavilion, an undulating roof that simulates sand dunes, and a green roof with nearly two million native plants and habitat for several endangered species. At the new University of Guelph-Humber in Toronto, a four-story "living wall" of orchids, ferns, ivy, and hibiscus serves as a super biofilter, using microbe action to break down hundreds of contaminants found in indoor air.

In 2003, designer Mick Pearce was awarded the international Prince Claus Award for the design of an office complex and shopping mall in Zimbabwe, which is ventilated, cooled, and heated entirely through natural means. This approach, inspired by termite mounds (more about that later) not only saves energy, but is more comfortable than the typical sealed and air-conditioned office. Such nature-friendly offices not only encourage more productive workers, but also result in more direct economic benefits. At the office complex and mall in Zimbabwe, ventilation reportedly costs one-tenth that of comparable air-conditioned structures; the complex uses 35 percent less energy than six conventional buildings combined, which saved the owner $3.5 million in energy costs in the first five years alone.

In *Natural Capitalism: Creating the Next Industrial Revolution*, Paul Hawken describes how a Lockheed building in Sunnyvale, California, reduced its lighting bill by three-fourths through better use of natural light. That also resulted in a 15 percent reduction in absenteeism and increased productivity. "Moreover, the lower overhead gave the company the edge in a tough contract competition, and the profits from that unexpected contract earned Lockheed more than it had paid for the whole building," according to Hawken. He also offers an intriguing explanation of a variant of the restorative approach: "The typical Western mechanical engineer strives to *eliminate* variability in human-made environments with thermostats and humidistats and photosensors. . . . But some Japanese designers use computer technology to replicate a more natural environment, subtly delivering air in seemingly random gusts. They may even inject subliminal whiffs of jasmine or sandalwood scent into the ventilation system to stimulate the senses."[5]

Some companies are actively promoting on-site gardens to beef up morale as more traditional benefits evaporate. In the *New York Times*, Kim Severson writes about employees at PepsiCo headquarters in New York raising carrots and squash on company plots, tending plants during lunch or other breaks. They're not alone. There also are organic gardens in plots or raised planting beds in buildings owned by Google, Yahoo, and *Sunset* magazine, spaces that might otherwise have been allotted to standard trimmed lawn and shrubs, or assigned as designated smoking areas. "At Aveda, which offers on-site massage and organic cafeteria food at its headquarters near Minneapolis, the garden is a chance for its seven hundred employees to take a break from their desks and take home fresh produce. Workers pay ten dollars for the season and, in return, they get a share of the bounty. Picking up a hoe is optional, but encouraged," Severson writes. "In many cases, employee groups asked for the gardens. Sometimes, managers suggested them to help supply a food bank or as a team-building activity. It turns out that building tomato trellises together can help erase office hierarchies."[6]

The man who gave us the biophilia hypothesis may have best captured the spirit of the restorative office building. In a PBS interview on *Nova*, while commenting on nature-deficit disorder, E. O. Wilson said: "A lot of architects are saying this is the next big thing." He mused: maybe we've had enough with "buildings and monuments to ourselves . . . gigantic phalli, huge arches, forbidding terraces and walkways . . . neo-Soviet buildings. . . . How great we are! But maybe what we really need down deep is to get closer to where we came from." Naturalizing our workplaces isn't a step back toward the primitive, he added, but rather a way to feel better. He described visiting an office building in North Carolina, which was designed biophilically: "[The designer] had to cut some trees, but he left the rest on this little knoll overlooking a stream. And you sit there with a glassed-in wall endlessly looking out, while chipmunks and warblers and so on are all over the place and the stream is flowing by. And you're at peace."[7]

Some office workers take nature into their own hands by wildscaping their offices. That's what Nancy Herron has done. Herron manages nature and fishing education programs for the Texas Parks and Wildlife Department. "Oddly, our office is a typical prairie-dog town of antiproductivity pods with heads popping over dividers," she says. Herron surrounds her office space with plants to soften the edges and "give my brain some separation from goings-on next door." She and several office mates even planted a wildscape of native plants in front of the building. People sit out there now to talk. She takes her staff to the state park adjacent to the building. "Outside, our creative juices start flowing. We solve problems, we volunteer for solutions, we are no longer in the box. We can talk openly, honestly; we're in an open environment, literally."

Universe Design

Where once the dominant business ethic was to make buildings and products bigger, today the rules of design for electronic gadgets include: make it smaller; make it smarter; make it indispensable; make it usable everywhere; make it prematurely obsolete. At least for those first two goals, E. F. Schumacher, the author of *Small Is Beautiful*, would have nodded his head in agreement.

The Nature Principle offers its own set of design rules: use natural systems to enhance human beings' physical, psychological, and spiritual life; preserve or plant nature everywhere; rather than plan for obsolescence, plan for long-term organic growth. (Frederick Law Olmsted, the father of American landscape architecture, drove some of his patrons to distraction. In their initial form, his parks often looked stunted and spare, and that was because he designed parks to reach their mature beauty decades into the future; he planned for growth.) The current central theory of technology is efficiency, but the guiding theory of a human/nature reunion is restoration of body, mind, spirit.

Whereas technology immersion results in walls that become screens, and machines that enter our bodies, more nature in our lives offers us homes and workplaces and natural communities that produce human energy. A related concept is universal design, which recognizes that human physical abilities range over a wide spectrum. Universal design erases the notion of "design for the disabled"—because all of us eventually face such obstacles and opportunities—and instead produces products and environments that make life more comfortable for people as they move through life.

As our society ages, disabilities will become more common, posing a growing barrier between older people and the outdoors. Does this mean that more hiking trails should be paved and ski runs railed? That's one approach. Other solutions are available. Peter Axelson, who became a paraplegic after a rock-climbing accident, designed the "sit ski," which today allows many disabled people to enjoy skiing and enabled him to become a world champion mono-skier. His Nevada-based company is developing technologies to help people with disabilities engage with nature, including off-road wheelchairs, walkers, and power scooters. The notion of nature-assisted aging, discussed earlier, also presents opportunities for designers of residential developments, assisted-living centers, and nursing homes, as well as for gerontologists, physical therapists, and other health providers. As a philosophy, universal design acknowledges that the best design encompasses the full human community.

An extended universal design philosophy would further broaden the concept of community, suggesting that the design of human products and environment should be about not just the effect on the individual human, but also the effect on other species, and could even incorporate things we have learned from observing other species. Such design takes into consideration all members—thus, the emergence of what might be called *universe design.*

Biomimicry, also called "respectful imitation," is a growing industrial field. Janine Benyus, a natural sciences writer and president of the nonprofit Biomimicry Institute, has written a half-dozen books on the subject. Among her honors is the 2009 Champion of the Earth award in Science and Innovation from the United Nations Environment Programme (UNEP).[8] Her 1997 book, *Biomimicry: Innovation Inspired by Nature,* brought wide attention to the field. Benyus argues that all human inventions have already appeared in nature, in more elegant form and at less cost to the environment: "Our most stealthy radar is hard of hearing compared to the bat's multifrequency transmission: Bioluminescent algae splash chemicals together to light their body lanterns. Arctic fish and frogs freeze solid and then spring to life, having protected their organs from ice damage. [Polar bears] stay active, with a coat of transparent hollow hairs covering their skins like the panes of a greenhouse. . . . The inner shell of a sea creature called an abalone is twice as tough as our high-tech ceramics. Spider silk, ounce for ounce, is five times as strong as steel. . . . Rhino horn manages to repair itself though it has no living cells." In terms of design, nature rejects what humans usually consider "limits," says Benyus.

While "the conscious emulation of life's genius," can be weaponized and abused, and become destructive to nature itself, the basic idea behind biomimicry is derived from awe and respect for the natural world. Biomimicry encompasses the view that nature is not an enemy to be vanquished, but our design partner; not the problem, but the solution.

For example, engineers from the car manufacturer Nissan, citing research into how fish move in schools, have announced their intention "to improve migration efficiency of a group of vehicles and contribute to an environmentally friendly and traffic jam–free driving environment." Nissan's experimental Episode Zero Robot, or EPORO, uses laser sensors, which may someday have practical use in a "Safety Shield" accident-avoidance system installed in cars.[9] The Shinkansen Bullet Train of the West Japan Railway Company travels two hundred miles per hour but, in the beginning, air pressure changes produced thunderclaps when the train emerged from a tunnel. Eiji Nakatsu, the train's chief engineer, who also happened to be a birder, recommended remodeling the front end of the train in the shape of a kingfisher's beak, resulting not only in a quieter train but also in a 15 percent reduction in the train's electricity use and a 10 percent increase in speed.[10]

As Michael Silverberg writes in the *New York Times Magazine*, various treelike contraptions are on the drawing board.[11] One product would target carbon—"100,000 such trees could mop up half the United Kingdom's carbon emissions"—and another would capture energy from sun and wind through "leaflike modules" that could be attached to a building. As the many leaves move in the wind, miniature generators would each produce tiny amounts of electricity. (Still, more *real* forests would do the job better and at less expense.)

Remember the award-winning office complex and shopping mall inspired by termite mounds? The designer recognized the genius of certain African and Australian termite species that create mounds taller than human beings, with special rooms for gardens and water collection, and a mysterious form of air-conditioning. Writing in *Natural History*, J. Scott Turner, a biology professor at the State University of New York's College of Environmental Science and Forestry, describes the process: "By building the mound upward into the stiffer breezes higher off the ground, the termites harness the wind to drive air movements in the mound's tunnels. The flow of the wind pushes air through the porous soil on the windward side and sucks it out on the leeward side, allowing the nest atmosphere to mix with fresh air from the outside world. . . . What is remarkable is the pattern of ventilation, an in-and-out movement very similar to the way air flows into and out of our own lungs."[12] To the designer, the mounds raise the question of where "animate" ends and "inanimate" begins.

When businesses engage nature as a partner, the benefits do not stop at the workplace, or with employee retreats, or even design, but extend directly to the marketplace, the service economy, and retail trade, which can in turn reshape cities and commercial areas. Kathleen L. Wolf, projects director at the College of the Environment, University of Washington, investigates how natural environments in an urban setting—that is, trees and other plants—influence the behavior and perceptions of shoppers and others.[13] She reviewed research on the role of trees in several large cities, including Austin, Seattle, and Washington DC, and found plantings attract consumers and tourists in business districts. The report, "Trees Mean Business," states: "Across all studies, consumer ratings increased steadily with the presence of trees. Visual preference scores were lower for places without trees and much higher for places with trees. . . . Images of business district settings with tidy sidewalks and quality buildings, but no trees, were at the low end of the scores, while the images of districts with well-tended large trees received the highest preference ratings, particularly when large trees formed a canopy over the sidewalk and street." And retailers take note: "Respondents were presented with a list of goods and services and asked to state prices for each. Price response varied somewhat between different-sized cities, yet trees were consistently associated with higher price points. Consumers claimed they were willing to pay 9 percent more in small cities and 12 percent more in large cities for equivalent goods and services in business districts having trees."[14]

The proof will be in the purchases. If future neighborhood shopping areas are immersed in nature, will people really avoid the big-box stores? Probably not. Price still rules. (Green roofs or solar farms on the big boxes would help.) But all things being equal, when the public is given a choice between a generic, marginal strip mall and a pleasant, tree-lined shopping area, the smart money would be on the trees.

Techno-Naturalists

One of the clichés about business and nature is that there's no profit to be made. Not true. Putting the Nature Principle to work for business isn't only a matter of workplace or commercial design, but of new products, too. Many people believe that technology is the antithesis of nature. Understandable. But here's an alternative view: A fishing rod is technology. So is that fancy backpack. Or a compass. Or a tent. When boomers my age ran through the woods with play guns, they were using technology as an entry tool to nature. Today, the family that goes geocaching or wildlife photographing with their digital cameras, or collecting pond samples, is doing something as legitimate as backpacking; these gadgets offer an excuse to get outside. The attitude of young citizen naturalists toward technology is bound to be different from that of many older people—and that could be an advantage.

Not long ago, I received a note from Jim Levine, who happens to be my literary agent, and who also has written several books about fatherhood and family life. He and his wife, Joan, were staying at their getaway cabin in Massachusetts. Jim was on his way out the door to take their four-year-old grandson, Elijah, on a walk through a nature preserve and to gather pond samples "to look at under the very cool microscope I got him," Jim wrote. Jim, who is a bit too attached to his own smartphone, was excited about the microscope: "It hooks up to my computer (desktop or laptop) and lets us both see the images on screen and record them as still photos or as movies. So from our last outing, I have pix of the outing, pix of him setting up the microscope, and then a video of what he actually saw— paramecium and all—when he looked through. Elijah just got done explaining to Joan that we won't necessarily retrieve a paramecium in our sample! At age 4!" And Jim and Joan—as grandparents—were connecting to nature, too.

Personally, I'm not keen on the kind of gadgets that go over the line—to the point where we become more aware of the gadget than of nature (iPod-guided tours of natural areas, for example). But tech-nonaturalists are here to stay. Of course, any gadget can distract from nature. People can become so transfixed by the camera screen that they never look past it to see the stream. In the same way, some fishermen are so intent on their gear, or on winning the tournament trophy, that they miss much of the environment around them, except for the rod, the reel, the feel of monofilament. The worth of any nature-oriented getaway gadget should be related to how long it takes the person to put down the gadget. Hopefully, they'll still want to look around and use their unaided eyes and all the other senses.

"How do we create experiences for people, particularly in cities, that foster awareness of the natural world?" asks Janis Dickinson, director of Citizen Science at Cornell Lab of Ornithology, which offers the Celebrate Urban Birds project. "It is possible, even likely, that a new generation of technonaturalists will document their outdoor experiences not with paper and pen but with electronic data, digital images, and video, creating new communities of action and meaning. Celebrate Urban Birds is exploring these ideas while remaining grounded in the real world. It is our overriding belief that spending real time in real nature, with its rhythms, sights, smells, and sounds, may be facilitated with technology but cannot be fabricated!"

We live in a goal-oriented society, and most people need some goal in mind when entering the natural world, whether it's to live out a fantasy or to hunt and gather. Shouldering that toy gun as a ten-year-old and heading for the woods was one way to enter nature. I have an imaginary new "toy" in mind, one that kids *and* adults might enjoy. Is it a pretend gun? Or a long-lens camera? Take your pick; the device could visually be mistaken for either. (Most of us who raised boys have realized that, even when toy guns are discouraged, children will often turn sticks into guns. So let's offer something new to express that hunter-gatherer instinct.) Boys, girls, adults (think paintball) could take this gadget on explorations in nature. Within this device would be a digital camera, a microphone, and a wireless phone connection. Point this device at a bird and click, and the image is immediately sent to your own Web-based life list, and to a Web site that maps and tracks species migrations and sightings. Using image and sound recognition, the bird would be identified and registered, thus aiding scientists and citizen naturalists working to understand migration patterns and population distribution. In fact, something like this service already exists for iPhone users—and by the time you read this entry, some more sophisticated version may be available. In this way, play becomes purposeful and participatory science. A related business idea emerged in 2010: a $1,200 digital scope that hunters can use for deer hunting—without actually shooting the deer. The scope includes a memory card that stores 10-second video clips recording accurate "shots." The plan is for the scope to be used in competitions broadcast by the Outdoor Channel.

Enthusiasm for such products is a matter of personal taste, but they do get people outdoors. When I asked some of my colleagues and friends for suggestions for other imaginary or existing products and services that could connect people of all ages to nature, they offered dozens of suggestions for entrepreneurs, with a certain thematic crossover between the sustainable and the restorative.

Ideas for new product lines, or ones that exist but could be marketed more widely to people of all ages, include: wildscape kits with guides, seeds and plants to naturalize your backyard (with coupons to local native-plant nurseries); nature tourism and walking guides (and smartphone apps); night cameras and video traps to "catch" seldom-seen animals in nearby nature. (San Diego Zoo conservationist Ron Swaisgood says, "Prices are falling and quality is improving. Purchase one, mount it to a tree in your local canyon and see what's going on. Upload the video to your Facebook page.")

Among the services: roof gardeners for hire; indoor fish-farm installers; forest kindergartens, where the kids learn outside all day; raising mushrooms to be used as packing material (this idea started as a classroom project and has grown into a full-scale business); roof painters who paint your roof white in summer months for heat reflection and black in the colder months for heat absorption; mobile bike tune-up guy and bike taxi services. My friend Jon Wurtmann suggests this novel idea: "People Walker. We have dog walkers—why not a service that takes your kids, your aging parents, the infirm, and walks them at their pace through a safe park, local trails . . ."

A third category: business-building restorative services, including business-sponsored annual competitions in birding, hiking, and other outdoor activities. Nancy Herron of Texas Parks and Wildlife reports: "We have an annual competition with business-sponsored teams who compete for how many different species of birds they see or hear over a week's time and the winning team's prize is selecting a conservation project to receive funding."

Once the entrepreneurial spirit kicks in, it's easy to start thinking of products and services. Some of these may not be your cup of organic tea—and yes, there's a certain contradiction between preserving nature and consumer products, but let's give ourselves a break. Would we rather that the commercial world emphasize everything *but* a connection to the natural world?

Business can, with nature as partner, become more productive and profitable; in fact, a nature-smart business has certain natural advantages over companies that continue to destroy the human connection to nature. Those advantages are sustainable only within a larger moral and societal context, suggesting this rule: If a business with nature adds more to the natural world than it subtracts, if it strengthens human care for nature, while enhancing human intelligence, health, and well-being, then that relationship—that business—is not only moral, but *truly* nature smart.

CHAPTER 16

Living in a Restorative City

The Natural Renewal of Our Urban Lives

WHEN TRAVELING, I walk to restore myself. Even in the loudest, most congested cities I usually find remnants of the natural world hiding in plain sight. I take photographs with my mobile-phone camera of moving water and light and sky, and critters—a groundhog shimmying across the greens of a university campus in upstate New York, a tangle of trout in a Connecticut stream, a fox slipping through downtown Little Rock—and as I stand there, I send these photographs to my wife. The camera gives me the excuse to stop, look, and listen.

One November afternoon in Fort Wayne, Indiana, in search of lunch, I walked out the front door of a Holiday Inn and ambled north along a commercial strip.

There were no sidewalks, so I kept to a grass berm, walking through parking lots, across gravel, to a street with no pedestrian crosswalk or pedestrian light. The drivers were mad with desire, the traffic an endless knot. I waited for a long time at a stoplight, then made my dive across the road. I trudged past Hooters (packed) and a Dream Girls strip joint (not so packed), to another intersection. I crossed the pavement of a gas station, then went down a grass slope to an Applebee's. I ate while reading the news on my phone, surrounded by flat screens.

Sports announcers were drowned out by the recorded song of the generic male bodice-ripping rocker. I paid up. Outside, I noticed a side street and a hint of woods, so I headed in that direction. I still heard the heavy traffic beyond the trees, and an occasional car went by, but this piece of the natural world slowly found me.

I looked up through bare branches at the gray cirrus, and watched a red-tailed hawk circle and swoop. I recalled something I had recently learned: Filmmakers will often dub the prosaic red tail's haunting cry over the image of the more exotic bald eagle, because the nation's symbol sometimes sounds like a dog's squeak toy. I wondered what the hawk sees, and I already knew the answer: anything it wants to see. Above the trees, above the hawk, leaves were falling from the sky. Maybe they were sent aloft this afternoon by the same upwell that supported the hawk, or perhaps they were captured by a whirlwind weeks ago, and only now are coming back to the earth.

I continued walking. I came to a chain across a path buried in leaves. A No Trespassing sign hung there. Stepping over the chain, I followed the path deep into the woods. A few minutes later, I came to a concrete bridge over a slow-running creek, where I stood and peered into the water. Leaves rolled along the brown mud. As I watched the current, I recalled using Google Earth to locate the creek of my boyhood, and finding it, or what was left of it, as I looked down from a virtual sky.

Now something heavy and frantic burst through the tangle of vines. A fleeting brown flank. The thud of hooves. Then silence. I held my breath, looking for the deer — it was there but I couldn't see it, like the mouse in *Goodnight Moon*. A sound like rain came from the nearly bare limbs above and I looked up to see leaves still clinging to the high branches, or shaking as they let go. The wind rose, the clattering grew, the sound and smell of water and earth and sky and deer and me and the whole world beyond Hooters spiraled upward into the gray-blue sky.

Urban Is the New Rural

Opportunities to find the natural world are all around us, even in the densest cities. But, unless we act quickly to conserve and restore these places, and create new ones, then nearby nature will become a quaint artifact of another time. The alternative is that nearby nature can become a central organizing principle of modern life. Earlier, we explored the importance of the role of the bioregion in our personal and regional identities, the importance of reinhabiting the places in which we live. We also looked at our homes and gardens, and how they can be re-natured. The challenge we turn to now is the larger built environment, our neighborhoods, suburbs, and countryside. Whether we're individuals, city planners, architects, wildlife specialists, or conservationists, we can all help reshape that environment. And some of us can make a living doing it.

Not long ago, I spent a pleasant afternoon with students at Cornell University who were studying for careers in botanical gardens. I accompanied several of them and their instructors on a walk through the adjacent Cornell Plantations, the university's home for an arboretum and 4,300 acres of natural areas, including bogs, gorges, glens, and woodlands. As we sat in an open-air shelter for lunch, we discussed the Garden Cities movement of the early twentieth century, which was infused with the idea that nature experience was connected to human health, and we talked about how that connection has been all but scrubbed from public consciousness and urban planning.

The education of these students was focused on creating botanical gardens to enhance city life. I asked them if they had ever considered careers that could lead to turning entire cities into botanical landscapes. They were intrigued by the question, and no, they had not considered that career path—yet.

Now comes a *natural* urban renewal movement. For half a century, governments have attempted to revive decaying inner cities, with mixed results. What was once called "urban renewal" often made life worse, as planners razed blighted neighborhoods and replaced architecture of character with massive projects that, through their poor design, undermined a sense of community. But in the twenty-first century, the most vibrant cities will be those that integrate the population into an urban environment enriched by both natural and re-natured habitat. Even for cities ravaged by the economy, perhaps especially there, the potential for greatness presents itself. With the natural world at the center of an emerging design philosophy, cities could once again be seen as gardens. In fact, they could become gardens.

In urban neighborhoods, thousands of redundant shopping centers could be replaced by mixed-use ecovillages, with both higher residential density and more habitat for nature. Fanciful thinking? Not if some of the most advanced community and architectural design techniques prove replicable. Enlightened public policy will offer special incentives to developers who build ecovillages in the inner neighborhoods and in those outer suburbs that are in need of renovation. Whenever possible, these green urban villages should include parks with native vegetation and be connected by wildlife corridors that allow animals, including people, to travel through neighborhoods.

Timothy Beatley, in his book *Green Urbanism: Learning from European Cities* and his film *The Nature of Cities*, points to several ecovillages and urban plans that are transforming parts of older European urban areas.[1] In Hammarby Sjöstad in Stockholm, Sweden, for example, a densely built community is connected to a grove of ancient oaks. A car-limited housing project in Amsterdam was planned to allow space for residents to plant gardens in the common area, and another neighborhood features a "free range" habitat for children. In Malmö, Sweden, the Western Harbor community features green roofs and rainwater retention in courtyard ponds and channels to support plants and wildlife within an urban setting. With solar collectors, wind turbines, and

other measures, the community now draws all of its energy from locally produced renewable sources.

In the United States, a handful of dense urban neighborhoods have
been resurrected as ecovillages, including Cleveland EcoVillage, two
miles west of downtown Cleveland, Ohio, which has twenty-four
energy-efficient town houses, cottages, and homes. The revitalization
of this urban district came about through a partnership of nonprofits,
the regional transit authority, local residents, and private developers.
The EcoVillage organic garden, on what had been unmaintained vacant lots, offers abundant produce from raised beds. And the community includes a park on a former gas station site, now planted with
drought-resistant species.[2] Not far from downtown Cincinnati, Ohio,
Enright Ridge Urban Ecovillage includes a sixteen-acre nature preserve, a community greenhouse, residential and community gardens,
and a two-mile trail through a park called Hundred-Acre Wood.
Residents boast of having nearby wildlife, chickens in the backyard,
friendly neighbors, and services within walking distance.[3]

The Incredible Edible City

Inevitably, cities will grow up. Literally. Residential towers and increased urban density are a given for those urban regions predicted
to expand rapidly. Architect Prakash M. Apte, a Fellow of the Indian
Institute of Architects and the Institute of Town Planners, sees this
brand of high-rise development as dehumanizing, a tearing of the
cultural fabric. "Case studies all over the world have documented the
inappropriateness of high-rise resettlement projects in poor areas,"
Apte writes. "The social and economic networks which the poor rely
on for subsistence can hardly be sustained in high-rise structures."[4]
But what if we built different kinds of skyscrapers: residential high-
rises and towering office buildings as vertical farms? In 1999, Dickson
Despommier, a professor of public health at Columbia University,

began to promote the concept of dedicated, high-rise hydroponic farms, which draw energy from the sun, wind, and wastewater. He estimates a thirty-story tower could feed fifty thousand people. In 2007, a lower-rise design for a vertical farm for Seattle won a green building contest. Theoretically, this design would supply about a third of the food needed for four hundred residents of the building.[5]

More extravagant plans call for spearlike skyscrapers, wrapped in spiraling agridecks that vine top to bottom, capturing rain or piped-in water and recycling it down the spiral to irrigate crops and flowers. Office workers or residents would see the outside world through rich gardens, or be able to walk outside to tend the plants, or simply to enjoy them. In New York, a plan for a 202-apartment complex called Via Verde, or the Green Way, includes an eighteen-story tower, a midrise building with duplex apartments, and town houses. Sixty-three units would be co-op apartments, and expensive; the rest would be lower-cost rentals. Starting at ground level, the complex's garden would spiral upward to a series of roof gardens and a sky terrace.

Even without vertical farms, urban agriculture is looking up. Every available roof and wall could provide natural habitat for humans and other critters. Aztec cities had their lush rooftops; so can we. Green roofs not only reduce heating and cooling costs and last longer than the typical roof; they can also absorb rainwater, provide habitat for wildlife, and help lower urban air temperatures. Green roofs and living walls can produce food and be used to purify polluted water. Obviously, they also add beauty.

In coming years, vast sections of existing urban neighborhoods will require renewal. Consider Detroit. In recent decades, that city was devastated by factory shutdowns, suburban growth, and disinvestment. "Just about a third of Detroit, some forty square miles, evolved past decrepitude into vacancy and prairie — an urban void nearly the size of San Francisco," Rebecca Solnit reports in *Harper's Magazine*. She describes wandering through one of the neighborhoods, "or rather a former neighborhood," where "approximately one tattered charred house still stood per block." Much of this area is usually depicted as a postapocalyptic urban wasteland, but something remarkable has occurred in Detroit, and it goes beyond, and deeper than, traditional, energy-efficient green design.

In 1989, a nonprofit organization, The Greening of Detroit, formed with a goal of combating the loss of a half-million city trees to Dutch elm disease.[6] The group also uses reclaimed vacant lots as growing grounds for trees that will eventually be replanted in the community. Their projects now include neighborhood vegetation restoration, park plantings, and the promotion of small-scale vegetable gardens. The organization reports on its Web site: "For each neighborhood nursery, we clean the lot, then build berms, spread mulch and plant trees. We install landscape plants, fencing and signage to improve the appearance of the lot and create a signature look, helping to reduce vandalism. The nurseries are initially planted with small tree stock that is allowed to grow for 3-5 years while it is cared for by the community and The Greening's Green Corps." The nonprofit has hired more than five hundred Detroit youths since 1998 to help maintain plantings and learn about urban ecology. This Green Corps program has been expanded, opening its doors to adults who want work experience and on-the-job training.

One example of the group's effectiveness is Romanowski Park, a twenty-six-acre urban park that includes a farm, playground, teaching pavilion, walking trail, sugar maple grove, and, yes, athletic fields for the soccer kids. During the growing season, the organization teams with neighborhood schools to teach students about gardening and nutrition. There's more: "The Greening of Detroit has inspired its volunteers and community partners to transform miles of public and private open space—including some of Detroit's 60,000 vacant lots—into usable, productive resources," the organization reports. "We've helped our planting partners to create hundreds of vegetable gardens and numerous perennial gardens and neighborhood tree nurseries throughout the city. These production greenspaces produce hundreds of trees and tons of produce for use in Detroit's neighborhoods each year."

None of this makes up for the economic devastation of Detroit. But Solnit was cheered after exploring what used to be the dense urban core and finding truck farms, where everyday people tilled the soil in abandoned lots to produce food for the table. She writes: "The future, at least the sustainable one, the one in which we will survive, isn't going to be invented by people who are happily surrendering selective bits and pieces of environmentally unsound privilege. It's going to be made by those who had all that taken away from them or never had it in the first place."[7]

Many urban and suburban dwellers are independently transforming their own homes and neighborhoods, much the way Karen Harwell enhanced her property, creating Dana Meadows Garden. Even beekeepers in Manhattan recently stepped out of the shadows and are now allowed to tend their hives legally, thanks to a long-sought health department ruling. In Gresham, Oregon, the city council in 2010 reversed an ordinance that excluded chickens from the city. Katy Skinner had raised chickens in Portland, and she started the Web site TheCityChicken.com, before relocating to Yacolt, Washington. "I like chickens because they are the easiest of pets next to a goldfish; there aren't many downsides to them," she says. Some families are finding that they prefer chickens to dogs or cats as pets, partly because they can be less work. And (until breeders correct this oversight) dogs and cats don't lay eggs. In *Backyard Poultry* magazine (that's right, there's a magazine devoted to this) Frank Hyman reports his experience successfully working to change city policy toward urban chickens in Durham, North Carolina: "In 30 years as a political activist I've won four races as a campaign manager, served on a city council, helped start political organizations, been president of a neighborhood association and worked on issues like affordable housing, living wage and recycling. But I never once imagined I would be working to change the laws to allow people to have backyard chickens." Hyman's wife, Chris, "thinks of hens as 'pets with benefits.' "[8]

The dream of an edible city sounds a lot like the marginalized community gardens movement of decades past—until you consider the booming organic food industry. Then add another ingredient: the Slow Food movement. This movement was launched in 1986 by Carlo Petrini, an Italian who took one look at a new McDonald's restaurant being built at St. Peter's Square in Rome and decided the way to fight fast food was with better taste. He created the first Slow Food campaign, in northern Italy, to protect "the pleasures of the table from the homogenization of modern fast food and life." Since then, Slow Food conviviums (from the Latin word for feast or entertainment) have sprouted everywhere.

The potential for the growth of urban agriculture is even greater than it might seem. A report by Rutgers University and members of the Community Food Security Coalition's North American Initiative on Urban Agriculture charts the national trend: across the country, "significant amounts of food" are cultivated by entrepreneurial producers, community gardeners, backyard gardeners, food banks in vacant lots, parks, greenhouses, rooftops, balconies, windowsills, ponds, rivers, and estuaries. A third of the two million farms in the United States alone are already located within metropolitan areas and produce 35 percent of U.S. vegetables, fruit, livestock, poultry, and fish (little surprise given urban sprawl). "The potential to expand urban production is enormous," according to the report. Add to this the growing concern about food security: "Times of war and conflict render tenuous our dependence on distant food sources, especially in this post-9/11 world." Although fear is a motivator, pleasure's more the point—the pleasure of a connected community.

After a conference of urban arborists held in Berkeley, I was walking down a street with Nancy Hughes, a leader in urban forestry. She pointed to a tree hemmed in by a tight container. "Once you start noticing shade patterns, you're never the same." Hughes believes we need aggressive municipal greenscaping policies to help clean the air, reduce surface heat, and please the senses. Trees absorb atmospheric carbon. Urban forests also retain and filter water. Creating an effective urban forest requires a good deal more knowledge and a larger investment than some policymakers might think.

Here's one example of the complexity: when planting trees to control air pollution, not just any tree will do, since some spread a little pollution of their own. Take your California sycamore or liquidambar. These trees are the arboreal equivalent to that '66 Imperial my Uncle Horton used to drive. Well, maybe not that bad, but they do emit chemical compounds that play a role in tropospheric ozone formation and aerosol production, according to research done at the Washington State University Laboratory for Atmospheric Research. Meanwhile, the avocado, peach, ash, sawleaf zelkova, and eastern redbud trees are low-ozone emitters. They're fine air-purifiers, the good citizens of treedom.

Sacramento's regional effort has led the way in California. The Sacramento Tree Foundation educates the public about the benefits of tree planting, pointing to a 270 percent return on investment in the urban forest. In 2005, the foundation launched its regional Greenprint initiative that hoped to double the region's urban tree canopy by planting five million new trees in twenty-two cities and four counties by 2025. Meeting that goal would mean a welcome three-degree drop in the city of Sacramento's average temperature during summer months and an estimated $7 billion in long-term savings on energy, air-pollution clean-up, and stormwater management. Another benefit is health. Sacramento has the second-highest skin cancer rate in California. The region has lost countless native oaks to housing developments, even though its residents need the shade.

Toronto also hopes to double its tree canopy, but officials there decided that achieving that goal would be impossible without more public involvement. Andy Kenney, a professor of urban forestry at the University of Toronto, started a campaign called Neighbourwoods that trains homeowners to identify, plant, and care for trees in their neighborhoods and on their own properties. Meanwhile, some cities are developing new approaches to parkland, lengthening or creating natural networks that connect parks with trails and neighborhoods. Examples include the BeltLine, Atlanta's planned streetcar or light-rail line circling the downtown core. The park will use existing rail-track easements to link green space with a walking and biking trail to forty new and existing parks. In Scottsdale, Arizona, Indian Bend Wash is a string of interconnected desert and grassy parks and recreation trails, known collectively as the Greenbelt. In Copenhagen, where one-third of the residents commute to work by bike, the city's green cycle routes initiative, which connects close-in suburbs with more urban neighborhoods, provides some seventy miles of paths through parks, and along the water, with bridges over roadways that have heavy car traffic. These green networks, combined with the increasing number of wildlife corridors being created in cities, are important components in an emerging standard, the modern urban greenprint.

Their influence can seep into surrounding neighborhoods. Along with other community leaders, Mike Stepner, principal of the Stepner Design Group and a professor at the NewSchool of Architecture and Design in San Diego, argues that the city's natural canyons (in aerial photographs, the complex pattern of canyons looks like the region's lungs and bronchi) offer a unique opportunity to use restorative design as a central organizing principle for the region's future. Stepner believes in bringing the canyons to the neighborhoods, not just bringing the neighbors to the canyons. Urban planners and canyon protectors could extend the look and feel of the canyons by adding native canyon plants and other natural elements to surrounding neighborhoods, as well as along boulevards, in parks, plazas, and other found spaces. Every one of these canyons within walking distance of a public school is a potential outdoor classroom.

A De-Central Park in Every City;
A Button Park in Every Neighborhood

When I met Harlem's Classie Parker, she practically raced across the community garden she oversees in New York City. She handed me a cluster of leaves from an herb she and her neighbors grow on this quarter-acre wedge between brownstones on West 121st Street in Harlem. "Don't you just feel happy in this place?" she asked, beaming. Her fellow gardeners were in the midst of a beauty and productivity makeover of their garden, which has been here for well over a decade. They grow food for more than five hundred families on this little piece of land. She's not an environmentalist, she told me. She's a farmer.

Every day her father, going on ninety, sits on a bench in the garden, gnarled hands on his cane, the perfect image of a peaceful urban farmer.

"Don't you feel like my dad is your dad?" she asked me.

That sentence has stayed with me since.

I was introduced to Classie by representatives of the Trust for Public Land (TPL), through their work to protect pieces of urban nature across the nation. Later, they took me to a public elementary schoolyard, where students had transformed bare asphalt into their own school garden. The teacher who oversees the garden told me that his students had begun to go beyond their garden, to study the street trees, comparing them with trees in other neighborhoods on the island of Manhattan. He also told me how some of his students had never seen the Harlem River, which flowed just beyond the buildings that front the river. I recall standing in that remarkable green space, still in Classie Parker's spell of hope and healing and the sheer pleasure of life itself. I thought about the threatened, fragmented chaparral canyons in my own city, and how some of us hope to protect them by giving them a collective identity and name: the San Diego Regional Urban Canyonlands Park. Hurt one and you've hurt them all.

In New York City, there are hundreds, perhaps thousands, of green places, even green roofs, that could be stitched together politically and protected. What would such a network be called? There will never be another Central Park, but New Yorkers could make urban history by creating a park comprised of thousands of small play areas landscaped with native plants, a galaxy of urban emeralds on the ground and on the roofs. Perhaps call it by one name: New York City's De-Central Park.

Play spaces—where adults as well as children spend time—could certainly be part of De-Central Park. Even in a city already dotted with parks, New York City's children don't have that many chances to interact with nature. To counteract this problem, a number of planners and educators are creating play areas where children and adults can roll down green slopes and climb rocks sheltered by trees. Surprisingly, green play areas can be designed to survive thousands of feet. During the last two decades, natural-play-area designers have become skilled at creating living landscapes that use specialized soil and plants, as well as new irrigation technologies; they design slopes to resist erosion; they cover walls with hanging gardens. To reflect sunlight and dispel gloom, designers place mirrors on nearby light-blocking buildings. Some of these techniques are now incorporated in Teardrop Park in Battery Park City, and are being planned for the larger Brooklyn Bridge Park. Plenty of opportunities are available to transform decaying asphalt playgrounds or vacant lots into natural play areas.

What better city than New York to go beyond the typical roof garden and create energy-efficient, habitat-providing green roofs, adapted for use as natural play areas? Says Yale's Stephen Kellert, "There's no reason why green roofs can't be experientially more positive and aesthetically rich environments, especially given that rooftops represent the largest available habitat in most metropolitan areas for the photosynthetic effects of sunlight. The possibility of doing something with that habitat is exciting."[9]

We also need to be more creative about what space is appropriate for nature experience, particularly because people have very different views about how existing open space and parkland should be used. In Australia, Peter Ker, environmental reporter for *The Age*, one of the country's national newspapers, describes how, in Melbourne, "meddling with parks has always been easier said than done." Plans to establish a community garden within one park sparked local anger. "One group of locals wanted the space to grow plants, while others saw the move as a reduction of existing park space for the benefit of few." The passion evoked by the debate caught local officials by surprise. With that controversy in mind, Deakin University associate professor Mardie Townsend suggested to Ker the "scouring (of) the urban environment for places to establish new parks and community gardens," including "taking advantage of laneways, disused blocks of land and river frontages that are unsuitable for housing developments." In the long term, she added, private companies could turn some of their land into public recreation spaces. "Think of a place like Chadstone [shopping center], where they have miles of car-parking and have two or three layers. Why not make the top one a [nature] park, which keeps everything cool under that roof and provides a wonderful open space for people? People are far more likely to go to Chadstone if there's a nice park there, where they can sit and have their lunch before going in to shop, so it becomes an economic attractor to business."[10]

Neighborhoods can be more creative, too. In recent years, the land-trust movement has been a roaring success, especially when compared to the large national environmental organizations, which are facing barriers to increasing funding and membership. But, of course, large land-trust organizations can't do it all. What if individuals and neighborhood groups were to step forward to protect the small green places closest to home, and then link them to an even larger green network? Remember the special place in nature that you had as a child—that wooded lot at the end of the cul-de-sac, that ravine behind your housing tract? What if adults had cared just as much about that special place as you did, when you were a child? Here's an idea whose time may be coming: the creation of neighborhood "nearby-nature trusts." Land-trust organizations could develop and distribute tool kits, and perhaps offer consulting services, to show neighborhood residents how they can band together to cut through red tape and protect those precious parcels of nearby nature—and these could be symbolically combined into de-central parks.

In Denver, when the Trust for Public Land, working with the Colorado Health Foundation, brought together groups concerned about the disconnect of people from nature, TPL leaders and I brainstormed on the future of land trusts in tough economic times. One of the TPL people suggested that neighborhood leaders might also identify abandoned houses, buy them, raze them, and turn the lots into re-natured parkland or community gardens. "We really do have to think about creating nature, not just preserving it," he said.

Here's an illustration of that kind of thinking. In Charlotte, North Carolina, the Catawba Lands Conservancy, a regional land trust, has protected seventy-five hundred acres. Catawba is also the lead agency for the Carolina Thread Trail, a trail network that will eventually weave through a huge area of North Carolina and South Carolina, reach into fifteen counties and serve over two million people. On its Web site, the Catawba organization describes the Thread Trail this way: "Simply put, it will link people and places. It will link cities, towns, and attractions. More than a hiking trail, more than a bike path, the Carolina Thread Trail will preserve our natural areas and will be a place for exploration of nature, culture, science, and history, for family adventures and celebrations of friendship."[11] If the full concept survives the legal and political challenges that are inevitable any time people pursue a vision this large, the Thread Trail will be one example of how regions can address a growing hunger for the health and well-being that nature provides human beings. To be sure, the availability of nearby nature is or should be seen as an integral element of our future health care system, for reasons related to both physical and mental health.

The central organizing principle of nearby-nature trusts would be *do it yourself, do it now*, with a little help and information from friends who know about land trusts.

What might these little parcels be called? Here's my suggestion: *button parks. Pocket park* is the term for small parks created by governments or developers; button parks—well, people can sew those on themselves. The term makes particular sense in the Carolinas. The reason that the Carolina Thread Trail is called a *thread* trail is not only because of the image that word evokes, but also because of the Carolinas' long dependence on the textile industries. In past decades, stitching shirts has given way to high-tech industries, but the regional sense of this history remains. While visiting with the good folks of Catawba, it occurred to me that the Carolina Thread Trail would be strengthened over time, politically and socially, if the people who live adjacent to the trail were to become more directly involved not only in the use of the trail but also in the embrace of button parks. These spaces wouldn't need to be physically connected to the trail, but would serve as small extensions of the trail throughout the region.

There would be objections, no doubt, some based on the fear of liability and possible loss of privacy. But precedents do exist around the country. In Fort Wayne, Indiana, Jason Kissel, the executive director of ACRES Land Trust, suggests an intriguing possibility. ACRES has protected natural habitats throughout northeast Indiana, southern Michigan, and northwest Ohio. Kissel thought that button parks could be created by neighborhood associations, and that, at least in Indiana public use of private land left in its natural state poses less danger of future litigation than land that has been "improved."

By going through the process of creating button parks, people would learn about the growing importance of the land-trust movement and support it.

Getting Along with the Neighbors

Creating livable cities isn't only about green infrastructure; it's also about how to consciously increase the urban wildlife population, and then how to get along with the new neighbors. In Portland, Oregon, wildscaper Mike Houck helps lead the growing national movement to rewild cities, and he describes the challenges that presents.

In Portland, developers and road builders chipped away for decades at urban wildness habitat. At the same time, invasive species such as Himalayan blackberry and English ivy overtook much of the publicly owned open space. Between 1990 and 2000, the city's population increased by 20.7 percent,[12] but consumption of open land went up only 4 percent.[13] That was the reverse of the trend in most U.S. metropolitan regions. The threats, including a weakening of the state's pioneering urban boundary limits, continue. Nonetheless, some elected officials, public agencies, and voters have quietly accepted a new paradigm of nature in the city, a shift in perception, from urban nature blindness to "wilder in the mind's eye," as Houck puts it. Portland officials are preserving more habitat within the urban boundaries and working to restore native vegetation. As a result, Houck happily reports a return of wildlife to the city. "The most productive peregrine falcon nest in Oregon is on the Fremont Bridge in Portland," he says. Fifteen years ago, there were no bald eagles in Portland. Now they, too, nest in the middle of the city. "While it's true the rebound of eagles and osprey is attributable to the ban on DDT, if the habitat were not in Portland they would not be here."

Other cities are following Portland's lead. Through the Intertwine Alliance, Portland formed an "alliance of alliances" with Chicago Wilderness, Houston Wilderness, the Lake Erie Allegheny Partnership for Biodiversity, and Amigos de los Rios in Los Angeles to lobby at the national level for funding for large regional biodiversity conservation that is focused on the urban environment.[14] Similar efforts exist in the Seattle region with the Cascade Land Conservancy, and with the East Bay Regional Park District in Contra Costa and Alameda Counties in the Bay Area in California. Austin, Texas, has protected an urban bat colony, and celebrates it as a source of economic development. Every evening, crowds gather to watch the bats swarm up from their home beneath a major city bridge; the living funnels are visible for miles. These bats not only help control the mosquito population, but also generate tourism dollars. The Texas highway department is building bridges with bat-attraction designs.

Other cities report different successes. Though many species remain threatened by pollution, development, and newly introduced invasive species, lake sturgeons are now spawning on an artificial reef in the Detroit River. "Think of this: 35 years ago we had major oil slicks on the Detroit River, elevated phosphorus levels, much more raw sewage, much more contaminants like DDT, PCP and mercury," writes John Hartig (no relation to researcher Terry Hartig), refuge manager of the Detroit River International Wildlife Refuge. And it's not only fish that are returning to the cities. The beavers are back, too.[15] Even New York is becoming wilder. "The 2007 wintertime appearance of a beaver in New York's Bronx River, the first in two centuries, added to the interest in reconnecting the region's 16 million residents with nature," he adds. And most recently, bald eagles, down to one pair in New York State in 1976, have returned in respectable numbers, even in Manhattan.

Rewilding our cities and suburbs does come with risk. Especially in the northeastern United States, deer overpopulation is a real problem for motorists and gardeners. Their dominance is also a threat to balanced biodiversity. Proposed solutions, all of them controversial, range from controlled hunting to deer birth control. Another issue is tick-borne disease, which is related to deer population. In Southern California, Colorado, and other growing regions, encounters between humans and mountain lions or bears have increased as housing developments have crept deeper into the backcountry.

This trend requires clear thinking about risk. Approximately thirty thousand people die every year in auto accidents, but only about 130 die each year because of deer encounters—and most of these deer-related human deaths involve automobiles. In fact, horses kill more people—more than two hundred annually—than deer do. The odds are 50,000 to 1 that you'll be killed by a large animal; by lightning, 56,000 to 1. Such statistics are small comfort to the relative handful of people who have encountered, say, an aggressive mountain lion, or who have had a child attacked by a coyote or fox—as has happened in recent years in the United States and the UK. But consider the risk from domestic pets. An American has a 1 in 50 chance of being bitten by a dog each year, according to the Centers for Disease Control.[16] Some eight hundred thousand Americans annually require medical attention for their injuries, half of them children.[17] Page through the nation's papers, and the headlines horrify. They tell of children killed by packs of pit bull terriers, the elderly mauled by their own guard dogs, joggers brought down by rottweilers. This is not to say that our pets aren't worth the risk. In fact many breeds are underemployed. If mentally balanced dogs were given an expanded role as protective hiking companions for young people and adults, in those areas where they're welcome, many people who might not otherwise enjoy outdoor experiences would feel comfortable going for outings in canyons, woods, and other natural areas.

A related issue: if we kept our cats indoors, we'd save the lives of countless songbirds, and we would protect our cats from coyotes, other wild predators, and outdoor hazards.

"Some people want a risk-free world. It's not going to happen," says Walter Boyce, wildlife veterinarian and executive director of the Wildlife Health Center at the University of California–Davis. Boyce is not unfamiliar with the personal pain that can occur during a close encounter with a wild animal. Three years ago, a deer attacked him. "We used to keep a captive deer herd here at the center," he told me recently. "From twenty or thirty feet away, a buck charged me. It thrashed me with its big rack for thirty to forty-five seconds." The deer damaged his thumb, possibly permanently, and pushed one antler deep into his leg. What invited the attack? Boyce made the mistake of crouching on one knee when the buck was in rut; such a submissive posture caused the buck to demonstrate dominance, "to prove he was the baddest boy on the block." While the public can learn general rules about living in close proximity to wild animals, the limitations of that approach are illustrated by the fact that Boyce, an expert in animal behavior, could unintentionally invite a deer attack.

Wild animals are not, by definition, entirely predictable, which for human beings is both cause for caution and joy. Still, Boyce argues that public education is one way to reduce risk. We can also learn to view that risk in the context that media headlines seldom offer: the enrichment of our everyday lives.

Here are some basics for living with urban wildlife: Relocating wild animals generally doesn't work; others move back into the territory. Feed your pets indoors, and do not feed wild animals. Try to get your neighbors to agree on this policy. Plant for wildlife: by planting native vegetation and leaving natural shelters intact, unwanted interactions with wild animals can be avoided and their company enjoyed. "One of the animals that has moved back into the Portland urban area is the beaver," says Houck. "They're wonderful to have around. On the other hand, they can be a pain in the butt if they dam up the wrong culvert. So we use a device called the 'beaver deceiver,' which allows the beaver to travel through a culvert, but prevents them from damming it." As for ticks, Thomas N. Mather, professor and director for the University of Rhode Island Center for Vector-Borne Disease, recommends increasing the use of clothing repellents. He says that this single strategy, if used more regularly, could reduce tick bites and infection by five times or more. And, of course, adults and kids should do a physical check after an outing in tick country: around the head, neck, waistband, groin, under the tops of socks, and so on. Parents should seek advice from their pediatrician or from Web sites that specifically address nature risks.[18]

Public education will help, but wisely designed development patterns also buffer human–wild animal contacts in our cities. This is one reason Michael Soule, a key promoter of the field of conservation biology and former chairman of environmental studies at UC–Santa Cruz, has argued for a lengthy wildlife corridor system in Southern California that, he says, should go from the Mexican border to the Transverse Range, from the Mojave Desert to the Santa Barbara coast. Soule writes, "Otherwise, eventually, I'm afraid, we'll lose the mountain lions in Southern California and that part of our mystery, of our wildness." And that loss would present its own psychological and spiritual risks to human beings.

Greenification

The Nature Principle is not anti-urban. In fact, it's pro-city—it's about growing the seeds of nature and authenticity that have already been planted and planting new ones. This morning I am in San Francisco, a unique domain within the Extranet. Stepping out of the Majestic Hotel, which was built in 1902 and has survived earthquakes and fire, I can see fog rappelling down the sides of the newer buildings and creeping along Sutter Street. I head out on an early morning walk toward the Fillmore District and Nihonmachi, also known as Japantown, depleted first by forced internment in the 1940s and then by redevelopment in the 1950s that widened Geary Boulevard and destroyed dozens of Victorian buildings. This is a place rich in human and natural history. As the San Francisco fog slips away to where fog lives in its off-hours, I think about my son Jason, now twenty-eight. He has lived in London, New York City, and Los Angeles—though recently he has been thinking about moving to Taos or Santa Fe. An urban guy, he has worked tirelessly for environmental causes, and he is sensitized to the physical world and what exists behind its surfaces and facades. He learned to surf the Extranet on slopes of California chaparral, so that now, even in a city, he finds wonder beneath the surfaces. I believe, and he agrees, that spending those many hours in the canyons of San Diego enabled him to become more observant of his surroundings and gave him the ability to look deeper into the organic terrain, even if mostly man-made. When he's my age, or older, he'll still have that ability, and the reassurance of the natural world when he needs it, especially if our cities become richer in nature.

A cautionary note about a risk that sometimes follows progress. In the past, as urban residents improved their lot, people with higher incomes moved in, and gentrification often pushed the pioneers out. The same thing could happen as urban gardeners green their neighborhoods. Greenification could push lower-income people further toward the fringes. Nearby nature could become a perk for the privileged. Some of the most impressive efforts to re-nature cities are, as we've seen, in lower-income neighborhoods. Public policies must assure that these efforts, including the ad hoc work by green guerillas—who have even torn up old asphalt to plant community gardens—aren't displaced by their own success. These policies must also require that new urban developments aren't just green fiefdoms for the wealthy. To an extent, this is occurring. For example, at this writing, Cincinnati's Enright Ridge Urban Ecovillage does include affordable housing. One can buy a two-story, two-bedroom home with a full basement and large deck overlooking protected woods for sixty thousand dollars. That's a start, but it's not enough.

Again, the fiercest protectors of equity are not likely to be urban officials, but the people who live in and help create re-natured neighborhoods. Natural capacity isn't only defined by the strengths that a culture brings to the creation of nearby nature. It's also about a people's capacity to marshal community organizing tools. Re-naturing the neighborhood is one challenge; protecting it is quite another. To be a sustainable garden, a city must be both biodiverse and economically diverse. The same is true for the new suburb.

CHAPTER 17

Little Suburb on the Prairie

New Edge Country

ONE WEEKEND IN 1991, Steve Nygren, a restaurateur, and his wife, Marie, took a weekend drive in the country. They had read an advertisement in a preservation newsletter about a property for sale, barely thirty minutes from Atlanta's Hartsfield-Jackson International Airport, and they were curious.

Wandering through the fields and deep woods, they fell in love with the sixty-acre farm and bought it. "We started coming out on weekends. And when we saw the effect it had on the kids and also on us, it changed our priorities," Nygren recalls. At the time, their kids were three, five, and seven, and the Nygrens lived in Atlanta's prestigious Ansley Park neighborhood, in the center of the city. "We had all these material things, all that anyone could imagine needing, and yet we found ourselves packing up every Friday night, anxious to get out to the country. We rented out the big main farmhouse and fixed up a little cottage nearby. Out there, the kids had one box of puzzles and toys for rainy weather, and that was all they had, except nature—which was a bigger draw to them than we had ever imagined." After three years of weekend visits, they put their city house on the market. Steve sold his group of thirty-four restaurants, took early retirement, and they moved to the country full-time. The family planted an organic garden, cut trails into the woods, started restoring the 1905 farmhouse, and converted an old horse barn into guest rooms. "We found that no matter how stressful life gets, or how difficult certain talks can be with your kids, a walk in the woods can change the whole tone of life," Nygren says.

Then one day while jogging, Nygren was horrified to see bulldozers chewing across an adjacent piece of farmland. So he bought nine hundred more acres. The restaurateur became an activist, then a developer. He began by contacting most of the landowners in the forty-thousand-acre Chattahoochee Hill Country region, "all told more than five hundred individuals, including "a mix of generational landowners, land speculators, and developers," Nygren says. "A leadership body was needed to shepherd the process of finding a balanced solution; thusly the Chattahoochee Hill Country Alliance was formed." After two years and countless public meetings, the county adopted a new land-use regulation precluding large-acreage estates in favor of a series of hamlets, tightly clustered villages surrounded by forest, farms, and meadows.

Today, Nygren, a youngish sixty-four-year-old with a shock of white hair, is a soft-spoken evangelist for a new—or, rather, old—kind of suburban development. His Serenbe, with 240 residents, is organized around principles of land preservation, local food production, energy efficiency, walkability, clustered buildings, arts, culture, community, and most of all, immersion in nature. Serenbe (a play on the words *be serene*) is one example of what suburban life might look like in the future. In a modified form, it could also be applied in the redevelopment of decaying urban and suburban neighborhoods.

This approach extends beyond traditional green design, which is essentially about conserving energy and leaving a small footprint on the Earth; the emerging design philosophy is about conserving energy *and* producing human energy.

In his book *Building for Life: Designing and Understanding the*

Human-Nature Connection, Stephen Kellert uses the term "restorative environmental design," which he says "incorporates the complementary goals of minimizing harm and damage to natural systems and human health as well as enriching the human body, mind, and spirit."[1]

Serenbe is the name of the full one thousand acres, including planned and current hamlets, the nineteen-room inn, organic farms, and planned art farm. So far, two hamlets have been built, Selborne, with a focus on the arts, and Grange, with an emphasis on agriculture. A planned third hamlet will focus on health and healing. Nearly all of the residences are directly adjacent to natural or agricultural land. Post boxes are stationed in the central commercial district; front porches are placed within six to eight feet of the sidewalk; walking paths connect the homes.

One might argue that any impact on the natural world, especially on valuable farmland, is too much impact. But this prime land would otherwise have been targeted by developers favoring either large estates or grading and filling the roll of the earth and packing in as many interchangeable units as possible. Instead, Serenbe leaves 70 percent of the woods and rural acreage intact, and devotes thirty acres to the Serenbe farm. Certified as organic and biodynamic, the farm produces more than 350 varieties of vegetables, herbs, flowers, fruits, and mushrooms, and sells all of this within forty miles of the farm through a 110-member Community Supported Agriculture program, a Serenbe Farmers and Artists Market, and local restaurants. The community's wastewater is treated using bioretention and constructed wetlands. The designers claim that monthly water usage for Serenbe is 25 percent lower than the national average. The compact little town, with no strip mall, will eventually accommodate as many or more people on 30 percent of the total land as would a traditional development using 80 percent of the land. This high-tech/high-nature configuration is arguably more economically sustainable than the current rural American landscape, which is emptying out as farming consolidates and rural tax bases deteriorate.

Nygren believes Serenbe has already stabilized the local tax base. Still, he faced lender disbelief in the economic model. "I tried to tell them we were creating the premium of a golf-course lot without the negative impacts of a golf course. They weren't buying it." Eventually, Nygren and his family financed Serenbe's development themselves. "We ended up having to pledge our real-estate holdings in Atlanta, in addition to the land at Serenbe, as collateral to guarantee the development loans," he said. "We had a family meeting, when it became obvious this was our only choice if the development was to move forward, and I presented to Marie and the girls the situation we were in. I had their college funds in a safe account, but other than that, we would have to put the balance of our financial holding at stake. They all voted to move forward, and we have." Now Nygren hopes to prove the economic viability of this kind of development.

Others share that hope. In 2006, the *New York Times* reported on a small but rapidly growing brand of second-home communities targeted at baby boomers who prefer nature trails to golf courses and tennis courts. Amenities offered by the 3 Creek Ranch in Jackson, Wyoming, for example, include raptor rehabilitation and bird-banding programs. In South Carolina, the Spring Island community offers mountain biking trails, plant and bird identification, and nocturnal wildlife walks.[2]

Are these just dude developments for the rich? Nygren acknowledges that most of the residences in Serenbe are executive homes, but a few smaller cottages are now available. I reminded him that many of the planned communities of the sixties and seventies were built with government subsidies, based on the promise that they would include modest-income housing. That promise was seldom kept. But Nygren contends that most developers and financial institutions will refuse to move in this direction until they see ample proof that wealthy people will forgo a large rural estate in favor of a town home on an eighth of an acre adjacent to large tracts of natural land.

Another danger is that such attractive communities will be Trojan Horse developments, literally paving the way for a deluge of traditional housing tracts. That, in fact, is a likely outcome, unless residential zoning regulations are rewritten to promote compact hamlets surrounded by natural or agricultural areas.

Nygren points to the English countryside as his development model, with its combination of nature, local farming, and village living. I recently traveled by train and car from the southwest corner of England to the middle of Scotland. Contemporary English countryside draws strict lines around old villages and newer cities so that farms and forests closely encircle nearly every residential area. The preserved countryside is a legacy of feudal landownership and post–World War II greenbelt laws enacted in part to direct new development into the bombed urban centers. With few exceptions, one rarely sees that pattern in America. However, in Britain, dense cities are filling up and nearby nature is disappearing. So some movement of population into the countryside is probably inevitable. Two scenarios seem likely, either the kind of suburban sprawl common in the United States or the creation of more rural villages, similar to Serenbe. In the UK and the United States, such settlements could combine local food production and preserved natural areas with high-tech communications, including more advanced teleconferencing. This would theoretically decrease some of the need for car travel.

The Urban Land Institute (ULI), a major U.S. nonprofit education and research institute focused on "smart growth," envisions such a future. A ULI report, published in 2004, projects that by 2025 the U.S. population will have grown by almost fifty-eight million people.[3] Infilling—adding households within revitalized city neighborhoods or inner suburbs—will meet some of the demand for housing, according to Jim Heid, a sustainable-development expert and the report's author. But development will still occur on and beyond the edges of cities. Portland, Oregon, projects in its metropolitan regional plan that 70 percent of near-term growth will be greenfield development (urban planner jargon for open land), and other U.S. jurisdictions predict numbers closer to 90 percent. "While it is often lumped with sprawl, greenfield development offers the most practical, affordable, and achievable chance to build without sprawl, given its potential to create large-scale, conserved open lands and sustainable modern infrastructure," writes Heid. Good greenfield development relies on three prerequisites: a region-wide system of sustainable open space; more and higher concentrations of walkable, bikeable, mixed-use development; and a diverse mix of housing types, sizes, and prices.

To these requirements, Nygren would add close access to nature, local food production, and sometimes looser restrictions. Serenbe avoids the typical standardization of housing styles by encouraging multiple builders to offer variety. The community does have constraints, including one stating that every house must have a front porch at least eight feet deep that spans 70 percent of the first floor. "We determined that's the size that you can get a good rocking chair on. Even with indoor air-conditioning, people will use these porches when they're large enough and close enough to the sidewalks." Serenbe is far less restrictive of children's play than many planned communities. "We purposefully have no playground," Nygren says. "We've got ball fields, natural woods and streams, and miles of hiking trails, picnic tables, tire swings and horseshoe pits and a tree house."

Could a child build his or her own tree house or fort in the woods? "Absolutely. Interestingly, we've not had one child injured in the woods."

Some environmental visionaries consider such developments counterproductive, for one main reason: they still depend on the automobile. Serenbe-ings may walk more locally, but who's going to tell them they can't drive to Atlanta?

Richard Register has been promoting the idea of ecocities for nearly four decades. By ecocities, he means cities upzoned "for more density and diversity in the centers," a wholesale rejection of the automobile, and a complete withdrawal from the addiction to sprawl. The author of several books on the topic, including *Ecocities: Rebuilding Cities in Balance with Nature*, Register rejects the New Urbanism and Smart Growth movements because, he told the Web site Treehugger, many of the proponents of those urban planning philosophies "speak out of both sides of their mouth saying transit, especially rail, is great (it is), and cars have to be accommodated too (they don't). . . . Cars or car-free cities. Choose." In Register's view, as long as we plan for automobiles, we'll be out of balance with nature, whether in re-natured cities or new edge country.

Restorative Transportation

Ironically, a motorized machine was one of the first twenty-first-century signals of a potential human-nature reunion. For many hybrid drivers, at least the early ones, the definition of the good driving experience shifted from speed and muscle to other measures of experience.

In 2003, a friend of mine, a dedicated conservationist, parked in our driveway to show off his new hybrid Toyota Prius. For some, at the time, hybrids were rolling bumper stickers that said, "Go to war for oil? Not in my name." You almost expected the GPS unit to tell you, in Ralph Nader's disembodied growl: "Turn Left at the next available election." I admired the car and wanted one. The last time I had applied my ecological views to car buying was in the 1970s, when I bought the first edition of the low-emission, rotary-engine Mazda. That engine melted. Nonetheless, I was willing to try again. Today, Kathy and I share one car, a hybrid.

There's room for debate about the environmental righteousness of hybrids, or the all-electric or hydrogen-powered cars. Register and other like-minded visionaries worry about, well, Trojan horsepower. The more efficient our cars become, the more likely we'll live in suburbia or farther from cities, even as fuel prices rise.

Unintended consequences aside, from the moment my friend parked his Prius in our driveway, I considered hybrid engines good news. Fighting global warming finally seemed . . . cool. Not just environmentally, but psychologically, the Prius spelled gain. To many, before the Prius, the work of someone like designer William McDonough, who proposed that we could create factories that would turn out cleaner water and air than they take in, would have seemed like fuzzy-thinking utopianism. After the Prius, not so much.

My friend, by the way, began to drive his wife nuts with his new driving habits. He watched the dashboard indicators like a nurse watches the instrument panel on a life-support system. He took pleasure in racking up more miles per gallon than advertised. This gain was not just a product of a different engine, but of his revised technique, which the hybrid's psychological imperative encouraged. At the time, I laughed at his obsession. But when we bought our own hybrid, I caught the bug. I've scoured Web sites devoted to this "new" kind of driving: to maximize mpg, the hybrid driver should "surge and coast" and "feather" the gas pedal, and so on. One might assume that such driving habits would deflect attention from the road and the environment around us. But for me, the opposite has proven to be true. One day, I realized that I was even aware of headwinds and tailwinds, and their impact on the dashboard readout on average mpg. I learned that the contour of the terrain, outdoor heat and cold, and other environmental factors also affected the mpg. The usual numbness of driving was replaced by a different mental state, both calmer and more aware. Call it the Zen of Prius, or the Hybrid High.

Well, slow driving only lasted a few months for me. Today, my wife still practices it, but I'm pretty much back to speed, though with reasonable gas mileage.

Despite a few glitches along the way, hybrid engines and other new technologies do encourage a different view of transportation. Hope rolls. But Register is right. It won't roll far without a more complete transportation transformation, including environmentally cleaner, quieter public and private vehicles in walkable cities and suburbs, with transportation pathways, including hiking and biking paths, through natural corridors.

Dan Burden describes his bicycle as the "learning machine." "As a child, I was skinny as a rail, had severely impaired physical coordination, scoliosis, myopia, and shyness," he recalls. His physical and mental condition began to change when he began to ride a bike. This learning machine transported him "to distant places never seen by car, foot or any other means. From nearly sunup to sundown the city and the countryside, as far as I could go, were mine."

By the time he was eighteen, he was off riding through farmlands, river valleys, and nearby woodlands. He learned how to find quiet roads, old farm paths, and trails. He rode in all weather, into foggy farmland nights and pelting rain. On warm summer nights, he could feel the layers of cooler air. He inhaled the scents of nature while descending or climbing undulating farm roads. He came to know the small changes in geography, in the seasons and even subseasons. "I became an acute observer of all things that made up the Ohio countryside," he says. "With the bike, and later my feet, I began to explore everything rural, everything urban, to appreciate what made each unique and distinct." On a bike, he adds, "You go at nature-speed."

When it comes to outdoor exercise, Burden wants us to think beyond physical health, to mental acuity and more. He argues passionately that free-range exploration, on foot or by bike, expands our civility and confidence, and our humanity.

Today, Burden is director of the Walkable and Livable Communities Institute, a Washington State–based national organization. He has worked as a bicycle consultant to the United Nations in China, served as bicycle and pedestrian coordinator for the state of Florida, and has photographed transit conditions in more than twenty-five hundred cities around the world. He promotes urban traffic-calming practices, better intersection design, waterfront trails, parks, land-sensitive clusters of homes, shops, and work centers.

Throughout human history, and up until around 1925, cities and suburbs were designed to accommodate the human foot, says Burden. "Then the city pattern and scale became extended with the combined added mobility of the car and the desire to embrace Modernism." After World War II, the United States had sufficient money to dismantle city cores and move outward. In time, all cities became vast land consumers as they abandoned their inner layers of Main Streets, downtowns, and historic centers. "This added mobility paved the way to filling in vast [parcels of] land with parking lots, taking out nature and farm fields as they were extended. Creeks were buried, estuaries filled in, many nearby woods taken out."

Baby boomers may be the last generation to remember the Sunday drive, that staple of family life that lasted into the early sixties, when mom and dad piled the kids, grandma, and the family dog into the car, perhaps after church, and went on a leisurely drive out of the city. Windows down, the dog's muzzle into the wind, dad's elbow on the car's windowsill, maybe a picnic basket in the trunk. The point was to slow down, take time to see the countryside, breathe it all in. Perhaps we could bring back a refined version of the Sunday drive. Imagine regenerative mass transit—alternatively fueled buses, trolleys, and trains—slipping quietly through a city, traveling transit corridors naturally buffered by forest and into the countryside, connecting inner-city neighborhoods with exurban ecovillages. Instead of taking that Sunday drive by car, you could take it by biophilic transit. Bring your picnic basket.

When I first considered that scenario, it seemed like another utopian dream. Then I visited a new nature center at Oregon's Tualatin River National Wildlife Refuge, a few miles southwest of downtown Portland. I noticed a public bus stop at the refuge's entrance. Not long after, the *Oregonian* newspaper reported that an AmeriCorps volunteer at the refuge was translating plant and animal names into Spanish, and planned a similar project in Russian, since at least sixty thousand Russian-speaking residents live in Portland, where an increasingly diverse population works in the region's booming plant nursery/grass seed industry. Tualatin River Wildlife Refuge, as it turned out, had "partnered with the regional transit system to provide a bus stop exclusively to access the refuge." Kim Strassburg, outdoor recreation planner at the refuge, also told the reporter, "Now anyone can hop on a bus in downtown Portland and be on the refuge trails in less than an hour."[4]

For decades, Burden has remained devoted to his learning machine, and to creating new ways for others to ride theirs in cities. He's about to make a radical change. A reversion, actually.

He and his wife, Lys, were car-free until they were in their thirties. As a young Navy man, he found it easy to live in Pensacola, Florida, without a car. On forest and swamp trails, he daily trekked two and a half miles from his base, Ellyson Field, to the University of West Florida campus. "My walk to school prepped me for unfettered thinking; my walk back, almost always under star-studded skies, was energizing, enriching my soul," he recalls.

He and Lys married in Ohio in 1970, and hitchhiked to Missoula, Montana. Unable to afford a car then, they walked and biked everywhere. The social circle they established there decades ago is still stronger than in any place they have lived since. He credits their feet. And their bikes. Now, Dan and Lys plan to return to the car-free lifestyle. Later this year, they'll move to Port Townsend, an eminently walkable, nature-immersed seaport in Washington, that calls itself the launching pad to the Olympic Peninsula and beyond. "Okay, there will be a truck for Lys's community gardening," he admits. "I'll still drive, of course, for my national and international work. But, as city designers and city planners we're duty-bound to try to live in and build great places—where living car-free does not mean a loss of independence, but new freedom, fitness, and happiness."

Burden's next move illustrates a conundrum of our time. At core, we now that dense but re-natured cities are essential—but small towns nd suburbs, or what suburbia could be, still call.

Subutopia and the Rule of Beauty

The creation of new towns such as Serenbe will help, but only the re-development of suburbia, the re-naturing of existing neighborhoods, along with the creation of restorative transportation, will result in meaningful progress.

The words *urban* and *suburban* are losing their meaning. Growth of the original suburbs offered the illusion of healthy country living. Even before that, late-nineteenth- and early-twentieth-century planners believed that cities and suburbs could and should be places rich with nature. That philosophy inspired the urban parks movement. The industrialists who pushed for the creation of New York's Central Park weren't concerned with gas prices. Their priority was worker productivity, linked to the health benefits of nearby nature. Unfortunately, planners and consumers lost touch with that philosophy. Today, too many of our urban and suburban neighborhoods are de-natured, and in some cases decaying, and that pushes many people even deeper into exurbia. Suburbs are a fact, and, just like inner-city cores, they can be improved.

"Postwar American suburbia is the largest and most costly undertaking in world history," says Tom Martinson, author of *American Dreamscape: The Pursuit of Happiness in Postwar Suburbia*. "It is high time we moved the suburbs to center stage of our national attention." The need for suburban redevelopment is increasing; the growth rate of suburban poverty is now twice that of cities.

In Subutopia, as I'll call it, aging shopping malls are replaced by or refashioned into more economically viable mixed-use centers; affordable and even luxury housing is placed on top of stores and in parking lots; "hedges" of small shops circle the blank walls of the big-box outlets; disconnected streets are stitched together and narrowed to discourage speeding; mom-and-pop corner groceries and other pedestrian amenities are placed throughout the residential neighborhoods. Martinson suggests that mixed-use strip malls and residential neighborhoods incorporate "architectural imagery—sculpture, art—that comes from the place itself." Subutopian redevelopers will plant a lush landscape, reminiscent of older neighborhoods, but redevelopment will also incorporate native plants, home or nearby production of food, and new and more unobtrusive solar technologies that will make each home as energy-independent as possible.

To encourage creativity and variety, we'll need to loosen the draconian covenants and restrictions imposed by developers and enforced by excitable community associations. One woman tells me the community association of her planned community decided that there were too many potted plants in front of their homes, so it came up with a new, private regulation: no more than two flower pots allowed, and they could only be ten inches across. Flower pots: the enemy within. In Subutopia, life is better but less than perfect.

To argue for suburban redevelopment is not to argue for sprawl or against the density seen in some urban settings—but *for* neighborhoods that have both higher human density *and* more natural habitat, rooftop gardens, walkability and hike-ability, and so forth. Traditional zoning has seldom encouraged a mix of nature, homes, and workplaces. As rings of suburbia begin to decay, natural community redevelopment zones could be established to encourage redevelopment that would combine the best features of, say, Serenbe, with the more compacted ecovillages of Western Europe. An endorsement of this approach comes with a caveat. How unfortunate if the rigidity of some current suburban developments were to be replaced by a greener, more efficient rigidity.

I once met Navajo rug weavers in the far, high desert of the Southwest—from Two Grey Hills, Ganado, Wide Ruins, Chinle—and looking closely at one of their rugs, I noticed they often were missing a line of wool on one edge. One woman explained: "The weaver places a spirit line in the rug, an imperfection through which all labor and concentration can escape." A spirit line is needed in the weaving of these greener, re-natured neighborhoods. Once the Nature Principle is brought into play, fear and compulsive order should give way to variance, to biodiversity and cultural diversity; there are no neat rows in the rain forest, no tight clustering of same-species life. The pattern is fractal—complex beyond the understanding of the science of economics. A tree gives us comfort not because its branches and leaves are formed in perfect and predictable order, but because it is unique within a larger, unseen pattern—like us.

The larger pattern is sensed; we feel it but do not see it, says artist and home designer James Hubbell. Hubbell and I were walking one day along a path through his family enclave of houses and studios. He showed me the first structure he had built, a diminutive cavern made of adobe with cedar beams. Now over eighty, he and his wife, Anne, live in a complex of hobbit-friendly structures near Julian, a mountain town east of San Diego that is nestled in pines, manzanita, and live oaks. This was the place where I spent time in shared solitude with my younger son. He began to build these structures, which seem to bubble out of the earth, over four decades ago. His place, burned once by wildfire and rebuilt, is touched with whimsy. Everything is curved, flowing, almost free-form. Stained-glass windows filter light so it seems you are on another planet; sculptures made of the local rocks and mud anchor the place. His art and architecture are praised around the world as examples of how to do what Frank Lloyd Wright advised, but did not always do: create human habitats that blend into nature, but do not disappear. As we walked, he suggested that the people who live in suburban neighborhoods could declare their individuality through signs and pieces of public art that spring from nature and the idiosyncrasies of their own cultures. "Each neighborhood is like a person: unique," he said. "For people and neighborhoods, small changes count."

Hubbell's approach reflects his respect for beauty and organic complexity.

It also suggests the role that artists can have in reconnecting humans to nature. Some artists now thrust masks on sticks, and other pieces of art, into the ground of urban lots that have been allowed to return to a natural state. In addition to linking the idea of art to the reality of nature, these art pieces and installations protect the land. People may dismiss open space — throw trash into it, ignore it, see it as something without value. However, the art changes perceptions and behavior by signaling that this is a place of value to human beings.

"I believe a culture builds what it believes," Hubbell said. "Right now, in our culture, we believe mainly in fear. In the beginning of [the twentieth] century, in art and architecture, you saw such beautiful, imaginative, organic expressionism in Germany and Austria." Then came the Bauhaus movement, all glass and steel boxes. Everything changed. "The feeling in Europe then was that something was wrong — something was coming. When you're afraid, you regulate. You make the angles equal."

Thinking of our highly regulated walled communities across America, Hubbell asks: "Can there be a sustainable future without beauty?" He has written: "The context that sustainability must exist in, is an infinite compassion for the world we live in, and a balance of the many parts. Beauty can be an arbiter of the myriad decisions needed to build a whole, ecological, truly sustainable solution, whether it is a building, a sewage system, an agricultural plan, or a wilderness system. . . . We have lived in a century that has made technology and information, and what we think are its benefits, God. Technology devoid of a sense of the whole is an attempt to dominate life, nature and knowledge. Can we build a sustainable world and leave out the mystery of our world?"

Hubbell believes that the best thing an architect or planner can do s communicate that the universe is exciting, and that mystery should e sought: "If we somehow find that feeling again, we would stop doing ated communities, because we wouldn't need them."

Eternity with a View

Here's one more way—a final way for some—to slow urban sprawl, to e rooted in the land, to repurpose our role with nature. This is not or everyone.

Edward Abbey, the great contrarian writer, author of the classic *Desert Solitaire*, knew how he wanted to be buried. He asked that no undertakers be hired, no embalming be done, that his body be transported in the back of a pickup truck, and that state laws be disregarded. Bagpipes would be played, corn on the cob served along "a flood of beer" and "singing, dancing, talking, hollering, laughing, and lovemaking." His friends and family made sure it happened. One friend, Doug Peacock, wrote an account of the send-off, which was published in *Outside* magazine.[5] "He'd wanted to nourish a plant, a cactus or a tree. He was buried illegally, deep in the desert, and just moments before we laid him to rest, I lay down in the grave to check out the view. There was blue sky and a faint desert breeze stirring the blossoms of a brittlebush. We should all be so blessed." A rock near the grave is said to be chiseled with this message:

EDWARD PAUL ABBEY
January 29, 1927–March 14, 1989
NO COMMENT

Billy Campbell, a physician, proposes something similar. I walked with him one day among the coastal live oaks above the valley of Santa Ysabel, California. With its gentle, grassy hills, clusters of oak and rock upheavals, this is one of the most beautiful spots in my county.

The nonprofit Nature Conservancy had recently bought a ranch here and optioned another, and intended to turn it into a nature preserve. Campbell hoped to convince the Nature Conservancy to acquire additional adjacent land and establish a combination nature preserve and memorial park. The time is right for a new approach. Space is so tight in Greece, for example, that people lease grave space; after six months, bones are dug up and moved to packed storage vaults. The British Home Office has considered mass exhumation of graves over one hundred years old, disposal of the remains, and reuse of the land. Cemeteries in the United States now favor higher-density mausoleums or double-occupancy graves. ("They're like bunk beds. If you're the first to die, you get the bottom bunk for eternity," said Campbell.) Some cemeteries only have room for ashes.

So Campbell believes new space can be found by protecting natural space in cities, suburbs, or the countryside. "You could buy a plot here, say over along that little trail, and you'd know it would never be touched," said Campbell. If developers ever wanted to turn this land into another Rolling Hills Estates, they'd have to do it over your dead body. By choosing to be buried in such preserves, people would be able to stand up for their environmental values long after death. Well, maybe not stand up.

By the time I spoke with him, Campbell's company, Memorial Ecosystems, had already created one such park in his home state of South Carolina. His goal was then, and remains, to establish similar burial preserves around the country, using the generated profits to help preserve threatened habitat elsewhere. Natural burials (sometimes called green burials) cost half the typical rate of a traditional funeral and burial. His company uses no crypts and requires biodegradable coffins. Natural burials don't use embalming fluids, which include carcinogenic chemicals.

In a nature preserve/memorial park, protected from development, grave plots or ash interments would be marked by small, engraved tones, if anything. The graves would be located at the fringes, or along existing trails.

Campbell envisioned a chapel for burial services, a "native plant propagation center" instead of the typical flower shop, and a small visitor's center. Weddings could also be held there. Computerized kiosks would provide information about the land's natural history, the native tribes that once lived there, and profiles of the people buried in the preserve. Visitors would wear earphones, much like those worn at art galleries, or carry handheld computers or smartphones equipped with GPS, which would guide them to the exact location where their relative is buried, thus avoiding the need for a marker. The GPS device would then offer a menu of memories: photos, videos, maybe a piano piece played by the deceased. An e-commerce Web site might offer virtual tours and online plot reservations. Campbell isn't the only entrepreneur thinking this way. At the far edge, a new Georgia company called Eternal Reefs uses human cremains mixed with concrete to help create artificial ocean reefs, which attract life.

Though the Santa Ysabel plan never became a reality, Chris Khoury, an Escondido psychiatrist and former president of the San Dieguito River Valley Land Conservancy, was rooting for it at the time. He hoped that money from a memorial park would help his organization buy additional land adjacent to the preserve. "I find the notion 'dust to dust' a comforting thought," he said. "This could be one way to bring back a sense of sacredness to our relationship with the earth." Khoury remembers trying to convince a recalcitrant landowner to sell his land to the park as part of a natural burial area by arguing: "Just think, you could make money burying dead environmentalists."

Campbell remains committed to his cause: natural burial grounds as a way to protect open space from development while offering a way for citizen naturalists to be, like Ed Abbey, part of the land they love for a long time. Maybe forever.

PART FIVE

The High-Performance Human

Making a Living, a Life, and a Future

When we walk upon Mother Earth, we always plant our feet carefully because we know the faces of our future generations are looking up at us from beneath the ground. We never forget them.

—Oren Lyons, Onondaga Nation

CHAPTER 18

Vitamin N for the Soul

Searching for Kindred Spirits

S OME PEOPLE WORSHIP nature. Others consider such worship blasphemous. Most of us are less direct; just beyond the veil of rain, we feel a presence for which we have no name. Or no presence at all, except beauty and terror. Whatever form wonder takes, nature gives us, at the very least, kinship.

"At my office, I look out and see the ocean, waves breaking on the beach, the endless horizon," says the oceanographer Wolf Berger, who speaks easily of his garden and the vast Pacific in the same sentence. He sees both as one address, his one true place. "Coming home from the office, I greet familiar plants in the front yard. Most of them are natives. They feel at home in our climate: Earth citizens, like myself. I know them as my cousins. The experience, then, is feeling at home, and being part of a very large family."

This family is larger than science can measure.

For years, I knew little about the ocean, though I lived minutes from the Pacific. My friend Louie Zimm helped me finally see the sea. One Sunday morning, Louie, my son Matthew, and I headed out to sea in Louie's twenty-foot boat. We went not to worship nature, or even to praise it, but to immerse ourselves in it. We moved above the great kelp forest, saw the leaves and trunks winding down into the other civilizations below. We moved on. To the west, a storm cloud grew darker as we turned toward it. Louie, a retired expedition captain for the Scripps Institution of Oceanography, pointed to a series of white explosions on the dark horizon: dolphins chasing anchovies, he said.

Knowing the law and good sense, Louie did not interrupt the feeding dolphins, but later he positioned his boat behind them. As we clipped along at ten to fifteen knots, perhaps two dozen dolphins turned from their group of several hundred and circled back around to join us. As Louie steered, my son and I hung over the bow, where we could almost touch the racing mammals. They cut in and out, within inches of the hull. Then we sat on our haunches, watching our escorts swing away to rejoin the group.

"Look at yourselves," Louie said, laughing. We were drenched with seawater blown back by dolphin exhalations.

These were common Pacific dolphins. Scientists now know that another species, bottlenose dolphins, essentially identify themselves through repeated signature whistles and clicks. The scientists don't know why they do this, or why "they're so self-centered," as *Newsweek* put it, or if any of their messages are meant for us. But we do hear them.[1]

Recent neurological studies of whales have revealed that humans and whales share specialized neurons associated with higher cognitive functions, including self-awareness and compassion, and that these neurons may have developed in parallel evolution. In fact, they may have appeared in whales millions of years before they did in humans. In "Watching Whales Watching Us," a 2009 article in the *New York Times Magazine*, Charles Siebert reported the growing evidence that whales live in worlds of complex social structures and even in cultures that appear parallel to ours: they teach; they use cooperative hunting tactics and tools (one of them consciously produced a "net" of bubbles used to round up schools of fish); and their clans communicate in different dialects.

Siebert reported that some scientists are baffled as to why gray whales off of Baja California Sur, Mexico, now "can't seem to get enough of us humans." Once referred to as "hardheaded devil fish" because they were known to smash ships into splinters, gray whales were hunted into near extinction. A 1937 ban on gray-whale hunting helped the population rebound. "Still, the question of why present-day gray-whale mothers, some of whom still bear harpoon scars [some whales can live for a century], would take to seeking us out and gently shepherding their young into our arms is a mystery that now captivates whale researchers and watchers alike," Siebert writes. This behavior goes beyond the close breaching familiar to whale watchers. In some cases, whales have gently lifted fishing boats on their backs.

Conventionally, scientists have dismissed such behavior as reflexive, suggesting that the animals are attracted to the sound of the boats' motors, or are using the hulls to scratch their barnacled backs. But other scientists believe that something extraordinary, perhaps unprecedented, is occurring. A few observers have described the behavior as a form of forgiveness. That last notion may be hard to swallow, given the fact that these same whales are now threatened by a human technology that could prove deadlier than harpoons: deep-sea sonar. Still, as Siebert puts it, the whales' "overtures toward us" may suggest a larger message: that they, and we, are not alone — or at least we should not be.[2]

The Giftedness

When it comes to matters of the spirit, specificity is the enemy of truth. That's my view. But it's hard to fathom how any kind of spiritual intelligence is possible without an appreciation for nature.

Most of us intuitively understand that all spiritual life, however it is defined, begins with and is nourished by a sense of wonder. The natural world is one of our most reliable windows into wonder and, at least to some, into a spiritual intelligence. Someday, it would be fascinating to bring the religious proponents of intelligent design, who see God as the ultimate biophilic designer, together with those who believe in the Gaia Hypothesis, which holds that the biosphere and all the physical elements of the Earth, and all the life on and within and above it, are integrated into a complex, self-correcting system—a kind of superorganism.

Details aside, people will continue to practice all manner of older spiritual rituals in nature, as well as new ones they create.

Jonathan Stahl, the wilderness educator who went on the bonding trip with his fiancée, Amanda, feels spiritually connected when in nature. "I was brought up Jewish but never really identified with the religion (or any other for that matter)," he says. "I did, however, find my own way of incorporating some of the principles of the holiday Yom Kippur into my life." Yom Kippur, the Day of Atonement, is a time to pray for forgiveness for sins committed during the year, and to make a clean start for the new year. On Yom Kipper, Stahl heads for a local trail, preferably one that leads to a high viewpoint. "I find a rock and carry it in my hand, constantly meditating on anything I've done in the past year that I am not proud of or would like to improve upon in the following year," he says. "If ever my thoughts begin to drift, the rock in my hand brings my attention back to the reason for this special hike. I think through various aspects of my life: career, family, friends, relationships, personal wellness, etc., and carry the weight to the top of the mountain. There, I leave the rock and all it represents, and look to the new horizon to start the year fresh. It's symbolic and not at all traditional to Judaism, but it works for me." He's practiced this ritual for several years and has shared his tradition with Amanda. "It's a way of bringing nature into religion and at least some aspect of Judaism into my life," he says.

Thomas Berry would have loved that story.

I first met Berry in 2005. He was ninety-one and living in Greensboro, North Carolina. Caroline Toben, the founder of the nonprofit

Center for Education, Imagination, and the Natural World, invited me to lunch with Berry, who was her friend. A Catholic priest of the Passionist order, Berry founded the History of Religions Program at Fordham University and the Riverdale Center of Religious Research. His books, including *The Dream of the Earth*, remain influential throughout the world. Near the end of his life, the United Nations honored him as a leading voice for the Earth.

For the better part of a century, Berry argued, eloquently and elegantly, that our environmental problems are primarily issues of the spirit. He often spoke and wrote about the transcendent childhood experience that served as a touchstone for his future life and work. "It was an early afternoon in May when I first looked down over the scene and saw the meadow," he wrote. "A magic moment, this experience gave to my life something, I know not what, that seems to explain my life at a more profound level than almost any other experience I can remember." That moment never ended.

Minutes after we slid into his customary booth at the O. Henry Hotel restaurant, he began to talk about the future. He had clearly had enough of the twentieth century, with its industrialized violence and ecological destruction. "Everything we discuss now should be about the twenty-first century," he said softly. His face lit up when he considered the possibilities ahead, and our evolving relationship with nature. "Our species once had two sources of inspiration and meaning: religion and the universe, the natural world. But we have turned away from nature," he said. The great work of the twenty-first century will be to reconnect to the natural world as a source of meaning.

Berry articulated a view seldom witnessed in popular media; that we must move beyond the conflict between worlds. In one corner is science, steeped in the "Darwinian principle of natural selection, which involves no psychic or conscious purpose, but is instead a struggle for earthly survival." This view of reality "represents the universe as a random sequence of physical and biological interactions with no inherent meaning." In the other corner is the dominant Western religious tradition, which, he said, has moved too far from an older creation story and toward a redemption mystique, in which passage to the next world is paramount and the natural world is of little concern. Most of the time, these two worlds—science and religion—communicate politely but the antagonisms are deep. And yet, Berry wrote in *The Great Work*, we are moving into an extraordinary time: "As we enter the 21st Century, we are experiencing a moment of grace. Such moments are privileged moments." In Berry's twenty-first century, we return to Earth.

In 1999, an interviewer for the journal *Parabola* asked Berry if our relation to nature connected with our inner human development.

"The outer world is necessary for the inner world; they are not two worlds but a single world with two aspects: The outer and the inner," he answered. "If we don't have certain outer experiences, we don't have certain inner experiences, or at least, we don't have them in a profound way. We need the sun, the moon, the stars, the rivers and the mountains and birds, the fish in the sea, to evoke a world of mystery, to evoke the sacred. It gives us a sense of awe. This is a response to the cosmic liturgy, since the universe itself is a sacred liturgy."[3]

You can see the possibility of a new movement among faith-oriented environmentalists, eager to move beyond the old divide between Bible-based interpretations of dominion and stewardship. (Of course we have dominion, they say; look what we're doing to God's creation. Why would we want to hurt God's creation?) You can see the possibility in the young people who now dedicate their lives to sustainability, or to biophilic design. You can see it in the growing recognition that exposure to nature enhances health, improves cognitive functioning, and nurtures the spirit. You can see it among the religious and nonreligious alike.

The last time I visited Berry was in 2009, in his room at an assisted living home, not long before he died. He was amused by that phrase "assisted living." He could no longer walk. He sat deep in his chair wrapped in an Indian blanket. I asked him about aging and the architecture and ritual of retirement homes. He thought about this for a moment and then once again his face filled with joy when he considered the possibilities of this new century. "The whole routine of the year could be more localized, more re-natured in the architecture," he said. "I suspect that will be done in future years. Particularly as we feel we can make our houses any way we want to, and begin to recognize that there are ways of doing things that require paying attention to a world that is beyond the human mind." He told me he felt an urgency to "go out into the natural world every day, no matter what the conditions are." Then he said, "In our later years, we feel a return. To be gifted with delight as a child, the giftedness should continue. The aging process is full of excitement that comes along with the pain of going through the changes. The giftedness continues."

It does continue. Three miles off Point Loma, in a region of the ocean that may soon become a marine sanctuary off-limits to fishermen, my son and I saw an ominous-looking dorsal fin cutting the waves, moving toward us. The fin dipped loosely now and then, like a sleepy eyelid, and then we saw what appeared to be an eye—a flattened orb, a great blue pupil beneath a reflective skein of saltwater. The eye looked at us as if its owner were curious.

"Karma fish," said Louie. He was smiling broadly.

We had encountered one of the strangest fish in the sea, an ocean sunfish, or *Mola mola*. This sunfish appeared to weigh a few hundred pounds. It circled the boat, almost touching the hull, pausing now and then. "Good luck to see one. Bad luck to hurt them," said Louie.

The world's largest known bony fish (sharks and rays are cartilaginous), the ocean sunfish can weigh up to five thousand pounds. Its shape suggests a flat, floating eye—or a fish head that has lost its body. When seen basking flat on the ocean surface, the sunfish can appear motionless, contemplative. It cruises slowly, eating gelatinous zooplankton and algae. Because of the insubstantial items in its diet the sunfish must ration its energy, Louie explained, "so it takes its time."

Since then, the *Mola mola* often comes to mind. That slow, unafraid creature somehow offered a reminder that life's tide can be slowed, and that I must take more time to recognize the miraculous.

CHAPTER 19

All Rivers Run to the Future

The New Nature Movement

Nothing so important as an ethic is ever "written" . . .
it evolves in the minds of a thinking community.
—Aldo Leopold

INSIDE THE SHACK, as this place is known, I had the eerie feeling that someone had just left. Part of me expected to see a meal, still warm and waiting, on the bare wood table. In a few months, the Shack would be declared—finally—a National Historic Landmark. But for now, it remained unprotected, hiding in plain sight in trees along a country road. The Shack's single room is small, as befits the rebuilt chicken coop that it is.

A slab of native rock above the stone fireplace is soot-stained; two oil lanterns sit on the oak mantel. The fireplace contains a mound of ashes and half-burned logs. Corner shelves hold cooking pots and a blue metal coffee pot. On the floor next to the fireplace: iron cooking pots. On the whitewashed walls: frying pans, strainers, an egg beater, baskets, shovels, racks, a post-hole hand drill, a two-man lumberjack saw.

Two turtle shells decorate another shelf, along with the feathers of a hawk, a pencil in a drinking glass, and a disheveled row of old books, some slid down on their sides. The table is surrounded on three sides by rough, hand-hewn benches.

This is the shack and surrounding woods that Aldo Leopold wrote about in his classic, *A Sand County Almanac,* which ranks among the handful of seminal books that formed the modern environmental movement. In the book, Leopold articulated his now famous Land Ethic. "The land consists of soil, water, plants, and animals, but health is more than a sufficiency of these components," he wrote. "It is a state of vigorous self-renewal in each of them, and in all of them collectively." He argued that humans should treat nature as they would another human being, that "society is like a hypochondriac—so obsessed with its own economic health that it has lost the capacity to remain healthy." All human ethics, he argued, evolved "upon a single premise: that the individual is a member of a community of interdependent parts." The land ethic "simply enlarges the boundaries of the community to include soils, waters, plants, and animals, or collectively, the land." In other words, our relationship with nature is more than *preserving* land and water; it is also our *participation with*, our role as members of, this wider community.

Leopold lived this ethic. In 1912 he served as U.S. Forest Service supervisor of the million-acre Carson National Forest in New Mexico, and in 1924 became associate director of the U.S. Forest Products Laboratory in Madison, Wisconsin, at the time the principal research institution of the Forest Service. In 1933, he was appointed chair of Game Management at the University of Wisconsin. During this period, he bought this plot of land near Baraboo, Wisconsin, and converted the chicken coop.

The ground had been farmed to death, but Leopold and his wife and children planted a pine forest and a prairie, attempting to restore the acreage to its pre-European-settlement condition. Their forest grew.

An hour had passed since I had entered the Shack. The light was fading. I sat on a handmade bunk bed. A dozen eight-by-ten-inch photographs, stained and dust-covered, were stacked and scattered on a bench. I held an image of Leopold standing outside the Shack. In the photograph, he tended burning logs. His wife looked into the smoke

I leafed through more of the photographs, restacking them as I went. Some of family, others of the Shack, but most were of the land itself.

Lingering, I studied my favorite photograph: Leopold's daughter Estella, perhaps nine years old, crouched at water's edge, wearing an oversized felt slouch hat, brim turned up on one side. She is launching a toy boat. Around her the sand is scalloped in little dunes. She is looking at the camera with a slight smile. I put the photo back on the bench and walked out of the Shack and down a path through the woods to the banks of the Wisconsin River, where Estella and her sisters and brothers played long ago. I thought about how enriched their lives were, on this land, among these trees.

A black Labrador moseyed down from the woods and fell in step. At the bank, the dog plunged ecstatically into the river, and paddled into clear water.

Headwaters and Converging Currents

A Sand County Almanac was published several months after Leopold's death in 1948, when he was sixty-one. He died of a heart attack shortly after fighting a fire on a neighbor's land not far from the Shack. The new, energy-efficient Leopold Center, made from trees culled from that forest, now sits on that land, up the road, past the wetlands where sandhill cranes step delicately. The Center's inaugural conference brought me here in April 2007. I was privileged to be one of a dozen people invited to consider how the Land Ethic could be applied anew in the twenty-first century. Leopold's daughters, Nina and Estella, and surviving son, Carl, now in their seventies and eighties, were our hosts. Our group made slight progress that day. We agreed that a *new* ethic—built on the ideas of Leopold and others, and shaped by a host of new practices and realities—is gathering.

In the early days of American conservationism, the influence of the natural world on the human organism was discussed as much as the human impact on nature, perhaps more. Douglas Brinkley, a recent Theodore Roosevelt biographer, writes, "Underlying President Roosevelt's love of pelicans and other birds was a staunch belief in the healing powers of nature. That he had a mighty strong Thoreauvian 'back to nature' aesthetic strain coursing through his veins becomes evident when we read his correspondence . . . with leading naturalists of his day." And, Brinkley writes, Roosevelt argued in his later years "that parents had a moral obligation to make sure their children didn't suffer from nature deficiency."[1] Roosevelt's emphasis on direct, personal experience in nature overlapped the nature study movement in the late nineteenth and early twentieth centuries, pioneered by, among others, Anna Botsford Comstock, who, with her husband John Henry Comstock, headed the Department of Nature Study at Cornell University and wrote the popular *Handbook of Nature Study*. The movement steered the education of children toward the use of nature experiences, not only for scientific learning, but for a deeper appreciation of the human experience. The nature study movement also changed the lives of countless adults, but critics began to dismiss that movement as soft and sentimental. Its power faded.[2]

By the late twentieth century, the emphasis of environmentalism had shifted strongly toward protection of the environment and preservation—to the point where the words *conservation* and *environmentalism* began to take on nuanced meanings in the public consciousness. Even now, many people consider conservationists more conservative: conservationists hunt and fish and think in terms of natural resources. Environmentalists—in the minds of some people, particularly their opponents—wish to protect nature from people; environmentalists are more likely to see nature in broad strokes, such as the impact of climate change.

These stereotypes are not entirely true or fair, but they do exist, to the extent that journalists tread this linguistic territory with care and confusion. There are no hard-and-fast rules on how to use these terms. Some people, of more conservative bent, will insist, "I'm no environmentalist—one of those tree-huggers. I'm a conservationist." And they'll know exactly what they mean by that. Some self-identified environmentalists are wary of "conservationists," whom they associate with hunting and tree cutting. (Those belonging to a third group, Conservationists Formerly Known as Environmentalists, haven't changed their basic outlook, but have come to the conclusion that the word *environmentalist* carries too much political baggage.)

These divisions were foreshadowed by a disagreement between Rachel Carson, the author of *Silent Spring*, and Leopold. Carson faulted Leopold because, as she interpreted his work, he had emerged from a tradition of using nature as a resource to be managed and harvested—he hunted and he logged. His youngest daughter, Estella, now emeritus professor of botany at the University of Washington, tells me that, in retrospect, this disagreement was overplayed, and that these two views of our relationship with nature—preservation and participation—are in the process of renewal. Today, such semantics are beginning to fade. Inevitably, the context is shifting from humans *and* nature, to humans *in* nature, and humans *as* nature.

Before he cofounded the Center for Whole Communities, Peter Forbes worked for eighteen years to lead conservation projects for the Trust for Public Land. He helped to protect threatened portions of Thoreau's Walden Woods, launched a program to protect and revitalize urban gardens and farms across New England, and worked to add twenty thousand acres of wild lands to New Hampshire's White Mountain National Forest, among other major efforts. He is a leading proponent of a brand of what he calls community-based conservation, which holds equal the health of the people and the health of the land. He argues that we're moving into an era in which the protection of nature, more than ever, must be placed in the larger sphere of relationships. "For example, a bit more than one-third of all the privately owned land in America is posted No Trespassing but 78 percent of all publicly owned land in America is posted No Trespassing," he says. "I know there are many good reasons to keep people off conserved land, but . . . that is not, nor ever can be, the basis for a broad social movement." Millions of acres of natural habitat have been protected in recent years; this is good but not sufficient. Even with such protection, are Americans "closer to that land or to the values that the land teaches?"

A healthy, whole community, he argues, begins with people in relationship to one another and to the land, and with this underlying assumption: *"Relationship to place is as important as the place itself."* As part of a new land movement, we "must focus on the human heart as much as the land itself. And what the human heart needs and craves today, and has through the ages, is relationship and connection to the larger, more meaningful diversity of life."

Such thinking is gaining strength in mainstream environmental and conservation groups. Carl Pope, chairman of the Sierra Club, tells this parable: "Once there was a man who tended and nurtured a beautiful garden all of his life. When the time came for him to leave this earth, he gathered his children and said to them, 'I have loved my garden. Now it is yours to care for.' To this, his children said, 'Why should we care for your garden? You never let us in it!'"

Sustainability is a primary goal, no doubt about it, but to some the word suggests *stasis*. As more than one person has asked, who wants a *sustainable* marriage? Sustainability is necessary, but it's not enough. Our language has not kept pace with the changing realities of the human relationship with nature. In fact, even the most basic descriptive words are endangered, in part because daily associations with nature have faded. In 2008, the new edition of the *Oxford Junior Dictionary* deleted the names of over ninety common plants and animals, among them nouns such as *acorn, beaver, canary, clover, dandelion, ivy, sycamore, vine, violet, willow,* and *blackberry*. What words were added? *MP3 players, voicemail, blogs, chat rooms,* and *BlackBerry*, a smartphone. Rather than letting the language of nature slip away or grow stale, we must add to it; we need new or refreshed ways to describe a hybrid world in which technology and nature are balanced, in which we experience the deeper powers of nature in our everyday lives.

A good friend of mine retrofitted his house with a state-of-the-art solar-cell system. His reveries about this accomplishment are impressive on one level. By going solar, he now spends about five dollars a year on his electricity bill (not counting the sixty-five dollars a month energy fee required by the state of California, even if he doesn't use that much energy—it's complicated); and he will soon start selling electricity to the state. As admirable as this is, my friend can veer into a mind-numbing recitation of technical terms and calculations. When talking about the more generalized "environment," he favors technical jargon. Only when pressed does he describe what this does for his *own* energy—his health, soul, and psyche.

"Well . . ." he said. "I do feel a . . ." He struggled for words. "Independence, I guess . . . but remember, I'm not off the grid. I don't want to be. I want to feed energy into the grid." He fell silent for a moment. Then he began to talk about relationship. He described his sense of becoming a "good ancestor, plugged into deep time."

This truly conservative idea, of honoring the role of ancestor, may itself seem out of time, but that is only because today's culture is frozen in time, obsessed with the immediate, and fearful of the future. My friend's words are given added meaning by his actions beyond his solar-powered house. He has spent years helping create an ocean-to-mountains regional conservancy, a vast nature park that his descendents may well enjoy seven generations from now. When he talks about his solar panels, in the context of generations past and future, his voice softens, he speaks with deeper passion, and he becomes more convincing. He is a good ancestor.

Through the use of tense and other linguistic idiosyncrasies, American Indian storytellers often describe their people's historic events as if they were, or are, *there* — in deep time. Similarly, they sometimes speak of the future as if it has already happened, and they have helped shape it. Recently, I encountered something similar in Australia. It's a relatively new custom there, one that we in the United States should emulate. At the opening of most major conferences, indigenous people are asked to give an invocation, and the first person to speak offers a brief statement honoring the original inhabitants of that particular site and the land itself.

What struck me about this ritual was that, by showing respect for the ancestors and for generations to come, the tone subtly shifted. Respect is contagious. This simple act, while not banishing racism, places it in a larger relationship. It offers a moment of reconciliation not only between humans, but between humans and land, and between generations.

Beyond Sustainability

In recent years, the environmental movement has become highly self-critical, which can be seen as a sign of movement strength. It's too easy to forget that just three decades ago few people talked about recycling; that in the 1950s and '60s, intelligent people thought nothing of throwing empty beer cans or hamburger wrappers out the car window, and how common it was to see rusted hulks of automobiles dumped into riverbeds or roadside ravines. Such scenes are rare today. Rivers that once caught fire are now fishable. The bald eagle is back. But these successes, and more, did not prepare us for even larger global challenges, including the human distancing from the natural world.

Now a river gathers force, growing from many tributaries: American Indian thought and tradition; Thoreau and Emerson; Theodore Roosevelt's faith in the restorative powers of nature; the work of Frederick Law Olmsted, whose designs gave America its great urban parks; the healthy cities movement at the turn of the nineteenth century; parts of many of our religious texts; and, of course, the writings of Leopold, Rachel Carson, and others.

Science is nourishing the headwaters; an expanding body of evidence links the human experience in the natural world to better physical health and enhanced cognitive abilities. New branches reach outward. Among them, as we have seen, are biophilic design, reconciliation ecology, green exercise, ecopsychology and other forms of nature therapy; place-based learning, the "whole communities" movement, Slow Food and organic gardening; the walkable cities movement; and the movement to reconnect children with the outdoors.

On the banks of this river, conversation is becoming more interesting, moving beyond protection and participation, and even beyond sustainability, to creation—not the biblical kind, but creation nonetheless.

On this topic, Leopold was prescient. He thought long and hard about creation. "To plant a pine, for example, one need be neither god nor poet; one need only own a good shovel," he wrote. "By virtue of this curious loophole in the rules, any clodhopper may say: Let there be a tree—and there will be one. If his back be strong and his shovel sharp, there may eventually be ten thousand. And in the seventh year he may lean upon his shovel, and look upon his trees, and find them good."[3] As suggested earlier in this book, environmentalism's motto should become *to conserve and create.* In addition to conserving resources and preserving wilderness, we must create new, regenerative environments. By the old way of thinking, a botanical garden should be in every city. By the new way of thinking, every city should be *in* a botanical garden.

Recognizing the mind/body/nature connection will be one of the most important actions that a revitalized environmental movement can take.

Leopold foresaw much of this, but so have others. In 1996, Thomas Berry (writing in more metaphysical terms) described what he called the Ecozoic era: "In the sequence of biological periods of Earth development we are presently in the terminal phase of the Cenozoic and the emerging phase of the Ecozoic era. The Cenozoic is the period of biological development that has taken place during these past

65 million years. The Ecozoic is the period when human conduct will be guided by the ideal of an integral earth community, a period when humans will be present upon the Earth in a mutually enhancing manner." He went on: "The Cenozoic period is being terminated by a massive extinction of living forms that is taking place on a scale equaled only by the extinctions that took place at the end of the Paleozoic around 220 million years ago and at the end of the Mesozoic some 65 million years ago. The only viable choice before us is to enter into an Ecozoic period."

There is still much we need to learn about the natural world, including more detailed knowledge about the benefits to health, cognition, and community; how much nature contact and what kind is optimal; and how best to re-nature our communities. But, as Howard Frumkin, dean of the School of Public Health at the University of Washington, often says, we may need more research, "but we know enough to act."

We can, in fact, build a new nature movement, a people-and-nature movement. The people who have spoken in the pages of this book suggest that such a movement has already begun. As it grows, health care professionals will prescribe green exercise and other nature experiences. Developers and urban planners will create homes, neighborhoods, suburbs, and cities that are nature-inclusive — and they will pursue nature-based urban and suburban renewal. This movement will dramatically increase the amount of nearby nature, resulting in greater biodiversity and increased food production closer to where we live. The movement will promote the creation of "de-central parks" and restorative transportation. New government policies will encourage greater human/nature social capital and build regional and personal identity. In education, this movement will push school districts and legislatures to incorporate nature's ability to enhance learning and creativity, and redefine the classroom in grade schools as well as universities. Both business and education will support the creation and promotion of career paths that extend beyond sustainability to include careers that connect people to nature.

All of these changes, and more, can be accelerated by government policymakers. Business, conservation groups, foundations, civic groups, and places of worship can work to develop those polices. But at the personal level, we can move more quickly to restore our lives through nature. And there is another way to move ahead, an old tradition in new clothes.

The Third Ring

Remember those cardboard kaleidoscopes we had when we were kids—how, when you twisted the cylinders, the pieces of colored plastic would snap into a vivid pattern? Sometimes the future comes into focus, just like that. For me, one such moment occurred at a conference held in New Hampshire in 2007. On that day, over a thousand people from across the state traveled to chart the course of the statewide effort to connect families with nature.

As hours of productive meetings came to an end, a father stood up, complimented the attendees' creativity, and then cut to the chase. "We've been talking a lot about programs today," he said. "Yes, we need to support the programs that connect people to nature, and yes, we need more programs. But the truth is," he added, "we've always had programs to get people outside and kids still aren't going outside in their own neighborhoods." Neither, for that matter, are that many adults. He described his own experience. "A creek runs through my neighborhood, and I would love it if my girls could go down and play along that creek," he said. "But here's the deal. My neighbors' yards back up to the creek, and I have yet to go to my neighbors and ask them to give permission to my kids to play along the creek. So here's my question. What will it take for me to go to my neighbors and ask them for that permission?"

The New Hampshire dad was raising a fundamental question for people of all ages.

What *will* it take?

The goal is deep, self-replicating cultural change, a leap forward in what a society considers normal and expected. But how to get there from here? Let me offer my Three Ring Theory. The First Ring is comprised of traditionally funded, direct-service programs (nonprofits, community organizing groups, conservation organizations, schools, park services, nature centers, and so on) that do the heavy institutional lifting of connecting people to nature. The Second Ring is made up of individual docents and other volunteers, the traditional glue that holds together so much of society. These two Rings are vital, but each has limitations. A direct-service program can extend only as far as its funding will allow. Volunteers are constrained by the resources available for recruitment, training, management, and fund-raising. Many good programs are competing for the same dollars from the same funding sources, a process with its own price. Particularly during difficult economic times, the leaders of direct-service programs often come to view other groups doing similar work as competitors. Good ideas become proprietary; vision is reduced. This response is understandable.

The best programs and volunteer organizations transcend these limitations, but doing so is always a struggle.

Now for the Third Ring: a potentially vast orbit of networked associations, individuals, and families. This Ring is based on peer-to-peer contagion, people helping people creating change in their own lives and their own communities, without waiting for funding. This may sound like traditional volunteerism, but it's more than that. In the Third Ring, individuals, families, associations, and communities use the sophisticated tools of social networking, both personal and technological, to connect to nature and one another.

Family nature clubs, described in an earlier chapter, offer one on-the-ground example. Using blog pages, social networking sites, and the old-fashioned instrument called the telephone (or smartphone), families are reaching out to other families to create virtual clubs that arrange multifamily hikes and other nature activities. An array of free organizing and activity tools is now available on the Internet for these clubs. They're not waiting for funding or permission; they're doing it themselves, doing it now.

Family nature clubs are only one example. The California-based organization Hooked on Nature, also described earlier, networks people who form "nature circles" to explore their own bioregions. In the San Francisco Bay Area, Exploring a Sense of Place organizes groups of adults who meet on weekends to go on hikes with botanists, biologists, geologists, and other experts on their regions' natural world. Similarly, the Sierra Club has networked hikers for years.

New Third Ring networks could connect people who are rewilding their homes, yards, gardens, and neighborhoods; neighbors creating their own button parks; businesspeople and professionals, including developers, hoping to apply biophilic principles. These networks, unlimited in their ability to grow, could transform future policies of more traditional professional societies. For example, today's influential Green Building Certification Institute's LEED certification for buildings is almost exclusively focused on energy efficiency and low-environmental-impact design. It's overdue for an update that would accommodate but go beyond energy conservation to include the benefits of more natural environments to human health and well-being. For the proponents of that change, going the conventional route to achieve such a policy change could take years. But an expanding network of individual professionals could accelerate that change—and as you read this, that may have happened already.

Similarly, networks of health care and wellness professionals already committed to the nature prescription could change elements of their professions without waiting for top-down pronouncements; peer-to-peer, they could change minds, hearts, and eventually official protocol, and they could, through this process, build a funding base for direct-service programs.

When I mentioned this Third Ring notion to the director of the Maricopa County Parks Department, the largest urban park district in the United States, he grew excited—not only about family nature clubs but about the broader context of the Third Ring. "I have programs right now in my park system for families, but they're underenrolled. This could be a way to change that," he said. Moreover, he faces new budget challenges. By encouraging families to create self-sustaining, self-organizing nature networks, he would be expanding the number of people who use his parks. Just as important, the growth of a Third Ring could translate into future political support for parks funding. Similarly, as large land-trust organizations and governments help neighborhoods create their own nearby-nature trusts, overhead would be small, but their reach would grow. So would the public's understanding of the importance of the land-trust concept. College students, those who hope to pursue careers connecting people to nature, could be similarly networked.

The Third Ring could be especially effective in changing the closed system of public education. At this writing, efforts are afoot to gather "natural teachers" into a national network. These educators, in primary and secondary schools, colleges and universities, are not necessarily environmental education teachers. They're the teachers who intuitively or experientially understand the role that nature experience can play in education. They're the art teachers, English teachers, science teachers, and many others who insist on taking their students outside to learn—to write poetry or paint or learn about science under the trees. I meet these teachers all over the country. Every school had one or two. And they feel alone.

What if thousands of these natural teachers were networked and, through this network, gained power and *identity?* Once connected, these educators could push for change within their own schools, colleges, and communities. Connected and honored, natural teachers could inspire other teachers; they could become a galvanizing—dare I say subversive?—force within their schools. In the process, they would contribute to their own psychological, physical, and spiritual health.

Third Ring networks can reach well beyond the immediate members. In Austin, Texas, a grade-school principal told me that he would love to include more nature experience in his school. "But you can't imagine the pressure I'm under now with the testing," he said. "We can't do everything." When I described the family nature club phenomenon, the principal was enthusiastic. Could he, I asked, provide tool kits—packed with educational material, guides to local parks, and so forth—and encouragement to children and parents to start their own nature clubs. "I could do that," he said, and he meant it. He immediately began to think of how the educational elements of these clubs might augment his curriculum.

Earlier that day, in a meeting of leaders from central Texas, a PTA president spoke movingly. "Listen, I'm really tired of going into a roomful of parents and telling them not to give their kids candy, because of child obesity," she said. "Recently I've started talking to them about getting their children, and themselves, outside in nature more often. You can't believe the different feeling in the room. In the room where I'm preaching about candy, the mood is rather unpleasant, but when I'm in a room with parents and we're talking about getting outside, then the mood is happy, even serene. Parents immediately relax when we talk about that." During our meeting, she began to make plans for her PTA to start encouraging family nature clubs.

Social networking, online and in person, has transformed the political world. Online tools are used to raise funds, to organize face-to-face house parties, and turn out voters. A nature-focused Third Ring using those same tools, and ones not yet imagined, could create a growing constituency for needed policy changes and business practices. It could, in fact, help create a re-natured culture.

What if family nature clubs *really* caught on, like book clubs did in recent years? What if there were ten thousand family nature clubs in the United States, created by families for families in the next few years? What if the same process in other spheres of influence moved nature to the center of human experience? In such a culture, that father in New Hampshire would be more likely to knock on his neighbor's door. Or, better yet, one of his neighbors will show up at *his* door, asking his family to join a new network of neighbors devoted to nature in their own neighborhood. Their first expedition: to explore the creek that runs through it.

To be clear, permanent cultural change will not take root without major institutional and legislative commitments to protect, restore, and create natural habitat on a global basis.

CHAPTER 20

The Right to a Walk in the Woods

A Twenty-First-Century Story

GENEROUS FUTURE HISTORIANS may someday write that our generation finally met the environmental challenges of our time—not only climate change, but the change of climate in the human heart, our society's nature-deficit disorder—and, because of these challenges, we purposefully entered one of the most creative periods in human history; that we did more than survive or sustain, that we laid the foundation for a new civilization, and that nature came to our workplaces, our neighborhoods, our homes, and our families.

Such a transformation, both cultural and political, will come only with a new consideration of human rights. Few today would question the notion that every person, especially every young person, has a right to access the Internet, whether through a school district, a library, or a city's public Wi-Fi program. We accept the idea that the "digital divide" between the digital haves and the digital have-nots must be closed. Recently I began asking friends this question: Do we have a right to a walk in the woods? Several people responded with puzzled ambivalence. Look at what our species is doing to the planet, they said. Based on that evidence alone, isn't the relationship between human beings and nature inherently oppositional? That point of view is understandable, given the destructiveness of human beings to nature. But consider the echo from folks who reside at another point on the political/ cultural spectrum, where nature is seen as an object under human dominion or as a distraction on the way to Paradise. In practice, these two views of nature are radically different. Yet there is also a striking similarity: nature remains the "other"; humans are in it, but not of it.

My mention of the basic concept of rights made some of the people I talked to uncomfortable. One friend said: "In a world in which millions of children are brutalized every day, can we spare time to forward a child's right to experience nature?" Good question. Others pointed out that we live in an era of litigation inflation and rights deflation; too many people believe they have a "right" to a parking spot, a "right" to cable TV, even a "right" to live in a neighborhood that bans children. As a consequence, the idea of rights is deflated. Do we really need to add more rights to our catalog of entitlements?

The answer to these questions is yes, if we can agree that the right at issue is fundamental to our humanity.

Several years, ago, while researching *Last Child in the Woods*, I visited Southwood Elementary, the grade school I attended when I was a boy growing up in Raytown, Missouri. There, I asked a classroom of children about their relationship with nature. Many of them offered the now-typical response: they preferred playing video games; they favored indoor activities—and when they were outside, they played soccer or some other adult-organized sport. But one fifth-grader, described by her teacher as "our little poet," wearing a plain print dress and an intensely serious expression, said, "When I'm in the woods, I feel like I'm in my mother's shoes." To her, nature represented beauty, refuge, and something else. "It's so peaceful out there and the air smells so good. For me, it's completely different there," she said. "It's your own time. Sometimes I go there when I'm mad—and then, just with the peacefulness, I'm better. I can come back home happy, and my mom doesn't even know why." She paused. "I had a place. There was a big waterfall and a creek on one side of it. I'd dug a big hole there, and sometimes I'd take a tent back there, or a blanket, and just lay down in the hole, and look up at the trees and sky. Sometimes I'd fall asleep back in there. I just felt free; it was like my place, and I could do what I wanted, with nobody to stop me. I used to go down there almost every day." The young poet's face flushed. Her voice thickened. "And then they just cut the woods down. It was like they cut down part of me."

I was struck by her last comment: "It was like they cut down part of me." If E. O. Wilson's biophilia hypothesis is right—that the human attraction to nature is hardwired—then our young poet's heartfelt statement was more than metaphor. When she referred to her woods as "part of me," she was describing something impossible to quantify: her primal biology, her sense of wonder, an essential part of her self.

To reverse the trends that disconnect human beings from nature, actions must be grounded in science, but also rooted in deeper earth. In 2007, an impressive collection of mayors, professors, conservationists, and business leaders met in Washington DC, to explore the disconnection between young people and nature. Their discussion— enlightening, at times passionate—was applicable to people of all ages, but as the hours passed, several of the attendees began to ask about quantification. Some were looking for a business model to apply to the challenge of introducing children to nature. Most saw the obvious need for more research.

"I appreciate this discussion, but I'd like to say something," announced Gerald L. Durley, senior pastor at Providence Missionary Baptist Church in Atlanta. Durley had helped found the Afro-American Cultural Organization and worked shoulder to shoulder with Martin Luther King Jr. He leaned forward and said, "A movement *moves*. It has life." Like every successful movement, the civil rights struggle was fueled by a strongly articulated moral principle, one that did not need to be proven again and again. The outcome of the civil rights movement might have been quite different, or at least delayed, Durley noted, had its leaders waited for more statistical proof to justify their cause, or focused on the metrics of lunch-counter sit-ins. Some efforts proved successful, some were counterproductive. But the movement moved.

"When making a moral argument, there are no hard-and-fast rules, and such arguments can always be contended," according to philosophy professor Larry Hinman. "But most moral arguments are made based on one or two points. These include a set of consequences and a first principle—for example, respect for human rights." Science sheds light on the measurable consequences of introducing people to nature; studies point to health and cognition benefits that are immediate and concrete. But a "first principle" emerges not only from what science can prove, but also from what it cannot fully reveal: a meaningful connection to nature is fundamental to our spirit and survival, as individuals and as a species.

In our time, Thomas Berry presented this inseparability most eloquently. Berry incorporated E. O. Wilson's biological view within a wider, cosmological context. In his book *The Great Work*, Berry wrote: "The present urgency is to begin thinking within the context of the whole planet, the integral Earth community with all its human and other-than-human components. When we discuss ethics we must understand it to mean the principles and values that govern that comprehensive community."[1] Berry believed that the natural world is the physical manifestation of the divine. The survival of both religion and science depends not on one winning (because then both would lose), but on the emergence of what he called a twenty-first-century story—a reunion between humans and nature.

Speaking of absolutes may make us uncomfortable, but surely this is true: As a society, we need to give nature back to our children and ourselves. To not do so is immoral. It is unethical. "A degraded habitat will produce degraded humans," Berry wrote. "If there is to be any true progress, then the entire life community must progress." In the formation of American ideals, nature was elemental to the idea of human rights, yet inherent in the thinking of the Founding Fathers was this assumption: with every right comes responsibility. Whether we are talking about democracy or nature, if we fail to serve as careful stewards, we will destroy the reason for our right, and the right itself. And if we do not use this right, we will lose it.

Van Jones, founder of Green for All and author of *The Green Collar Economy*, maintains that environmental justice groups are overly focused on "equal protection from bad stuff"—the toxins too often dumped in economically isolated neighborhoods. He calls for a new emphasis on equal access to the "good stuff"—the green jobs that could lift urban youths and others out of poverty. However, there's another category of "good stuff"—the benefits to physical, psychological, and spiritual health, and to cognitive development, that all of us receive from our experiences in the natural world.

Our society must do more than talk about the importance of nature; it must ensure that people in every kind of neighborhood have everyday access to natural spaces, places, and experiences. To make that happen, this truth must become evident: *We can truly care for nature and ourselves only if we see ourselves and nature as inseparable, only if we love ourselves as part of nature, only if we believe that human beings have a right to the gifts of nature, undestroyed.*[2]

The little girl in Raytown may not have a specific right to that particular tree in her chosen woods, but she does have the inalienable right to be with other life; to liberty, which cannot be realized under protective house arrest; and to the pursuit of happiness, which is made whole by the natural world.

So do you.

CHAPTER 21

Where Mountains Once Were
and Rivers Will Be

A Career Guide to Everyday Eden

J ANET KEATING AND I climbed to the top of a mountain in West
Virginia, through oak and hickory, hemlock, pines and tulip poplar, basswoods, maple and locust—one of the most biodiverse
forests in the world—or what is left of it. We stood for a moment
looking up at four or five bat houses, which had been mounted by a
coal company.

Our eyes moved from the little wood boxes to the decapitated landscape below us, the evidence of mountaintop removal, the vanishing of
much of the state's horizon.

Keating, a former public school teacher, is executive director of the
Ohio Valley Environmental Coalition, a group that waged a successful
region-wide fight to keep what would have been the largest chlorine-
based pulp mill in the United States out of West Virginia. She has
been fighting mountaintop removal for years. Until you've seen the
impact of this type of mining for yourself, it's hard to clearly imagine
the magnitude of the devastation. What was once an adjacent mountain is simply gone; what the great machines did to this mountain can
only be compared to glaciation's advances and withdrawals. Not only
are the rock and earth gone forever, but the understory, the original home of those bats, is scraped away. Some one hundred acres of

approximately 80 different tree species, including dogwood and red-bud and spicebush; 710 species of flowering plants; 42 species of ferns; 138 species of grasses and sedges are all gone, along with a thousand vertical feet of mountaintop. All of this is shoved into valley fills. Slurry, liquid waste from the coal-washing process, is stored in impoundments. Especially when built at the headwaters of a watershed, this waste can seep or spill into the lower valleys and hollows, choking stream life and flooding human settlements with carcinogenic chemicals, including arsenic and mercury. When one impoundment failed, in 2000, it released 306 million gallons—more than the number of gallons spilled in the Gulf disaster—buried the land under as much as ten feet of sludge, and killed all life in seventy-five miles of waterways. Another sludge slurry pond dam that broke in 1972 killed 125 people, injured 1,100, and left 4,000 homeless. The company referred to the event as "an act of God."

The Surface Mining Control and Reclamation Act of 1977 requires coal companies to "reclaim" the land by replacing topsoil (under waivers, the companies may use "topsoil substitutes"). Coal-mining outfits might argue that this method of extraction is the only cost-effective way to extract seams of coal not available through traditional mining methods. And they might remind us that we are an energy-hungry nation. On this last point, they would certainly be right.

As Keating and I looked down at the crater (the massive destruction, mostly hidden from public view by the forests around it, is difficult to assess unless one has looked at it from above), I wondered if such a place could ever be restored. She shook her head. "What we're looking at down there will be hydroseeded, which means they'll just spray it with grass seed, usually non-native, and some kind of chemical that helps the grass grow," she said. The scene below us reminded me of the disappearing horizon in my own city, where mammoth graders cut and fill the hills for development.

But what about those ads that the coal companies run describing their restoration projects? "They show their little showcase places, or they say, 'Isn't it wonderful? Now we have flat land available for development—for houses,'" Keating said. "Sometimes they reclaim it for fish and wildlife habitat. The aquatic system in the Appalachian region had some of the highest richness and endemic populations of mussels and fish. There's no way that it's going to come back, because they've changed the soil chemistry, they've changed the light regime. Nothing is going to be the same."

If money were no object, would it be possible to restore or reclaim the land that has been destroyed by mountaintop removal, truly reclaim it? "Not in our lifetime. One reason is we don't even know what we've lost. In southern West Virginia, where most of this is taking place, the state never fully inventoried the natural world. I think part of the reason was, as long as we don't know what we're destroying, it's free."

In addition to direct affronts to the natural world and human health, cultural memory is torn and lost. "All of our mountains have names," Keating said. "Or had them. And the creeks all have names, and people know, or knew, these places. *They had names.* People would go into these woods and hunt ginseng, and they would use the money from selling ginseng to buy their family's Christmas presents. They would use the herbs here, the goldenseal, the bloodroot, for medicines—now gone."

These mountains offer a warning. Nature restoration—even human/nature restoration—can be used as a cover for more destruction. As businesses become more productive and inventive through a deeper understanding of nature and its patterns, the need for a restorative business ethic will grow.

Paul Hawken, the author and entrepreneur, writes: "Business must change its perspective and its propaganda, which has successfully portrayed the idea of 'limits' as a pejorative concept. Limits and prosperity are intimately linked. Respecting limits means respecting the fact that the world and its minutiae are diverse beyond our comprehension and highly organized for their own ends, and that all facets connect in ways which are sometimes obvious, and at other times mysterious and complex."[1] Or, as John Muir put it: "When you tug on a string in Nature, you find it is connected to everything else." Nature's limits are akin to what a "blank canvas was to Cezanne or a flute to Jean-Pierre Rampal," writes Hawken. "It is precisely in the discipline imposed by the limitations of nature that we discover and imagine our lives."[2]

Despair is tempting, and the reasons for it may yet triumph over those for optimism. But models for a new business ethic are emerging everywhere, along with opportunities for a new sense of purpose within the business world, and, for individuals, the potential for new identity.

Traditionally, agriculture has created many, if not most, of the jobs related to the human connection to nature. A new movement in that arena, one that includes but goes beyond organic crops, could not only change the nature of cities, but could revive the family farm and the small towns that once served them. In this sector, a restorative business ethic is coming into focus.

The New Agrarians

One afternoon, I rode from Denver to Boulder with Page Lambert, one of the best writers of the West. She looked out at the "oil slick," as she put it, of housing developments spreading across the plains. 'People move here for the ambience, but because they don't fully understand the ranching culture, they end up stopping the beauty that drew them," she said. As we drove, Lambert described her relationship with cattle—the fifty cows that her family tended when they lived in Wyoming.

Her memoir, *In Search of Kinship*, records the experiences of living off that land. She also keeps a diary and recently sent me passages from it, describing the sensory wonder of the small family ranch: wading through waist-high snow, drifts ten feet deep in the draws, to feed th livestock; finding a coyote's den in a drift, mountain lion tracks up th canyon, a horse frozen solid in winter. She wonders what happens t a culture when it loses knowledge of such connections. Lambert an others struggle "in vain against the anti-ranching politics of the day against those who blame small family farms and ranches for the ba conservation ethics of corporate agriculture," she says. And she fear that many well-intentioned people still do not understand "the role o hoofed animals on the western grasslands, and the role of rural cultur in the nation's consciousness." In her diary, she writes, "I fly to Califor nia and spend five days beside my dying father. I stroke his body, spea softly to him, hold his hands." She phones home and speaks to her fam ily. Her children "are in the basement with a hypothermic newbor calf, birthed during a blizzard. She tells of how they "massage the calf" body, use hot water bottles and an electric blanket to warm him, spea softly to him. He dies within moments of my father, at high noon o the spring equinox." In that moment, despite her sorrow, she is gratefu that her children "view death, not impersonally as filtered through th media, but as a vital part of their own lives." As we drive, she consider the snow that still drifts across the land, and the lives that follow.

Lambert and other ranchers and farmers who value and hope t extend their heritage have a friend in Courtney White, cofounder an executive director of the Quivira Coalition, a nonprofit conservatio organization, based in Santa Fe, New Mexico, dedicated to the concep of land and health, and to building bridges between ranchers, environ mentalists, scientists, public land managers, and others. The organiza tion had adopted this Wendell Berry quote as its unofficial motto: "You can't save the land apart from the people, to save either you must sav both." One of the coalition's goals is to spread the concept of the Nev Ranch. Elements include progressive ranch management, scientifically guided riparian and upland restoration, local food production, lan health assessment, and monitoring.

I first met the lanky, friendly White at a Quivira Coalition conference in Albuquerque. Many of the five hundred or so people in the room wore cowboy hats, and most of the rest looked like REI shoppers just back from a wilderness hike. A decade ago, White, an ex–Sierra Club activist and former archaeologist, decided that environmentalism-as-we-know-it was fading and would soon be replaced by something he calls the "new agrarianism." "I wanted to push back a bit against a major paradigm of the environmental movement, of which I was a member at the time, which said that nature and people their work, specifically) needed to be kept as far apart as possible . . . that environmental problems could be solved with environmental solutions largely devoid of culture or economics," he wrote. "According to this line of thinking the natural world could be 'saved' apart from an effort to 'save' ourselves."[3] By contrast, he defines the new agrarianism as "an ecological economy centered on food and land wealth which builds resilience, encourages ethical relationships, and celebrates life." He points to the growing interest in local, family-scale sustainable food, fiber, and fuel production—in, near, and beyond cities. The surge, which began in the 1980s, is "collaborative watershed groups focused on restoring health to riparian areas, it's the innovative use of livestock to combat noxious weed infestations, it's the carbon-sequestering practices of good land stewardship, and much more."

Environmentalists are right when they criticize certain farming and ranching techniques. But re-natured ranching and farming practices are cultivating renewed ethical ground. For example, consider David and Kay James, who, with their kids, raise grass-fed beef (rather than cattle fattened on corn and agricultural by-products in a feedlot) on 20,000 acres of public land across parts of Colorado and New Mexico. During the agriculture depression of the 1970s, the ranch fell on hard times, but the James's adopted a complex grazing program, diversified into other organic businesses, and the ranch returned to life. Not only that, but four of the five James offspring came back to the ranch, and brought sustainable businesses with them—this, in an era when young people are often tempted to flee farming regions. The James family described to White the land and community standards they hope will create a new rural America: lands covered with biologically diverse vegetation; lands tuned to functioning water, mineral, and solar cycles; lands with abundant and diverse wildlife; a community benefiting from locally grown, healthy food; and a people aware of the importance of agriculture to the environment.[4]

Anthony Flaccavento, former executive director of the nonprofit Appalachian Sustainable Development (ASD), is another pioneer in vanguard agriculture. In the late 1990s, when tobacco farming went into a rapid decline, many small-scale growers, feeling under siege from health advocates, shrinking markets, and environmentalists, were ready to quit farming, even though their families had known no other life for generations. In 2000, recognizing the plight of these tobacco farmers and the simultaneous gap in the region's organic-produce supplies, ASD launched Appalachian Harvest, a co-op program for new and experienced organic farmers. Co-op participants now sell their fresh organic produce wholesale to major retail markets. "When people hear that tobacco farmers—the 'enemies' of health and environment—are switching to organic produce (and now livestock), they are amazed," he says. The co-op keeps local dollars at home by involving local people in the production, marketing, and consumption of goods.

"For many church and social-justice activists, the credo was, 'Think your way to a new way of living,'" he adds. "Over time, my philosophy evolved from there into 'Live your way to a new way of thinking.'" Immersion in the culture he serves, and in the nature that serves the culture, is the foundation of his activism. As part of his immersion philosophy, Flaccavento operates his own seven-acre, certified-organic farm. "Because I farm, too, if there's a generally bad year, my farm gets hit just like the others." Flaccavento recently founded SCALE nc. (Sequestering Carbon Accelerating Local Economies) and allows ublic visits to his land to help promote his vision of ecologically sound arming practices.

Other examples of vanguard agriculture scarcely resemble maintream farming. Teal Farm, in the foothills of Vermont's Green Mounain National Forest, offers one glimpse. The farm includes some 540 cres of northern hardwood watershed with streams and pastures. A armhouse and barn boast a renewable energy system, and eight acres f orchard "in sculpted micro-climates around the buildings." In the nline journal, *Reality Sandwich*, Anya Kamenetz describes the farm as looking less like the monoculture fields of traditional agriculture and ore like an enhanced wilderness."[5]

Meanwhile, in eastern Montana, organic farmers and free-range anchers comprise "a new breed of optimists," as *High Country News* uts it, and are creating co-ops and building their own mills and akeries and packing operations, without the federal subsidies that onventional farmers get. Some farmers are creating full-processing perations, "from seed to sandwich" under the same roof, similar to he microbreweries popular in hip urban centers."[6]

Someday, it may be common for farms and ranches to do doubleuty as schoolyards. Just as some ranchers charge fees for hunting on heir land, farmers and ranchers might attract extra income by providng space for hands-on business retreats, nature therapy, or education nd rural experiences for young city dwellers. In Norway, farmers and eachers are working together to create new curricula. Students there pend part of the school year on the farm, immersed in science, nature, nd food production. Alone, such practices would not be enough to ave a small farm. But utilizing a farm or ranch for education could elp a rural family remain on their land, create new jobs, and connect rban people to the sources of their food and to nature.

Courtney White takes this line of thinking further. He wants farmers) think of themselves as farmers of the future—literally. He proposes what he calls the "carbon ranch," which would use food and stewardship to build soil and fight climate change. In fact, he sees climate change as an opportunity. A new generation of agrarians could accomplish large-scale removal of greenhouse gases from the atmosphere through plant photosynthesis and other land-based carbon sequestration activities, old and new. They would also be growing an expanded sense of purpose and identity.

The challenges of urban and suburban sprawl will always be thorny, but the creation of re-natured cities and suburbs, the new agrarian-ism, and restorative transportation offer antidotes to sprawl. So will a revived rural life, the resurgence of job-producing, life-enhancing rural regions and small towns. The division between urban and rural agriculture will continue to dissolve. Jobs, meaning, and a new sense of identity will grow.

The Great Work

The creation of *personal identity*, the pride and meaning that come from what Thomas Berry called the Great Work—the re-naturing of life—is key to the next nature movement.

Corey Sue Hutchinson has found her true purpose by mending topographical wounds. Like Janet Keating and Courtney White, she cares deeply about land. A decade ago, Hutchinson arrived for our first meeting, at the One-Stop Market, in a spray of gravel. She was driving her F-150 Ford pickup, with its side panel advertising her company Aqua-Hab Aquatic Systems. She bounded out to meet me with a strong handshake: "Call me Corey Sue." At thirty-eight, she was tan and muscular, her arms scarred from physical labor. On this day, her hair was woven into a long braid. She wore designer sunglasses, earrings, jeans, work boots, and a stylish cotton ball cap that said "No B.S." I followed her in my car to northern New Mexico's La Plata River. Which she planned to move.

When Corey Sue was a sophomore at Northern Michigan University, she decided to become a marine biologist, so she packed a bag of clothes, jumped on her bicycle and, with only four hundred dollars in her pocket, rode some two thousand miles to Oregon State University—where she learned she was prone to violent seasickness. She shifted to watershed management. In 1989, she accepted a job as a biologist in southern Colorado's San Juan National Forest.

"I wanted to make a difference, to protect the environment," she said. But she grew impatient with the government habit of "having meetings to plan meetings, and accomplishing little." So in 1994, she gave up her plum job and generous pension and set out to join the growing number of private river restorers in the West.

During the past century, some—not all—ranchers and developers have dramatically altered and damaged rivers like this one, removing the thick vegetation and allowing cattle to collapse the banks with their hooves, which encourages erosion. One rancher even bulldozed his stretch of the La Plata into a straight line, making it more ditch than river. Now, gentleman ranchers, as some of the newcomers are called, have bought up parts of the West and often prevent public access. That's the bad news. The good news is that some of them have become riverkeepers. The family that bought this land, through which the La Plata runs and where I spoke with Corey Sue, hired her to return it to a natural, winding pattern.

As she walked through the cheat grass and willows on the bank, swinging a walking stick made from a broomstick and bike handlebar, she talked of the river as if it were a person. Corey Sue explained how she pores over old photographs, especially aerial photos, of the way the river once was—and then hypothesizes what the river would have been like by now, if left to its own devices. She builds grade-control structures, creates vortex weirs, stabilizes banks with native protection of cottonwood logs, root wads, and willow, and hauls in boulders

to reduce erosion. She operates the heavy equipment herself. "Client
seem to get a kick out of that, a little gal in the big D-9 bulldozer wh
actually knows what she's doing."

Corey Sue's work is about sustainability, but it's also about connect
ing people to nature, about creating—or re-creating—a purposefu
place. She has completed dozens of river projects like this over th
years. Her approach is part science, part art; she calls it "hydrologi
voodoo." Often, she operates more on gut instinct than from statistica
data. Essentially, she speeds up geologic time, accomplishing in a fe
weeks what nature might take a century or more to do. Acceleratin
the process, if only by fifty years, can potentially prevent the perma
nent loss of some kinds of watershed. Her understanding of a river'
desire is sometimes eerie. After she began the La Plata project, th
river flooded. "To my surprise, a new channel cut right where I wa
planning to put one. This river wants to get back to what it was."

No doubt about it, Corey Sue is making a difference. "But humilit
is a requirement for this job," she says. Once, the Animas, a river sh
worked hard to save from dumped cars and collapsed banks, shifted o
its own and washed out everything she had done. "Sometimes Mothe
Nature has other ideas."

I first wrote about Corey Sue years ago, so recently I called her u
to ask how the work was going. She said she was still in business. "Bu
now a lot more people are doing this. There's more competition i
river work and wetland restoration. So I feel like I was at the begin
ning of something, and now I'm surviving in a competitive world," sh
said with pride. Some of her most recent work was on Colorado's Wes
Fork of the Mancos River, on a stretch that had been damaged by
small mining operation. She paused. "I want to emphasize something
Rivers are dynamic. They can be nudged, but they can't be controlled.
There are, however, rivers of no return, she added. The ones that ar
so devastated by human industry and development that they can neve
be restored.

Like those mountaintops in West Virginia. Restoration has its limits.

The lesson here, though, is that resistance is not futile. Renewal is possible. Janet Keating and Corey Sue Hutchinson have made good lives for themselves. To paraphrase the ancient Greek ideal: one works to tame the savageness of man; the other works to make gentle the life of the world.

Making a Living and a Life

Young adults have always been drawn to the possibility of creating a new and better world. Those I meet often tell me that they would like to make a career of connecting people to nature. They want to know which college they should attend, what their opportunities for real careers might be. Such questions should be easier to answer.

Higher education has incorporated the lessons of sustainability into curricula, but the focus is primarily on efficiency, on sustaining the natural environment through smarter production and conservation of fuel. Less familiar is the approach of producing human intellectual and creative energy through the restorative and productive powers of the natural world. In the past, careers that connected humans to nature were either taken for granted (farming) or minimized, if recognized at all: forestry, park rangers, gardeners, landscape architects (sometimes), and after that, you could just about quit counting. At this writing, I'm not aware of any comprehensive career guide that offers information on the array of businesses that do or could reunite humans and the natural world: urban designers, teachers who use natural habitat as laboratory, health care workers, nature therapists, botanical gardeners, organic farmers, vanguard ranchers, nature-camp operators, gardening instructors, natural landscape architects, natural playscape designers, urban park planners, guides, outdoor play specialists, nature interpreters, and many others. When people begin to consider the career possibilities of human restoration through nature, their eyes light up: here is a positive, hopeful view of the human relationship with the Earth.

Many people would pursue such jobs, if career guides and other resources were available and widely known—and if these also described how any career can be molded in a way that restores both nature and human beings. Sooner or later, a school of higher education—perhaps a school that teaches teachers—is going to realize the potential and create an entire program devoted to connecting people to nature. Enter this program, learn about the benefits of human restoration through the natural world, and *then* decide what profession you will choose (law, education, urban planning, or any other) to apply that knowledge and intent. No matter what career is chosen as the *tool* to connect people to nature, this is a way to love the natural world and humanity, too, and make a living at it.

Having spent time with some who do pursue such careers or avocations, I am impressed with the infectious characteristic they seem to share. They're happy. And they feel alive. Most of the individuals I've met work primarily with children and nature, so I may be seeing a subset with a particular propensity. And, frankly, the number of professionals who can be classified as working in the broad field of human-nature restoration is relatively small. But that number could grow quickly, given the right conditions. Some schools are already edging in this direction.

Not long ago, Arno Chrispeels, a science teacher at Poway High School in California, invited me to talk with his students about the changed relationship between the young and the natural world. I was prepared for twenty or so students to attend the talk. To my surprise, the auditorium was packed with over two hundred students. (They were given extra credit.) I braced for gum popping and note passing. But as I spoke, the students became intently curious, and not because I am a great speaker—I am adequate—but because of something else. I talked about two topics. First, the growing body of scientific evidence showing how outdoor experiences can enhance their ability to learn and think, expand their senses, and improve their physical and mental health. *Their* health, not an abstraction. Second, I talked about the fact that, because of climate change and the other crushing environmental problems that we face, everything in the coming decades must change. We'll need new sources of energy; new types of agriculture; new urban design and new kinds of schools, workplaces, and health care. Whole new careers will emerge that have yet to be named.

As the students left the auditorium, I turned to Chrispeels and asked, "What was that about? Why were they paying such close attention? I didn't expect that reaction."

"Simple," he said. "You said something positive about the future of the environment. They never hear that."

A few weeks earlier, an expert on global climate change, from the University of California–San Diego, had addressed the same students. "Their eyes froze over," said Chrispeels, who asked these same students to write down the dominant messages that they hear about the environment from media, environmentalists, and the wider culture. Most of the comments described two messages: pick up after yourself (nature is a chore); and the planet is in big trouble (but it's too late to save it anyway). The students described the dominant tone they hear: "Humans are a bad environment for other humans." "Ozone hole getting larger, global warming." "The environment will die." "The dangers of nature." "Natural disaster." "People are inherently bad." "We will resort to artificial nature because we destroyed it all to make room for people." "You will see the Earth reach its end." And so on.

True, our relationship with the Earth is in deep trouble. Despair has become fashionable and is prescribed early. This is the primary media storyline: It's too late, game over. No wonder, then, that so many young people are reluctant to suit up. Yes, we hear other messages, and a significant number of people are working hard on major environmental issues, but many more are not. In 2010, a series of polls and studies showed that Americans under the age of thirty-five, as a group, remain less engaged than older Americans on the issue of climate change; that, among all Americans, public concern about many environmental issues is at a twenty-year low. As I was writing this book, the Gulf Coast suffered from one of the largest environmental disasters in our history, and we do not yet know if that event will affect long-term values. But we do know that, because of a generational disengagement from experiences in the natural world, intimate knowledge of nature is declining. For the young and the old, this trend shows some signs of improvement, including an uptick in national park attendance after years of decline. Some press accounts attribute this news to the pressures of the Great Recession; but some of us believe that it may also be related to the thousands of people who have worked tirelessly in recent years to connect children to nature. Now the movement must turn to adults as well.

My contention throughout this book is that reconnecting to nature is one key to growing a larger environmental movement. That reconnection is visceral and immediately useful to many people's lives. Encouraging personal reconnection does not mean less engagement with global environmental issues; it means more. To act, most of us need motivation beyond despair. EcoAmerica, a nonprofit group focused on changing environmental values, believes that the first-generation environmental argument (in recent decades) was about catastrophe; the second-generation arguments were about economic benefits—green jobs—and national security. If the polls are accurate, though, neither of these arguments worked well, on their own. We're entering the era of the third-generation argument, which will give added focus to the intrinsic importance of the natural world to our health, our ability to learn, our happiness, our spirit.

Several weeks after my visit, Chrispeels gave his students a different assignment: Find a place in nature, spend a half hour alone in it, and write a one-page essay about the experience. Chrispeels shared the results with me. A theme ran through many of these essays: the students came home feeling better than when they left. Among their comments: "I saw things I never saw before." "I heard new things." One young man said he could "smell the beauty." "When I sat down in nature to write this weekend I found myself reconnected, my insides and outsides." "Nature, how I've been separated from you for so long. . . . There was something there that made me so happy. . . . I've found it's so lost, it's so deep within me. . . . I try to resurface it but it's fading fast." Two of the students went outside at night. One wrote that after lightning lit up her yard, everything looked "dark and scary, but honestly I felt so much more peaceful and relaxed in this nature environment than I have in a very long time." A young woman wrote, "I saw more stars than I have probably ever seen in my entire life." She had lived her life in cities, "where parks are distinguished plots of land with green grass carefully watered and mowed." But now she noticed the sounds of birds and the wind in the trees, and she found that "it wasn't boring at all being alone."

Some of these students described their half hour as a life-changing experience. I wondered. After all, these young people had been prepped. During my visit to the school, I had described the scientific evidence suggesting that exposure to natural settings reduces stress, stimulates creativity and cognitive development, and tunes in all the senses. But these young people completed the connection on their own.

I would like to believe that they also caught a glimpse of a better future—that what they recalled or found new, during their half hour in nature, was a sense of the unnoticed world, of the possible, of hope.

And there is no practical alternative to hope.

A s the writing of this book came to a close, Kathy and I rented a cabin in the mountains east of our home for a week. When we arrived, we sat on the deck overlooking Lake Cuyamaca, an alpine lake in the high-desert mountains. Recent firestorms had taken most of the pines, but some remained on an island. We watched the shadows of clouds move across the water. Our eyes followed the changing light on Stonewall Peak, where we had first hiked before we were married.

That afternoon, she and I went for a walk to the lake and across a dam to the island, and then into the forest of oak and remnant pine, then along the stream that feeds the lake. Stonewall stood in the near distance. We walked back to the lake and sat on a bench under the trees at water's edge. A flotilla of Canada geese, a species known for fierce monogamy, moved out of a cove and along the shore, pausing in front of us to feed in the silt and water plants. The largest goose watched us closely, until it made some signal, imperceptible to us, and the other geese followed him to the next cove.

White egrets and two great blue herons stood in the shallows. One heron lifted into the air and flew toward the island's point, carved a long arc, and glided back to rejoin its mate. We watched a bass cruising the shallows, a curious ground squirrel, two dragonflies, a swarm of small shorebirds. We sat for a long time, letting all of this envelop us.

Later, as we recrossed the dam in the wind, we looked out over the green backwater pasture. Kathy asked if the boys had ever been on the island.

I said, yes, I brought them here when they were small: "We slept in the van and at dawn I was awake first and saw Jason's little hand hanging down from the top bunk." She smiled and the wind lifted the brim of her hat. "We would both feel better and be healthier if we could come here or places like it more often," I said. She bent to pick up some trash from the trailside.

"I agree. But I'm the one who resists. You married a city girl."

Truth is, we both have our excuses. Even with knowledge of the benefits of the natural world, our long-established life patterns sometimes get the better of us. Kathy's hesitancy comes in part from her earliest associations with nature, which were not always enjoyable. For my part, inertia is the main barrier. And too much work. At some deeper level, perhaps the fear that developers might sweep through like a fire and take the wild places that I love. It's happened before.

I walked Kathy to the cabin, then headed back to the lake, which was now gray in the rising wind. I rounded the point of the island and was startled by one of the great blue herons. It landed like a paratrooper on the shore, its long neck and head perfectly still. I watched it and it watched me, each of us looking for clues to the other's next move. The intensity of the heron's eyes was disconcerting. Then, without looking away, the bird lifted its wings and pushed its body up, held there for a second or two, and then floated higher and glided off across the water. I was filled, once again, with that sense of release and return, that *it* I had felt so many years ago under the cottonwood.

At moments like this, I need no proof of a greater intelligence beyond these gifts of sight, hearing, touch, smell, taste, and other senses still unnamed. This expression is not the worship of nature, but a celebration of kinship. Ours are the eyes of the watcher being watched.

An hour passed. I felt a presence above me. I looked up. A heron hovered directly above me, looking down. Then the wind shifted and the bird floated backward and to the side. It pumped its wings twice, and was gone. But I knew that if I waited patiently, it would return.

SUGGESTED READING

A partial listing of an expanding literature

Abram, David. *The Spell of the Sensuous.* New York: Vintage Books, 1997.

Ackerman, Diane. *A Natural History of the Senses.* New York: Vintage Books, 1990.

Adams, Cass, ed. *The Soul Unearthed.* New York: Tarcher, 1996.

Alexander, Christopher. *The Phenomenon of Life: The Nature of Order.* Berkeley, CA: The Center for Environmental Structure, 2002.

Alexander, Christopher, Sara Ishikawa, and Murray Silverstein. *A Pattern Language: Towns, Buildings, Construction.* New York: Oxford University Press, 1977.

Armitage, Kevin C. *The Nature Study Movement: The Forgotten Popularizer of America's Conservation Ethic.* Lawrence: University Press of Kansas, 2009.

Ausubel, Kenny, ed. *Nature's Operating Instructions: The True Biotechnologies.* San Francisco: Sierra Club Books, 2004.

Beatley, Timothy. *Biophilic Cities: Integrating Nature into Urban Design and Planning.* Washington, DC: Island Press, 2011.

———. *Green Urbanism: Learning from European Cities.* Washington, DC: Island Press, 2000. (His film *The Nature of Cities* is also recommended.)

Benyus, Janine M. *Biomimicry: Innovation Inspired by Nature.* New York: Harper Perennial, 2002.

Berry, Thomas. *The Dream of the Earth.* San Francisco: Sierra Club Books, 2006.

———. *The Great Work: Our Way into the Future.* New York: Bell Tower, 1999.

Berry, Wendell. *A Continuous Harmony: Essays Cultural and Agricultural.* New York: Harcourt Brace Jovanovich, 1972.

Buzzell, Linda, and Craig Chalquist, eds. *Ecotherapy: Healing with Nature in Mind.* San Francisco: Sierra Club Books, 2009.

Callenbach, Ernest. *Ecotopia.* Berkley, CA: Bantam Books, 1975.

Carson, Rachel. *Silent Spring.* Boston: Houghton Mifflin, 1962.

Charles, Cheryl, and Bob Samples. *Coming Home: Community, Creativity, and Consciousness.* Fawnskin, CA: Personhood Press, 2004.

Clinebell, Howard. *Ecotherapy: Healing Ourselves, Healing the Earth.* Minneapolis: Fortress Press, 1996.

Cohen, Michael J. *Reconnecting with Nature: Finding Wellness through Restoring Your Bond with the Earth.* Corvallis, OR: Ecopress, 1997.

Coleman, Mark. *Awake in the Wild: Mindfulness in Nature as a Path of Self-Discovery.* Maui, HI: Inner Ocean Publishing, 2006.

Dean, Amy E. *Natural Acts: Reconnecting with Nature to Recover Community, Spirit, and Self.* New York: M. Evans and Co., 1997.

De Botton, Alain. *The Architecture of Happiness.* London: Penguin Books, 2006.

Drew, Philip. *Touch This Earth Lightly: Glenn Murcutt in His Own Words.* Sydney: Duffy & Snellgrove, 2000.

Eiseley, Loren. *The Immense Journey.* New York: Vintage Books, 1959.

Eisenberg, Evan. *The Ecology of Eden.* New York: Knopf, 1998.

Farr, Douglas. *Sustainable Urbanism: Urban Design with Nature.* Hoboken, NJ: John Wiley & Sons, 2007.

Gallagher, Winifred. *The Power of Place: How Our Surroundings Shape Our Thoughts, Emotions, and Actions.* New York: Harper Perennial, 1994.

Gatty, Harold. *Nature Is Your Guide.* New York: Penguin Books, 1958.

Glacken, Clarence J. *Traces on the Rhodian Shore: Nature and Culture in Western Thought from Ancient Times to the End of the Eighteenth Century.* Berkeley: University of California Press, 1967.

Hadot, Pierre. *The Veil of Isis: An Essay on the History of the Idea of Nature.* Cambridge, MA: Belknap Press of Harvard University Press, 2006.

Hartley, Dorothy. *Lost Country Life.* New York: Pantheon Books, 1979.

Hawken, Paul. *The Ecology of Commerce.* New York: HarperCollins, 1993.

Hawken, Paul, Amory Lovins, and L. Hunter Lovins. *Natural Capitalism: Creating the Next Industrial Revolution.* Boston: Little, Brown and Co., 1999.

Henderson, Bob, and Nils Vikander. *Nature First: Outdoor Life the Friluftsliv Way.* Toronto: Natural Heritage Books, 2007.

Hiss, Tony. *The Experience of Place: A New Way of Looking At and Dealing With Our Radically Changing Cities and Countryside.* New York: Vintage Books, 1991.

Hoagland, Edward. *Tigers and Ice: Reflections on Nature and Life.* New York: Lyons Press, 1999.

Houck, Michael C., and M. J. Cody, eds. *Wild in the City: A Guide to Portland's Natural Areas.* Portland: Oregon Historical Society Press, 2000.

Jackson, Maggie. *Distracted: The Erosion of Attention and the Coming Dark Age.* New York: Prometheus Books, 2009.

Kahn, Peter H., Jr. *Technological Nature: Adaptation and the Future of Human Life.* Cambridge, MA: MIT Press, 2011.

———. *The Human Relationship with Nature: Development and Culture.* Cambridge, MA: MIT Press, 1999.

Kellert, Stephen R. *Building for Life: Designing and Understanding the Human-Nature Connection.* Washington, DC: Island Press, 2005.

———. *Kinship to Mastery: Biophilia in Human Evolution and Development.* Washington, DC: Island Press, 1997.

Kellert, Stephen R., Judith Heerwagen, and Martin Mador, eds. *Biophilic Design: The Theory, Science, and Practice of Bringing Buildings to Life.* Hoboken, NJ: John Wiley & Sons, 2008.

Kellert, Stephen R., and Edward O. Wilson, eds. *The Biophilia Hypothesis.* Washington, DC: Island Press, 1993.

Kemper, Kathi. *Mental Health, Naturally: The Family Guide to Holistic Care for a Healthy Mind and Body.* Elk Grove Village, IL: American Academy of Pediatrics, 2010.

Kooser, Ted. *Local Wonders: Seasons in the Bohemian Alps.* Lincoln: University of Nebraska Press, 2004.

Korngold, Rabbi James S. *God in the Wilderness: Rediscovering the Spirituality of the Great Outdoors with the Adventure Rabbi.* New York: Doubleday, 2007.

Leopold, Aldo. *A Sand County Almanac: And Sketches Here and There.* New York: Oxford University Press, 1949.

Lewis, Charles A. *Green Nature/Human Nature: The Meaning of Plants in Our Lives.* Urbana: University of Illinois Press, 1996.

Lopez, Barry, ed. *The Future of Nature: Writing on a Human Ecology from Orion Magazine.* Minneapolis, MN: Milkweed Editions, 2007.

MacGregor, Catriona. *Partnering with Nature: The Wild Path to Reconnecting with the Earth.* New York/Oregon: Atria Books/Beyond Words, 2010.

Manguel, Alberto, ed. *By the Light of the Glow-Worm Lamp: Three Centuries of Reflections on Nature.* New York: Plenum Trade, 1998.

Margulis, Lynn, and Dorion Sagan. *Dazzle Gradually: Reflections on the Nature of Nature*. White River Junction, VT: Chelsea Green Publishing, 2007.

Marinelli, Janet, and Paul Bierman-Lytle. *Your Natural Home: The Complete Sourcebook and Design Manual for Creating a Healthy, Beautiful, and Environmentally Sensitive Home*. Boston: Little, Brown, 1995.

McDonough, William, and Michael Braungart. *Cradle to Cradle: Remaking the Way We Make Things*. New York: North Point Press, 2002.

McKibben, Bill. *Deep Economy: The Wealth of Communities and the Durable Future*. New York: Henry Holt, 2007.

Meine, Curt D. *Aldo Leopold: His Life and Work*. Madison: University of Wisconsin Press, 1988.

Meyrowitz, Joshua. *No Sense of Place: The Impact of Electronic Media on Social Behavior*. New York: Oxford University Press, 1985.

Moore, Robin C., and Herb H. Wong. *Natural Learning: Creating Environments for Rediscovering Nature's Way of Teaching*. Berkeley, CA: MIG Communications, 1997.

Morris, Stephen. *The New Village Green: Living Light, Living Local, Living Large*. Gabriola Island, British Columbia: New Society Publishers, 2007.

Muir, John. *The Mountains of California*. Garden City, NY: American Museum of Natural History/Anchor Books, 1961.

Naisbitt, John. *High Tech/High Touch: Technology and Our Search for Meaning*. London: Nicholas Brealey Publishing, 2001.

Oelschlaeger, Max. *The Idea of Wilderness: From Prehistory to the Age of Ecology*. New Haven, CT: Yale University Press, 1991.

Orr, David W. *Earth in Mind: On Education, Environment, and the Human Prospect*. Washington, DC: Island Press, 2004.

———. *The Nature of Design: Ecology, Culture, and Human Intention*. New York: Oxford University Press, 2002.

Plotkin, Bill. *Nature and the Human Soul: Cultivating Wholeness and Community in a Fragmented World*. Novato, CA: New World Library, 2008.

Pretor-Pinney, Gavin. *The Cloudspotter's Guide: The Science, History, and Culture of Clouds*. New York: Perigee Trade, 2007.

Pretty, Jules N. *The Earth Only Endures: On Reconnecting with Nature and Our Place in It*. Sterling, VA: Earthscan, 2007.

Pyle, Robert Michael. *The Thunder Tree: Lessons from an Urban Wildland*. Corvallis: Oregon State University Press, 2011.

Register, Richard. *Ecocities: Building Cities in Balance with Nature*. Berkeley, CA: Berkeley Hills Books, 2002.

Reich, Charles A. *The Greening of America*. New York: Random House, 1970.

Rosenzweig, Michael L. *Win-Win Ecology: How the Earth's Species Can Survive in the Midst of Human Enterprise*. New York: Oxford University Press, 2003.

Roszak, Theodore. *Ecopsychology: Restoring the Earth, Healing the Mind*. Ed. Theodore Roszak, Mary Gomes, and Allen Kanner. New York: Sierra Club Books, 1999.

———. *The Voice of the Earth: An Exploration of Ecopsychology*. Grand Rapids, MI: Phanes Press, 2001.

Sabini, Meredith, ed. *The Earth Has a Soul: C. G. Jung on Nature, Technology, and Modern Life*. Berkeley, CA: North Atlantic Books, 2002.

Samples, Bob. *The Metaphoric Mind: A Celebration of Creative Consciousness*. Rolling Hills Estates, CA: Jalmar Press, 1993.

Schmitz-Gunther, Thomas, ed. *Living Spaces: Sustainable Building and Design*. Cologne: Konemann, 1998.

Schneider, Richard J., ed. *Thoreau's Sense of Place: Essays in American Environmental Writing.* Iowa City: University of Iowa Press, 2000.

Schumacher, E. F. *A Guide for the Perplexed.* New York: Harper and Row, 1978.

Shellenberger, Michael, and Ted Nordhaus. *Break Through: From the Death of Environmentalism to the Politics of Possibility.* New York: Houghton Mifflin, 2007.

Shepard, Paul. *Coming Home to the Pleistocene.* Washington, DC: Island Press, 1998.

———. *The Others: How Animals Made Us Human.* Washington, DC: Island Press, 1997.

Skutch, Alexander F. *Harmony and Conflict in the Living World.* Norman: University of Oklahoma Press, 2000.

Sobel, David. *Childhood and Nature.* Portland, ME: Stenhouse Publishers, 2008.

Solnit, Rebecca. *Wanderlust: A History of Walking.* New York: Penguin Books, 2000.

Sternberg, Esther H. *Healing Spaces: The Science of Health and Well-Being.* Cambridge, MA: Belknap Press of Harvard University Press, 2009.

Suzuki, David, Amanda McConnell, and Adrienne Mason. *The Sacred Balance: Rediscovering Our Place in Nature.* Vancouver: Greystone Books, 1997.

Tallamy, Douglas W. *Bringing Nature Home: How Native Plants Sustain Wildlife in Our Gardens.* Portland, OR: Timber Press, 2007.

Thomas, Elizabeth Marshall. *The Old Way: A Story of the First People.* New York: Farrar, Straus & Giroux, 2006.

Thomas, Keith. *Man and the Natural World: A History of the Modern Sensibility.* New York: Pantheon Books, 1983.

Tobias, Michael, ed. *Deep Ecology.* San Diego, CA: Avant Books, 1984.

Tuan, Yi-Fu. *Topophilia: A Study of Environmental Perception, Attitudes, and Values.* New York: Columbia University Press, 1974.

Venolia, Carol. *Healing Environments: Your Guide to Indoor Well-Being.* Berkeley, CA: Celestial Arts, 1995.

Venolia, Carol, and Kelly Lerner. *Natural Remodeling for the Not-So-Green House: Bringing Your Home into Harmony with Nature.* New York: Lark Books, 2006.

Vessel, Matthew F., and Herbert H. Wong. *Natural History of Vacant Lots.* Berkeley: University of California Press, 1987.

Vindum, Tina. *Tina Vindum's Outdoor Fitness: Step out of the Gym and into the BEST Shape of Your Life.* Guilford, CT: Globe Pequot Press, 2009.

White, Courtney. *Revolution on the Range: The Rise of a New Ranch in the American West.* Washington, DC: Island Press, 2008.

Whitfield, John. *In the Beat of a Heart: Life, Energy, and the Unity of Nature.* Washington, DC: Joseph Henry Press, 2006.

Wiland, Harry, and Dale Bell. *Edens Lost and Found: How Ordinary Citizens Are Restoring Our Great American Cities.* White River Junction, VT: Chelsea Green, 2006.

Wilson, Edward O. *Biophilia.* Cambridge, MA: Harvard University Press, 1984.

———. *The Creation: A Meeting of Science and Religion.* New York: Norton, 2006.

Young, Jon, Evan McGown, and Ellen Haas. *Coyote's Guide to Connecting with Nature.* Shelton, WA: Owlink Media, 2010.

NOTES

Introduction

1. United Nations Population Fund, www.unfpa.org/pds/urbanization.htm.

2. Steven Dick, "The Postbiological Universe," 57th International Astronautical Congress 006, National Aeronautics and Space Administration (NASA) Headquarters, www.setileague org/iaaseti/abst2006/IAC-06-A4.2.01.pdf.

3. Another term sometimes used is *transhumanist*. For more on these concepts, see Humanity+, a nonprofit organization, at humanityplus.org/.

. Singing for Bears

1. Diane Ackerman, *A Natural History of the Senses* (New York: Random House, 1990), xix.

2. J. Porter, B. Craven, R. Khan, et al., "Mechanisms of Scent-Tracking in Humans," *Nature Neuroscience* 10 (2007): 27, www.nature.com/neuro/journal/v10/n1/abs/nn1819.html.

3. Porter, Craven, Khan, et al., "Mechanisms of Scent-Tracking," 27–29.

4. Tom J. Wills, Francesca Cacucci, Neil Burgess, et al., "Development of the Hippocampal Cognitive Map in Preweanling Rats," *Science* 328, no. 5985 (2010): 1573–76, doi: 10.1126/science.1188224.

5. Juan Antonio Martínez Rojas, Jesús Alpuente Hermosilla, and Pablo Luis López Espí y Rocío Sánchez Montero, "Physical Analysis of Several Organic Signals for Human Echolocation: Oral Vacuum Pulses," *Acta Acustica United with Acustica* 95, no. 2 (2009): 325–30, www eurekalert.org/pub_releases/2009-06/f-sf-ssd063009.php.

6. Hundreds of thousands of Internet viewers have watched videos of young Ben Underwood, who lost his sight to cancer when a toddler, do amazing things through tongue-click echolocation. He could ride a bike, surf, and even shoot hoops with neighbor kids. He shared his methods with researchers and brought inspiration to many before he died of cancer early in 2009.

7. Quoted in Pallava Bagla, "Tsunami-Surviving Tribe Threatened by Land Invasion," *National Geographic News*, August 8, 2005, news.nationalgeographic.com/news/2005/08/ 808_050808_jarawa.html.

8. J. W. Brown and T. S. Braver, "Learned Predictions of Error Likelihood in the Anterior Cingulate Cortex," *Science* (2005). Retrieved from: "Brain Study Points to 'Sixth Sense,'" ScienceBlog, February 18, 2005, www.scienceblog.com/cms/node/7036.

9. Lea Winerman, "A 'Sixth Sense?' Or Merely Mindful Caution?" *Monitor* 36, no. 3 (2005): 62, www.apa.org/monitor/mar05/caution.aspx.

10. Erika Smishek, "Mapping the Sixth Sense," *UBC Reports* 50, no. 1 (2004), www.public affairs.ubc.ca/ubcreports/2004/04jan08/mindsight.html.

11. Tony Perry, "Some Troops Have a Sixth Sense for Bombs," *Los Angeles Times*, October 8, 2009.

12. K. A. Rose, I. G. Morgan, J. Ip, et al., "Outdoor Activity Reduces the Prevalence of Myopia in Children," *Ophthalmology* 115, no. 8 (2008) 1279–85.

. The Hybrid Mind

1. Robert Michael Pyle, "Pulling the Plug: Nothing Satisfies Like the World beyond the Screens," *Orion Magazine*, November/December 2007, www.orionmagazine.org/index php/articles/article/466/.

2. Louise Story, "Anywhere the Eye Can See, It's Likely to See an Ad," *New York Times* January 15, 2007, www.nytimes.com/2007/01/15/business/media/15everywhere.html.

3. See www.collisiondetection.net/mt/archives/2005/10/meet_the_life_h.php.

4. Maggie Jackson, "May We Have Your Attention, Please?" *Bloomberg Businessweek,* June 12, 2008, www.businessweek.com/magazine/content/08_25/b4089055162244.htm.

5. "The Modern American Family: Always in motion, Child-Dominated, Strained—and Losing Intimacy?" www.college.ucla.edu/news/05/elinorochsfamilies.html.

6. George Stix, "Turbocharging the Brain—Pills to Make You Smarter?" *Scientific American,* October 2009, www.scientificamerican.com/article.cfm?id_turbocharging-the-brain.

7. Rachel Kaplan and Stephen Kaplan, *The Experience of Nature: A Psychological Perspective* (New York: Cambridge University Press, 1989); Stephen Kaplan, "The Restorative Benefit of Nature: Toward an Integrative Framework," *Journal of Environmental Psychology* 15 (1995) 169–82.

8. Stephen Kaplan and Raymond De Young, "Toward a Better Understanding of Prosocial Behavior: The Role of Evolution and Directed Attention," *Behavioral and Brain Science* 25, no. 2 (2002):263–64. www-personal.umich.edu/~rdeyoung/publications/IFS_version_commentary_on_rachlin_bbs_%282003%29.html.

9. T. Hartig and M. Mang, "Restorative Effects of Natural Environment Experiences," *Environment and Behavior* 23, no. 1 (1991): 3–26. Also see: T. Hartig, G. W. Evans, L. D. Jamner, D. S. Davis, and T. Gärling, "Tracking Restoration in Natural and Urban Field Settings," *Journal of Environmental Psychology* 23 (2003): 109–23.

10. Marc G. Berman, John Jonides, and Stephen Kaplan, "The Cognitive Benefits of Interacting with Nature," *Psychological Science* 19, no. 12 (2008): 1207–12.

11. A. Faber Taylor, F. E. Kuo, and W. C. Sullivan, "Coping with ADD: The Surprising Connection to Green Play Settings," *Environment and Behavior* 33, no. 1 (2001): 54–77.

12. James Raffan. "Nature Nurtures: Investigating the Potential of School Grounds," The Evergreen Canada Initiative, evergreen.ca/en/lg/naturenurtures.pdf.

13. R. H. Matsuoka, "High School Landscapes and Student Performance," University of Michigan, Ann Arbor (2008), hdl.handle.net/2027.42/61641.

14. M. C. R. Harrington, "An Ethnographic Comparison of Real and Virtual Reality Field Trips to Trillium Trail: The Salamander Find as a Salient Event," *Children, Youth, and Environments* 19 no. 1 (2009): 74–101, www.colorado.edu/journals/cye/index_issues.htm.

15. American Institutes for Research, *Effects of Outdoor Education Programs for Children in California* (Palo Alto, CA: American Institutes for Research, 2005). Available on the Sierra Club Web site. Retrieved from www.air.org/files/outdoorschoolreport.pdf.

16. For full abstracts, see "Children's Contact with the Outdoors and Nature: A Focus on Educators and Educational Settings," and a collection of summaries taken from four volumes of research developed by the Children and Nature Network (C&NN) and available at www.childrenandnature.org/research/. These C&NN Annotated Bibliographies of Research and Studies were written by Cheryl Charles, president, Children and Nature Network, and Alicia Senauer, Yale University.

17. American Society for Microbiology, "Can Bacteria Make You Smarter?" *ScienceDaily* (May 24, 2010), www.eurekalert.org/pub_releases/2010-05/asfm-cbm052010.php.

18. *The Selected Writings of Ralph Waldo Emerson,* ed. Brooks Atkinson (New York: The Modern Library, 1964), 901.

19. Bent Vigsø and Vita Nielsen, "Children and Outdoors," CDE Western Press, 2006 www.udeskole.dk/site/84/427/. Reported in "Nature Makes Children Creative," *Copenhagen Post Online,* October 18, 2006, www.cphpost.dk/news/1-latest-news/7179.html?tmpl=component&print=1&page=.

20. Edith Cobb, *The Ecology of Imagination in Childhood* (New York: Columbia University Press, 1977).

21. Cecily Maller, Mardie Townsend, Lawrence St Leger, et al., "Healthy Parks, Healthy People," Deakin University and Parks Victoria, March 2008, 41, www.parkweb.vic.gov.au/resources/mhphp/pv1.pdf.

22. Ibid., in reference to writings by S. Yogendra.

23. "Hilary Mantel: The Novelist in Action," *Publishers Weekly*, October 5, 1998, 60–61.

24. Retrieved from artist Richard C. Harrington's blog, 100horsestudio.blogspot.com/2008_02_01_archive.html.

25. Gary Small and Gigi Vorgan, *iBrain: Surviving the Technological Alteration of the Modern Mind* (New York: William Morrow, 2008).

26. Functional MRI or functional Magnetic Resonance Imaging (fMRI) is a type of MRI scan that measures changes in blood flow associated with neural activity in the brain or spinal cord.

27. www2.macleans.ca/.

28. Lianne George, "Dumbed Down: The Troubling Science of How Technology Is Rewiring Kids' Brains," November 7, 2008, Macleans.ca.

4. Fountains of Life

1. Stephen R. Fox, *John Muir and His Legacy* (Boston: Little, Brown, 1981), 116.

2. In the United States, *Glamour* magazine offers a blog called Vitamin G, for Green. European public health officials also refer to vitamin G. For researchers in the Netherlands, the G stands for green; specifically the effect of green space on health and learning and feelings of social safety. The current, and still champion, definition of vitamin G is riboflavin (also known as B2). Vitamin N may be a bit problematic, as in some street parlance, the *N* refers to nicotine. Others have referred to vitamin N, as in *nature*, including Linda Buzzell-Saltzman, founder of the International Association for Ecotherapy, in a 2010 blog for *Huffington Post*, and Valerie Reiss in *Holistic Living* in 2009.

3. M. Wichrowski, J. Whiteson, F. Haas, A. Mola, and M. J. Rey, "Effects of Horticultural Therapy on Mood and Heart Rate in Patients Participating in an Inpatient Cardiopulmonary Rehabilitation Program," *Journal of Cardiopulmonary Rehabilitation* 25, no. 5 (2005): 270–74.

4. C. M. Gigliotti, S. E. Jarrott, and J. Yorgason, "Harvesting Health: Effects of Three Types of Horticultural Therapy Activities for Persons with Dementia," *Dementia: The International Journal of Social Research and Practice* 3, no. 2 (2004): 161–80.

5. Gene Rothert, "Using Plants for Human Health and Well-Being," *Palestra*, winter 2007, findarticles.com/p/articles/mi_hb6643/is_1_23/ai_n29335131/.

6. See R. S. Ulrich and R. F. Simons, "Recovery from Stress During Exposure to Everyday Outdoor Environments," in *Proceedings of the Seventeenth Annual Meetings of the Environmental Design Research Association* (Washington, DC: EDRA, 1986): 115–22; J. A. Wise and E. Rosenberg, "The Effects of Interior Treatments on Performance Stress in Three Types of Mental Tasks," *CIFR Technical Report No. 002-02* (1988), Ground Valley State University, Grand Rapids, MI; R. S. Ulrich, "View through a Window May Influence Recovery from Surgery," *Science* 224 (1984): 420–21.

7. G. Diette, M. Jenckes, N. Lechtzin, et al., "Predictors of Pain Control in Patients Undergoing Flexible Bronchoscopy," *American Journal of Respiratory and Critical Care Medicine* 162, no. 2 (2000): 440–45, ajrccm.atsjournals.org/cgi/content/abstract/162/2/440; Gregory B. Diette, Noah Lechtzin, Edward Haponik, Aline Devrotes, and Haya R. Rubin, "Distraction Therapy with Nature Sights and Sounds Reduces Pain During Flexible Bronchosopy," *Chest* 123, no. 3 (2003): 941–48, chestjournal.chestpubs.org/content/123/3/941.full.

8. J. F. Bell, J. S. Wilson, and G. C. Liu, "Neighborhood Greenness and Two-Year Changes in Children's Body Mass Index," *American Journal of Preventive Medicine* 35, no. 6 (2008): 547–53.

9. Jordan Lite, "Vitamin D Deficiency Soars in the U.S., Study Says," *Scientific American*, March 23, 2009, www.scientificamerican.com/article.cfm?id=vitamin-d-deficiency -united-states.

10. Cecily Maller, Mardie Townsend, Lawrence St Leger, et al., "Healthy Parks, Healthy People," Deakin University and Parks Victoria, March 2008, www.parkweb.vic.gov.au/ resources/mhphp/pv1.pdf.

11. R. Parsons, "The Potential Influences of Environmental Perception on Human Health," *Journal of Environmental Psychology* 11 (1991): 1–23; R. S. Ulrich, R. F. Simons, B. D. Losito, et al., "Stress Recovery During Exposure to Natural and Urban Environments," *Journal of Environmental Psychology* 11 (1991): 231–48; R. S. Ulrich, "View through a Window May Influence Recovery from Surgery," *Science* 224 (1984): 420–21.

12. N. R. Fawcett and E. Gullone, "Cute and Cuddly and a Whole Lot More? A Call for Empirical Investigation into the Therapeutic Benefits of Human-Animal Interaction for Children," *Behaviour Change* 18 (2001): 124–33; S. Crisp, and M. O'Donnell, "Wilderness-Adventure Therapy in Adolescent Mental Health," *Australian Journal of Outdoor Education* 3 (1998): 47–57; C. A. Lewis, *Green Nature/Human Nature: The Meaning of Plants in Our Lives* (Urbana: University of Illinois Press, 1996); K. C. Russell, J. C. Hendee, and D. Phillips-Miller, "How Wilderness Therapy Works: An Examination of the Wilderness Therapy Process to Treat Adolescents with Behavioural Problems and Addictions," in *Wilderness Science in a Time of Change*, ed. D. N. Cole and S. F. McCool (Ogden, UT: Department of Agriculture, Forest Service, Rocky Mountain Research Station, 1999); A. Beck, L. Seraydarian, and F. Hunter, "Use of Animals in the Rehabilitation of Psychiatric Inpatients," *Psychological Reports* 58 (1986): 63–66; A. H. Katcher and A. M. Beck, *New Perspectives on Our Lives with Companion Animals* (Philadelphia: University of Pennsylvania Press, 1983); B. M. Levinson, *Pet-Oriented Child Psychotherapy* (Springfield, IL: Charles C. Thomas, 1969).

13. Thomas Herzog, Eugene Herbert, Rachel Kaplan, and C. L. Crooks, "Cultural and Developmental Comparisons of Landscape Perceptions and Preferences," *Environment and Behavior* 32 (2000): 323–37; T. R. Herzog, A. M. Black, K. A. Fountaine, and D. J. Knotts, "Reflection and Attention Recovery as Distinctive Benefits of Restorative Environments," *Journal of Environmental Psychology* 17 (1997): 165–70; Patricia Newell, "A Cross-Cultural Examination of Favorite Places," *Environment and Behavior* 29 (1997): 495–514; Kalevi Korpela and Terry Hartig, "Restorative Qualities of Favorite Places," *Journal of Environmental Psychology* 16 (1996): 221–33. Kaplan and Kaplan, *The Experience of Nature: A Psychological Perspective*. New York: Cambridge University Press, 1989.

14. B. J. Park, Y. Tsunetsugu, T. Kasetani, T. Kagawa, and Y. Miyazaki, "The Physiological Effects of *Shinrin-yoku* (Taking in the Forest Atmosphere or Forest Bathing): Evidence from Field Experiments in Twenty-four Forests across Japan," *Environmental Health and Preventive Medicine* 15, no. 1 (2010): 18–26.

15. Q. Li, K. Morimoto, A. Nakadai, et al., "Forest Bathing Enhances Human Natural Killer Activity and Expression of Anti-Cancer Proteins," *International Journal of Immunopathology and Pharmacology* 20 (2007): 3–8.

16. In Peter H. Kahn's book *Technological Nature: Adaptation and the Future of Human Life* (Cambridge, MA: MIT Press, 2011), Kahn offers a brief history of the term *biophilia*: "This term was used as early as the 1960s by [Erich] Fromm . . . in his theory of psychopathology to describe a healthy, normal functioning individual, one who was attracted to life (human and non-human) as opposed to death. In the 1980s, [E. O.] Wilson . . . published a book titled

Biophilia. I have never seen Wilson cite Fromm's use of the term, so it is unclear whether Wilson was aware of this earlier usage. Either way, Wilson shaped the term from the perspective of an evolutionary biologist. He defined biophilia as an innate human tendency to affiliate with life and lifelike processes. Biophilia, according to Wilson, emerges in our cognition, emotions, art, and ethics, and unfolds 'in the predictable fantasies and responses of individuals from early childhood onward. It cascades into repetitive patterns of culture across most of all societies.'" See Edward O. Wilson, *Biophilia: The Human Bond with Other Species* (Cambridge, MA: Harvard University Press, 1984), 85.

17. Stephen Kellert and Edward O. Wilson, eds., *The Biophilia Hypothesis* (Washington, DC: Island Press, 1993), 31.

18. Gordon H. Orians, "Metaphors, Models, and Modularity," *Politics and Culture*, April 9, 2010, www.politicsandculture.org/2010/04/29/metaphors-models-and-modularity/.

19. William Bird, "Natural Thinking—Investigating the Links between the Natural Environment, Biodiversity, and Mental Health," *A Report for the Royal Society for the Protection of Birds* (June 2007): 40. www.rspb.org.uk/Images/naturalthinking_tcm9-161856.pdf.

Re-naturing the Psyche

1. Quoted in Peter Ker, "More Fertile Imagination," *The Age*, March 20, 2010.

2. J. Barton, R. Hine, and J. Pretty, "Green Exercise and Green Care: Evidence, Cohorts, Lifestyles, and Health Outcomes—Summary of Research Findings," Centre for Environment and Society, Department of Biological Sciences, University of Essex, 2009, www.essex.ac.uk/bs/staff/barton/Green_Exercise_Research_Feb09.pdf. (This is an unpublished review paper, available only at the Web site.)

3. "Ecotherapy: The Green Agenda for Mental Health," Mind Week Report, May 2007, www.mind.org.uk/assets/0000/2138/ecotherapy_report.pdf.

4. M. Bodin and T. Hartig, "Does the Outdoor Environment Matter for Psychological Restoration Gained Through Running?" *Psychology of Sport and Exercise* 4 (2003): 141–53.

5. Jo Barton and Jules Pretty, "What Is the Best Dose of Nature and Green Exercise for Improving Mental Health? A Multi-Study Analysis," *Environmental Science and Technology*, 44, no. 10 (2010): 3947–55.

6. C. A. Lowry, J. H. Hollis, A. de Vries, et al., "Identification of an Immune-Responsive Mesolimbocortical Serotonergic System: Potential Role in Regulation of Emotional Behavior," *Neuroscience* 146, no. 2 (2007): 756–72.

7. Quoted in Clint Tabot, "Depression Rx: Get Dirty, Get Warm," *Colorado Arts and Sciences Magazine*, University of Colorado at Boulder, artsandsciences.colorado.edu/magazine/2009/09/depression-rx-get-dirty-get-warm/.

8. Nancy E. Edwards and Alan M. Beck, "Animal-Assisted Therapy and Nutrition in Alzheimer's Disease," *Western Journal of Nursing Research* 24, no. 6 (2002): 697–712. wjn.sage-pub.com/content/24/6/697.abstract.

9. Bente Berget, Øivind Ekeberg, and Bjarne O. Braastad, "Animal-Assisted Therapy with Farm Animals for Persons with Psychiatric Disorders: Effects on Self-Efficacy, Coping Ability, and Quality of Life, a Randomized Controlled Trial," *Clinical Practice and Epidemiology in Mental Health* 4, no. 9 (2008), www.cpementalhealth.com/content/4/1/9.

10. C. Antonioli and M. Reveley, "Randomised Controlled Trial of Animal Facilitated Therapy with Dolphins in the Treatment of Depression," *British Medical Journal* 331 (2005): 1231.

11. A. Baverstock and F. Finlay, "Does Swimming with Dolphins Have Any Health Benefits for Children with Cerebral Palsy?" *Archives of Disease in Childhood* 93, no. 11 (2008).

12. Glenn Albrecht, "Solastalgia: A New Concept in Human Health and Identity," *Philosophy Activism Nature* 3 (2005): 41–44.

13. Quoted in Diana Yates, "The Science Suggests Access to Nature Is Essential to Human Health," *News Bureau*, University of Illinois–Urbana-Champaign, Feb. 12, 2009, news .illinois.edu/news/09/0213nature.html.

14. Linda Buzzell and Craig Chalquist, eds., *Ecotherapy: Healing with Nature in Mind* (San Francisco: Sierra Club Books/Counterpoint, 2009). Also see Buzzell's online "Ecotherapy News," www.huffingtonpost.com/linda-buzzell/.

15. Over time, the movement branched out to include other chronic illnesses and occupational therapy. In 1955, Michigan State University awarded the first graduate degree in horticultural/occupational therapy. In 1971, Kansas State University established the first horticultural therapy degree curriculum.

16. Mind chief executive Paul Farmer's quotes come from a press release regarding the May 2007 Mind-commissioned report "Ecotherapy—The Green Agenda for Mental Health." For more information on this charity, see www.mind.org.uk/.

17. Quoted in Daniel B. Smith, "Is There an Ecological Unconscious?" *New York Times Magazine*, January 30, 2010.

6. The Deep Green High

1. John Muir, "A Wind-Storm in the Forests," in *The Mountains of California*, ch. 10 (1894), as edited and condensed by Paul Richins Jr., Backcountry Resource Center, pweb.jp .net/~prichins/backcountry_resource_center.htm. For more on John Muir, including his writings, see www.sierraclub.org/john_muir_exhibit/default.aspx.

2. *Tina Vindum's Outdoor Fitness: Step out of the Gym and into the BEST Shape of Your Life* (Guilford, CT: Globe Pequot Press, 2009).

3. Kelli Calabrese, *Feminine, Firm, and Fit* (Ocala, FL: Great Atlantic Publishing Group, 2004).

4. Alison Freeman, "Working Out in the Green Gym," *BBC News Online*, October 29, 2004, news.bbc.co.uk/1/hi/england/london/3718626.stm.

5. See *Fly-Fishing for Sharks* (New York: Simon & Schuster, 2000), my book about the cultures of fishing.

6. "Runners' High Demonstrated: Brain Imaging Shows Release of Endorphins in Brain," *ScienceDaily*, University of Bonn, March 6, 2008, www.sciencedaily.com/releases 2008/03/080303101110.htm. Sourced from H. Boecker, T. Sprenger, M. E. Spilker, et al., "The Runner's High: Opioidergic Mechanisms in the Human Brain," *Cerebral Cortex* 18, no. 1 (2008), 2523–31.

7. The Nature Prescription

1. J. F. Talbot and R. Kaplan, "The Benefits of Nearby Nature for Elderly Apartment Residents," *International Aging and Human Development* 33, no. 2 (1991): 119–30.

2. Patrick F. Mooney and Stephen L. Milstein, "Assessing the Benefits of a Therapeutic Horticulture Program for Seniors in Intermediate Care," *The Healing Dimensions of People Plant Relations*, ed. Mark Francis, Patricia Lindsey, and Jay Stone Rice.

3. Candice Shoemaker, Mark Haub, and Sin-Ae Park, "Physical and Psychological Health Conditions of Older Adults Classified as Gardeners or Nongardeners," *Hortscience* 44 (2009): 206–10.

4. K. Day, D. Carreon, and C. Stump, "The Therapeutic Design of Environments for People with Dementia: A Review of the Empirical Research," *Gerontologist* 40, no. 4 (2000): 397–416.

5. Leon A. Simons, Judith Simons, John McCallum, and Yechiel Friedlander, "Lifestyle Factors and Risk of Dementia: Dubbo Study of the Eldery," *Medical Journal of Australia* 184, no. 2 (2006): 68–70.

6. The contents of the medicine bottle included a variety of information, including a Web address to National Wildlife Refuges, a guide to animal tracks, Leave No Trace tips, a link to information on planting native vegetation to help bring back butterfly and bird migration routes, a PowerBar, and other items—including a temporary tattoo of migratory birds.

7. Daphne Miller, "Benefits of Park Prescriptions," *Washington Post*, November 17, 2009.

8. Richard Goss, "Woodland Therapy Taking Root in UK," *Sunday Times*, September 14, 2008; C. Ward Thompson, P. Travlou, and J. Roe, "Free Range Teenagers: The Role of Wild Adventure Space in Young People's Lives," *OPENspace*, November 2006 (prepared for Natural England), www.openspace.eca.ac.uk/pdf/wasyp_finalreport5dec.pdf.

9. The National Trust, "Nature's Capital: Investing in the Nation's Natural Assets," www.nationaltrust.org.uk/main/w-global/w-news/w-news-nature_s_capital.htm.

8. Searching for Your One True Place

1. "Bye, Bye Boomers, Not Quite Yet," by Joel Kotkin and Mark Schill, *New Geography*, August 25, 2008, www.newgeography.com/content/00197-bye-bye-boomers-not-quite.

2. Christopher J. L. Murray, Sandeep Kulkarni, Catherine Michaud, et al., "Eight Americas: Investigating Mortality Disparities across Races, Counties, and Race-Counties in the United States," *Public Library of Science Medicine*, September 2006, www.plosmedicine.org/article/info%3Adoi%2F10.1371%2Fjournal.pmed.0030260.

3. Rita Healy, "Where You Will Live the Longest," *Time*, September 12, 2006, www.time.com/time/health/article/0,8599,1534241,00.html.

4. Catherine O'Brien, "A Footprint of Delight," *NCBW Forum Article*, October 2006, www.bikewalk.org/pdfs/forummarch1006footprint.pdf.

5. Catherine O'Brien, "Policies for Sustainable Happiness" (paper presented at the International Conference on Policies for Happiness, Siena, Italy, June 14–17, 2007), www.unisi.it/eventi/happiness/curriculum/obrien.pdf.

9. The Incredible Experience of Being Where You Are

1. Stefan D. Cherry and Erick C. M. Fernandes, "Live Fences," Department of Soil, Crop, and Atmospheric Sciences, Cornell University, 1997, www.ppath.cornell.edu/mba_project/livefence.html.

2. Karen Harwell and Joanna Reynolds, *Exploring a Sense of Place: How to Create Your Own Local Program for Reconnecting with Nature* (Palo Alto, CA: Conexions, 2006).

3. James H. Wandersee and Elisabeth E. Schussler, "Toward a Theory of Plant Blindness," *Plant Science Bulletin* 47, no. 1 (2001), www.botany.org/bsa/psb/2001/psb47-1.html.

4. Charles A. Lewis, *Green Nature/Human Nature: The Meaning of Plants in Our Lives* (Urbana: University of Illinois Press, 1996), 8.

5. Charles A. Lewis, *Green Nature/Human Nature*, 4, 6.

10. Welcome to the Neighborhood

1. Diane Mapes, "Looking at Nature Makes You Nicer," MSNBC, October 14, 2009, www.msnbc.msn.com/id/33243959/ns/health-behavior.

2. N. Weinstein, A. Przybylski, and R. Ryan, "Can Nature Make Us More Caring? Effects of Immersion in Nature on Intrinsic Aspirations and Generosity," *Personality and Social Psychology Bulletin* 35, no. 10 (2009): 1315–29.

3. "Nature Makes Us More Caring, Study Says," University of Rochester News, September 30, 2009, www.rochester.edu/news/show.php?id=3450.

4. F. E. Kuo and W. C. Sullivan, "Aggression and Violence in the Inner City: Impacts of Environment via Mental Fatigue," *Environment and Behavior* 33, no. 4 (2001): 543–71.

5. F. E. Kuo and W. C. Sullivan, "Environment and Crime in the Inner City: Does Vegetation Reduce Crime?" *Environment and Behavior* 33, no. 3 (2001): 343–67, www.herluiuc.edu

6. Cecily Maller, Mardie Townsend, Lawrence St Leger, et al., "Healthy Parks, Healthy People," Deakin University and Parks Victoria, March 2008, www.parkweb.vic.gov .au/resources/mhphp/pv1.pdf.

7. John Berger, *About Looking* (New York: Pantheon, 1980), 145.

11. The Purposeful Place

1. Peter Berg and Raymond F. Dasmann, "Reinhabiting California," *Ecologist* 7, no. 10 (1977): 6.

2. Among the books that put a foot in the door of "bioregional identity" are *Home Ground: Language for the American Landscape*, ed. Barry Lopez and Debra Gwartney (San Antonio, TX: Trinity University Press, 2006), and Arthur R. Kruckeberg, *The Natural History of Puget Sound Country* (Seattle: University of Washington Press, 1995).

3. Efforts are under way in Canada to declare 50 percent of all their public lands forever wild. See Canadian Parks and Wilderness Society, www.cpaws.org/. This U.S. group is working on a potential natural lands map: www.twp.org/. This group is working on a U.S./Canada biosphere approach: www.2ciforest.org/en/mainpageenglish.html.

4. See Sustainable Caerphilly, www.caerphilly.gov.uk/sustainable/english/home.html.

5. See www.happyplanetindex.org/public-data/files/happy-planet-index-2-0.pdf, and "Costa Rica Tops Happy Planet Index," http://www.happyplanetindex.org/news/archive/news-2.html.

6. See World Database of Happiness, worlddatabaseofhappiness.eur.nl/.

7. 2010 Environmental Performance Index, Yale Center for Environmental Law and Policy, Yale University, envirocenter.research.yale.edu, and Center for International Earth Science Information Network, Columbia University, ciesin.columbia.edu, February 2010.

8. Sergio Palleroni quoted in: Eric Corey Freed, "Five Questions about Our Future," *Natural Home*, May/June 2009.

9. For the UK's Springwatch, see www.bbc.co.uk/springwatch.

10. California Academy of Sciences, Bay Area Ant Survey, www.calacademy.org/science/citizen_science/ants/.

11. Project FeederWatch, www.birds.cornell.edu/pfw/.

12. James McCommons, "Last-Ditch Rescues," *Audubon*, March–April 2009, audubon magazine.org/features0903/grassroots.html.

13. Kirk Johnson, "Retirees Trade Work for Rent at Cash-Poor Parks," *New York Times*, February 17, 2010.

14. Dianne D. Glave, *Rooted in the Earth: Reclaiming the African American Environmental Heritage* (Chicago: Lawrence Hill Books, 2010), 3.

12. The Bonding

1. Martha Erickson, "Shared Nature Experience as a Pathway to Strong Family Bonds," Children and Nature Network Leadership Writing Series, www.childrenandnature.org/downloads/CNN_LWS_Vol1_01.pdf.

2. Martha Farrell Erickson and Karen Kurz-Riemer, *Infants, Toddlers, and Families: A Framework for Support and Intervention* (New York: Guilford Press, 1999).

13. The Nature Principle at Home

1. See Bruce Buck, "Ranch House Spectacular," *New York Times*, November 15, 2007.

2. Peter H. Kahn Jr., *Technological Nature: Adaptation and the Future of Human Life* (Cambridge, MA: MIT Press, 2011).

3. Quoted in Virginia Sole-Smith, "Nature on the Threshold," *New York Times*, September 7, 2006.

4. John Berger, *About Looking* (New York: Pantheon, 1980).

5. Michael L. Rosenzweig, *Win-Win Ecology: How the Earth's Species Can Survive in the Midst of Human Enterprise* (Oxford: Oxford University Press, 2003).

6. Douglas W. Tallamy, *Bringing Nature Home: How Native Plants Sustain Wildlife in Our Gardens*, expanded ed. (Portland, OR: Timber Press, 2009).

7. These tips are condensed from *Bringing Nature Home* and are used here with author Douglas Tallamy's permission.

14. Stop, Look Up, and Listen

1. Quote from Jack Troeger is from www.darkskyinitiative.org/.

2. See Verlyn Klinkenborg, "Our Vanishing Night," *National Geographic*, November 2008.

3. Itai Kloog, Abraham Haim, Richard G. Stevens, Micha Barchana, and Boris A. Portnov, "Light at Night Co-Distributes with Incident Breast but Not Lung Cancer in the Female Population of Israel," *Chronobiology International* 25, no. 1 (2008): 65–81.

4. Jack Greer, "Losing the Moonlight," *Daily Times* (Salisbury, MD) April 19, 2007.

5. Quoted in Jack Borden, "For Spacious Skies," *Boston Review* 8, no. 4 (1983).

6. cloudappreciationsociety.org/manifesto/.

15. Nature Neurons Go to Work

1. Mark Boulet and Anna Clabburn, "Retreat to Return: Reflections on Group-Based Nature Retreats," International Community for Ecopsychology, no. 8 (August 2003), www.ecopsychology.org/journal/gatherings8/html/sacred/retreat_boulet&clabburn.htlm. "Social Ecologist and Author Stephen R. Kellert Shares His Views of Sustainable Design," *Sustainable Ways: A Prescott College Publication* 2, no. 1 (2004), prescott.edu/academics/adp/programs/scd/sustainable_ways/vol_2_no_1/the_sw_interview.html.

2. "Social Ecologist and Author Stephen R. Kellert Shares His Views of Sustainable Design," *Sustainable Ways: A Prescott College Publication* 2, no. 1 (2004), prescott.edu/academics/adp/programs/scd/sustainable_ways/vol_2_no_1/the_sw_interview.html.

3. Vivian Loftness, as quoted in Richard Louv, *San Diego Union-Tribune* column, July 18, 2006.

4. David Steinman, "Millions of Workers Are 'Sick of Work,'" *The Architecture of Illness*, www.environmentalhealth.ca/fall93sick.html.

5. Paul Hawken, Amory Lovins, and L. Hunter Lovins, *Natural Capitalism: Creating the Next Industrial Revolution* (New York: Back Bay Books, 2008), 88.

6. Kim Severson, "The Rise of Company Gardens," *New York Times*, May 11, 2010.

7. "A Conversation with E. O. Wilson," PBS, *Nova*, April 1, 2008, www.pbs.org/wgbh/nova/beta/nature/conversation-eo-wilson.html.

8. www.biomimicryguild.com/. www.unep.org/NewsCentre/videos/player_new.asp?w=720&h=480&f=/newscentre/videos/shortfilms/2009-4-23_VTS_02_1.

9. Minoru Shinohara (from keynote speech, October 7, 2009), "Nissan EPORO Robot Car 'Goes to School' on Collision-Free Driving by Mimicking Fish Behavior," Nissan press release. www.autoblog.com/2009/10/02/nissans-robot-concept-cars-avoid-accidents-by-mimicking-fish/.

10. www.biomimicryinstitute.org/case-studies/case-studies/transportation.html.

11. Michael Silverberg, "Man-Made Greenery," *New York Times Magazine*, December 13, 2009.

12. J. Scott Turner, "A Superorganism's Fuzzy Boundaries," *Natural History*, July–August 2002, findarticles.com/p/articles/mi_m1134/is_6_111/ai_87854877/?tag=content;col1.

13. www.naturewithin.info/urban.html#contact.

14. Kathleen L. Wolf, "Trees Mean Business: City Trees and the Retail Streetscape," *Main Street News*, August 2009, 3–4.

16. Living in a Restorative City

1. Timothy Beatley, *Green Urbanism: Learning from European Cities* (Washington, DC: Island Press, 2000).

2. www.ecocitycleveland.org/ecologicaldesign/ecovillage/accomps.html.

3. enrightecovillage.org/.

4. Prakash M. Apte, "Dharavi: India's Model Slum," *Planetizen*, September 29, 2008, www.planetizen.com/node/35269.

5. Bina Venkataraman, "Country, the City Version: Farms in the Sky Gain New Interest," *New York Times*, July 15, 2008.

6. www.greeningofdetroit.com/3_1_featured_projects.php?link_id=1194537199.

7. Rebecca Solnit, "Detroit Arcadia: Exploring the Post-American Landscape," *Harper's Magazine*, July 2007, 73.

8. Frank Hyman, *Backyard Poultry* 4, no. 6 (December 2009–January 2010), www.cafepress.com/durhamhens.

9. Keller's comments are from a presentation on biophilic design, October 2009, at the University of Oregon–Eugene. Kellert's speech was reported by Camille Rasmussen and Jo-anna Wendel in the student newspaper *Oregon Daily Emerald*.

10. Peter Ker, "More Fertile Imagination," *The Age* (Australia), March 20, 2010.

11. www.carolinathreadtrail.org/index.php?id=24.

12. www.fairus.org/site/PageServer?pagename=research_researchf392.

13. www.sightline.org.

14. www.theintertwine.org.

15. Kelli Kavanaugh, "Green Space: Sturgeon Spawning Returns to the Detroit River," *Metromode*, June 4, 2009.

16. www.cdc.gov/HomeandRecreationalSafety/Dog-Bites/dogbite-factsheet.html.

17. J. J. Sacks, M. Kresnow, and B. Houston, "Dog Bites: How Big a Problem?" *Injury Prevention* 2 (1996): 52–54.

18. The Web site for the Audubon Society of Portland offers general information on living with a variety of urban wildlife: audubonportland.org/backyardwildlife/brochures. For other resources on outdoor safety, including information on ticks, see: the Centers for Disease Control Web site, www.cdc.gov/Features/StopTicks/. A site specific to ticks is: www.tickencounter.org/.

17. Little Suburb on the Prairie

1. Stephen Kellert, *Building for Life: Designing and Understanding the Human-Nature Connection* (Washington, DC: Island Press, 2005).

2. Joanne Kaufman, "Vacation Homes: Seeking Birds, Not Birdies," *New York Times*, October 6, 2006.

3. Jim Heid, *Greenfield Development without Sprawl: The Role of Planned Communities* (Washington, DC: Urban Land Institute, 2004).

4. *Oregonian*, March 4, 2008, www.oregonlive.com.

5. Doug Peacock, "Chasing Abbey," *Outside*, August 1997, outside.away.com/magazine/0897/9708abbey.html.

18. Vitamin N for the Soul

1. Mary Carmichael, *Newsweek*, 2007, www.msnbc.msn.com/id/12776739/site/newsweek.29042079.

2. Charles Siebert, "Watching Whales Watching Us," *New York Times Magazine*, July 8, 2009.

3. Nancy Stetson and Penny Morrell, "Belonging: An Interview with Thomas Berry," *Parabola* 21 (1999): 26–31.

19. All Rivers Run to the Future

1. Douglas Brinkley, *The Wilderness Warrior* (New York: Harper, 2009), 26 (photo caption).

2. Kevin C. Armitage of Miami University of Ohio has written an excellent history of the movement: *The Nature Study Movement: The Forgotten Popularizer of America's Conservation Ethic* (Lawrence: University of Kansas Press, 2009).

3. Aldo Leopold, *A Sand County Almanac, and Sketches Here and There* (1948; New York: Oxford University Press, 1987), 81.

20. The Right to a Walk in the Woods

1. Thomas Berry, *The Great Work: Our Way into the Future* (New York: Three Rivers Press, 2000), 105.

2. A proposal: If someone is destructive toward nature, whether a corporate president or an individual citizen, should that person lose their right to visit government-operated natural areas? The devil would be in the definition of *destructive*.

21. Where Mountains Once Were and Rivers Will Be

1. Paul Hawken, *The Ecology of Commerce* (New York: HarperCollins, 1993), 35.

2. Ibid., 35.

3. Courtney White, *Revolution on the Range: The Rise of the New Ranch in the American West* (Washington, DC: Island Press, 2008), 40.

4. Ibid., 12.

5. Anya Kamenetz, "Teal Farm: Living the Future Now," *Reality Sandwich*, www.realitysandwich.com/teal_farm.

6. *High Country News*, www.hcn.org/issues/313/16001.

INDEX

Center for Education, Imagination, and the Natural World, 244–245
Center for Whole Communities, 253
Center on Everyday Lives of Families, 23
Centers for Disease Control and Prevention, 85–86, 215
Chadstone shopping center, 210
Chadwick, Alan, 173
chaparral, 107, 108–109, 207–209
Chattahoochee Hill Country, 220–221
Chautauqua Festival, 35–36, 68–69
Chawla, Louise, 34, 146
Chiba University, 51, 86
Chicago Wilderness, 214
chickens, 204–205
Children and Nature Network, 137, 144
Children, Youth, and Family Consortium, 144
China, 114–115
chlorophyll, 108
Chrispeels, Arno, 282–285
citizen naturalists, 130, 131–135
civil rights, 267–269
civilization, 113–114
Clabburn, Anna, 183
Cleveland EcoVillage, 201
Cloud Appreciation Society, 180–181
Cloudspotter's Guide, The (Pretor-Pinney), 180–181
coal mining, 270–273
Cobb, Edith, 34
Colorado Department of Public Health and Environment, 95
Colorado Department of Veterans Affairs, 66
Colorado Health Foundation, 211
Columbia University, 128, 201
Commerzbank Tower, 185
community, 189
community-based conservation, 253–254
Community Food Security Coalition, 205
Comstock, Anna Botsford, 252
Comstock, John Henry, 252
Condor Recovery Team, 131
connecting people to nature, 258–264
conservation theories, 116, 251–253
Conservationists Formerly Known as Environmentalists, 253

continuous partial attention, 22–24
Cornell Plantations, 199
Cornell University, 133, 193, 199, 252
Costa Rica, 100–101, 128
Cox, Mike, 93
Coyote's Guide to Connecting with Nature (Young et al.), 31–32
creative genius, 33–36
culture, 54, 114, 234, 263, 274
cummings, e. e., 1
Cuyamaca Mountains, 140–144

Dana Meadows Organic Children's Garden, 157–159, 204
Daniel, Terry, 179
Dark Sky Initiative, 178
darkness, 177–181
Darwin, Charles, 245–246
Dasmann, Raymond, 122
DDT, 213, 214
death, 274
Deakin University, 34–35, 48, 56, 113, 210
De-Central Park, 209, 211
deep green exercise, 72–77
deep green high, 70–77
deer, 214–215
dehumanized life, 23–24
Delightful Places Survey, 96
Denver Trust for Public Land, 211
depression, 58–62
Desert Solitaire (Abbey), 235
despair, 283–284
Despommier, Dickson, 201–202
Detroit, 202–204
Detroit River, 214
"Devil's Teeth, The," 20
DeYoung, Raymond, 28
Diagnostic and Statistical Manual, 62
Dick, Steven, 4
Dickinson, Janis, 193–194
Dillane, James, 106–107
directed-attention fatigue, 27–29
dirt, 60, 65
disabilities, 83, 188–189
Distracted (Jackson), 22–23
dolphins, 61, 242
Donahue, Ashley, 148–150
Donahue, Chip, 148–150

Richard Louv is the author of eight books about family, nature, and community and founding chairman of the Children & Nature Network. He has written for numerous newspapers and magazines, including the *New York Times*, the *Times* of London, *Orion Magazine*, and *Parents* magazine. From 1983 to 2006 he was a columnist for the *San Diego Union-Tribune*. He has been an adviser to the Ford Foundation's Leadership for a Changing World award program and is a member of the Citistates Group, an organization of urban observers. In 2008 he was awarded the Audubon Medal by the National Audubon Society. Past recipients have included Rachel Carson, Robert Redford, Jimmy Carter, and E. O. Wilson.

Richard Louv may be reached via www.richardlouv.com.